FIGHTERS OF THE 20TH CENTURY

JIM WINCHESTER

Airlife

Royal Aircraft Factory B.E.2

United Kingdom
1912

This Armstrong Whitworth-built B.E.2c of the Royal Flying Corps served in France in 1915/16. Note the nationality markings on the fin. (Philip Jarrett collection)

The earliest military aircraft were not built for aerial fighting or bombing but for reconnaissance or 'scouting' missions. Air combat came about when opposing scouts happened to meet in the air. Later scouts were built with manoeuvrability and firepower in mind, but at the beginning of World War I, the Royal Flying Corps was equipped largely with poorly armed cumbersome machines like the Royal Aircraft Factory **B.E.2**. In fact, the B.E.2 dated from 1912 and was the first major design by Geoffrey de Havilland, who was at that time working for the R.A.F. at Farnborough. B.E. stood for 'Blériot Experimental', although this was because it embodied certain features of Blériot designs (such as wing warping) rather than having a direct connection with Louis Blériot.

The B.E.2 was a two-seat biplane, large for its day, with staggered wings and a narrow rear fuselage. Power came from a 70-hp (52-kW) Renault engine and it featured wing warping as its control method rather than ailerons. The improved **B.E.2a** was the first British aircraft to arrive in France at the outbreak of war and served mainly as an unarmed scout. The **B.E.2c**, developed in 1914, had a 90-hp (67.1-kW) engine and introduced ailerons for control. It was sometimes armed with a pilot-operated Lewis gun,

The B.E.2c appeared in 1914. It was large, slow and cumbersome, but was effective against German airships over England. (TRH Pictures)

mounted on the fuselage side at an angle in order to clear the propeller. Otherwise, the observer (who sat in the front seat) fired a backwards-facing gun attached to a centre-section strut. The B.E.2c was designed for inherent stability and this, combined with its useless armament, meant that many were destroyed by German Fokker monoplanes and other more nimble machines, resulting in the grim nickname 'Fokker fodder'. Despite this, the B.E.2c continued to be supplied to the front line until 1917 and a total of 1,216 were built.

The B.E.2c had more success in the home defence role. Usually modified as single-seaters with an upward-firing Lewis gun, the stately biplanes destroyed no fewer than five German airships over the UK in 1916. Lieutenant W.L. Leefe Robinson of No.39 Squadron received the Victoria Cross (VC) for destroying Schutte-Lanz airship *SL11* over Woolwich, London, in September 1916. Another VC was awarded to B.E.2c pilot Lieutenant F.K. McNamara for an action in Palestine. Many of the later **B.E.2d** had a 100-hp (74.6-kW) RAF engine.

The definitive version was the **B.E.2e**, first flown in February 1916 with a larger-span upper wing and a new tail design, 1,320 were built plus conversions.

Specification: RAF B.E.2c
Type: two-seat biplane fighter
Powerplant: one 90-hp (67.1-kW) RAF 1a V-8 piston
Dimensions: span 36 ft 10 in (11.23 m); length 27 ft 3 in (8.30 m); height 11 ft 4 in (3.45 m); wing area 396 sq ft (36.79 m²)
Weights: empty 1,370 lb (621 kg); max. take-off 2,142 lb (972 kg)
Performance: max. speed 72 mph (116 km/h); climb to 6,500 ft (1980 m) in 20 minutes; service ceiling 10,000 ft (3050 m); endurance 3 hours 15 minutes
Armament: one 0.303-in (7.7-mm) Lewis machine-gun

Airco D.H.1 and D.H.2

The legendary aircraft designer Geoffrey de Havilland joined the Aircraft Manufacturing Company (Airco) in 1914, having worked on a number of aircraft for the Royal Aircraft Factory at Farnborough. His first important design for Airco was the **D.H.1** fighter. In those days, British aircraft were usually named after the initials of the designer rather than a company designation. The D.H.1 was a two-seat scout biplane with a pusher engine. This allowed the pilot to fire the machine-gun unobstructed by the propeller or airframe. The wings and fuselage were attached to the tail surfaces by braced struts, but despite the D.H.1's flimsy appearance, it was a sturdy machine, fully capable of aerobatics. The D.H.1 appeared in January 1915 and featured a 70-hp (52-kW) Renault inline engine. The similar **D.H.1A** had a 120-hp (89-kW) Beardmore engine. A total of 100 of both versions were built, mainly for home defence and training units.

Seeking greater manoeuvrability, de Havilland scaled down the D.H.1 (which spanned 42 ft (12.50 m) and was 28 ft 11 in (8.83 m) long) to produce the single-seat **D.H.2** (dimensions below), which featured a smaller Gnome Monosoupape rotary engine. The prototype D.H.2 first flew on 1 June 1915 and was sent to France for operational evaluation in August. Unfortunately, it was captured by the Germans on the 15th, having fallen behind their lines. Nevertheless, production went ahead and the D.H.2 became operational with No. 24 Squadron early in 1916. Major

The two-seat D.H.1A had an inline Beardmore engine. Though not fitted here, the single gun was mounted on the pillar forward of the front cockpit. (TRH Pictures)

Lanoe Hawker VC soon proved the main exponent of the D.H.2 and by the time of the first Battle of the Somme, he and his fellow D.H.2 pilots had virtually rid the skies of Eindeckers, ending the first 'Fokker Scourge'. On 23 November 1916, Hawker's D.H.2 was shot down near Bapaume by an Albatros D.II flown by Manfred von Richthofen, and he was killed.

The D.H.2 was regarded as a difficult machine to fly, and this was not helped by the armament set-up, which required the pilot to move the machine-gun between two mounts depending on the bearing of the target. This arrangement was later replaced by a central pivoting mount, but this was often fixed, pilots aiming the whole aircraft at the target. Some late production D.H.2s were fitted with a 100-hp (74.6-kW) Le Rhône engine. In total, about 400 D.H.2s were built, 226 of which were issued to units on the Western Front. Others served in Macedonia and Palestine and some were still in service in the summer of 1918.

The pusher configuration of the D.H.2 overcame the problem of firing the gun through the propeller arc. This is the prototype D.H.1. (The Aviation Picture Library)

Specification: Airco D.H.2
Type: single-seat biplane fighter
Powerplant: one 100-hp Gnome Monosoupape 9-cylinder rotary
Dimensions: span 28 ft 3 in (8.61 m); length 25 ft 3 in (7.68 m); height 9 ft 7 in (2.91 m); wing area 249 sq ft (23.13 m²)
Weights: empty 943 lb (428 kg); max. take-off 1,441 lb (654 kg)
Performance: max. speed 93 mph (150 km/h); climb to 5,000 ft (1525 m) in 8.45 minutes; service ceiling 14,000 ft (4,267 m); endurance 2 hours 45 minutes
Armament: one 0.303-in (7.7-mm) Lewis machine-gun, up to 460 lb (208 kg) of bombs

Fokker E.I to E.IV Eindeckers

J ava-born Dutchman Anthony Fokker developed more than 60 distinct aircraft designs during World War I. He had established an aircraft factory in Berlin in 1912, building several fairly primitive types, which were bought by the German army and used mainly for training. The capture of French ace Roland Garros and his Morane-Saulnier Type L in April 1915 provided the inspiration for the first of many famous Fokker designs. The Type L was a monoplane with deflector plates to allow the Hotchkiss machine-gun to fire through the propeller arc. Fokker was charged with improving this crude system and reputedly developed his gun synchronisation system in 48 hours.

The first aircraft armed with a synchronised, forward-firing machine-gun was the Fokker **E.I**, which was delivered from June 1915 (E stood for Eindecker or monoplane). It was a mid-winged monoplane with externally braced wings and a tailskid landing gear. Power came from an 80-hp (59.7-kW) nine-cylinder Oberursel rotary engine. A total of 54 were produced for the German army and the Austro-Hungarian army by June 1916. The E.I was quickly followed by the refined and strengthened **E.II**, which was slightly larger and heavier. Built both in armed and unarmed versions, the E.I and E.II were first used for training, before the armed versions were re-engined with a

Fokker E.IIs such as this were built as trainers before being re-engined as the E.III. The arrival of the E.III on the front turned the tide of the air war. (TRH Pictures)

100-hp (74.6-kW) Oberursel rotary as the **E.III**.

A total of 72 E.IIs were converted to E.IIIs and 158 were built new, deliveries beginning in autumn 1915. With their speed, relative manoeuvrability and effective firepower, the E.IIIs tore through the ranks of the Royal Flying Corps' (RFC) B.E.2c scouts and other slow, cumbersome aircraft – the so-called 'Fokker Scourge' of winter 1915. The forward-firing armament of the Fokker Eindeckers gave them a major advantage when they appeared over the Western Front. At first they were not allowed to fly over Allied lines in case the secret of the gun synchronisation was captured. Two of the most famous aces of the war, Max Immelmann (the 'Eagle of Lille') and Oswald Boelcke, were extremely successful in E.IIIs. Both pilots developed new tactics. Immelmann scored 16 victories but was killed in combat in 1916, probably as a result of a gun synchronisation failure causing him to shoot off his own propeller.

The final production Eindecker was the **E.IV**. Despite a more powerful 160-hp (119.3-kW) engine and with twin machine-guns as standard (although some were noted with three), the slightly larger E.IV was by now facing better Allied designs and only 49 were delivered, the last in July 1916.

The E.IV was the last and best performing of the Eindeckers. By the time it appeared in 1916, it was outclassed by new Allied biplanes. (Aviation Picture Library)

Specification: Fokker E.III
Type: single-seat monoplane fighter
Powerplant: one 100-hp (74.6-kW) Oberursel U.I, 9-cylinder radial piston
Dimensions: span 31 ft 3 in (9.52 m); length; 23 ft 7.5 in (7.20 m); height 7 ft 10.5 in (2.40 m); wing area 165.77 sq ft (15.40m²)
Weights: empty 880 lb (399 kg); max take-off 1,345 lb (610 kg)
Performance: max. speed 87 mph (140 km/h); climb rate unknown; service ceiling 13,451 ft (4,100 m); range; 149 miles (240 km)
Armament: one or two Spandau 7.92-mm machine-guns

Nieuport 11 to 17

Edouard Nieuport's aeronautical company was founded in 1910. Nieuport himself was killed in 1911 and Gustave Délage became the chief designer. His first combat aircraft design was the Nieuport or Nie 10, a structurally lightweight biplane used by France, Britain, Russia and Italy, and licence-built in the last two countries in single- and two-seat versions.

The **Nieuport 11** that was delivered to the Aviation Militaire in January 1916 was similar to the Nie 10 and used the same 80-hp (59.7-kW) Le Rhône motor but was smaller in all dimensions and thus had better performance. Synchronisation problems were avoided by having the single Hotchkiss or Lewis gun fire over the wing outside the propeller arc. The Nie 11 was able to carry eight Le Prieur rockets, mainly for use against observation balloons and airships. These were really little more than glorified fireworks in design. Both wings were slightly swept back, the lower wing being much smaller than the upper wing (which made it a 'sesquiplane') and was a source of weakness, but the Nie 11 soon proved popular with pilots, who christened it the *Bébé* (baby) Nieuport or simply *Bébé*. It was licence-built in Holland, Russia and Italy.

By the time of the Battle of Verdun in February 1916, the Nie 11 equipped eleven *escadrilles* (squadrons) and cleared the skies of the less manoeuvrable Fokker monoplanes. One of the most enthusiastic users was French ace Charles Nungesser, who painted his macabre skull-and-coffin insignia on aircraft N880.

The Nieuport 17 was flown by many Allied aces including Guynemer, Bishop and Ball. This model has a single synchronised Lewis gun. (TRH Pictures)

The **Nieuport 12** was an enlarged version of the two-seat Nie 10 with a 110-hp (82.1-kW) Clerget engine, used mainly by France and the RNAS. The **Nieuport 16** was basically a Nie 11 with a 110-hp (82.1-kW) Le Rhône 9J engine and a synchronised gun. Although used by France, the Royal Naval Air Service (RNAS), RFC, Belgium and Russia, it was soon replaced by the definitive **Nieuport 17**.

The Nie 17, which entered service in mid-1916, was initially equipped with an overwing Lewis gun but was later fitted with a synchronised Vickers gun. Larger than the Nie 11, the Nie 17 was christened *Superbébé* by pilots and was regarded as one of the classic designs of the Great War. The German High Command ordered that its best features, notably the 'V' strut arrangement, be copied, resulting in the Albatros D.III and D.V series. The Nieuport 17 was the first mount of most fighter pilots of the American Expeditionary Force. A developed version, the **Nieuport 17bis**, was delivered in only small numbers and mainly used in the training role.

The Nieuport 11 was the first missile-armed fighter, armed with a battery of Le Prieur rockets as well as a machine-gun. (Philip Jarrett collection)

Specification: Nieuport 11
Type: single-seat biplane fighter
Powerplant: one 80-hp (59.7-kW) Le Rhône 9C 9-cylinder rotary piston
Dimensions: span 29 ft 6 in (9.00 m); length 22 ft 11.5 in (7.00 m); height 8 ft 10.25 in (2.70 m); wing area 236.81 sq ft (22.00 m²)
Weights: empty 705 lb (320 kg); loaded 1,058 lb (480 kg)
Performance: max. speed 104 mph (167 km/h); climb rate 660 ft (200 m); service ceiling 14,765 ft (4500 m); endurance 2 hours 30 minutes
Armament: one 0.303-in (7.7-mm) Lewis machine-gun, eight Le Prieur rockets

Sopwith Pup

United Kingdom
February 1916

Officially known as the **Scout**, but universally known as the **Pup**, Sopwith's first single-seat landplane fighter was designed to an Admiralty requirement. The chief designer was Herbert Smith, with input by test pilot Harry Hawker. The design was largely influenced by the Tabloid light bomber of 1914. The prototype Scout was first flown in February 1916 and ordered in April by the Royal Naval Air Service. It entered service in July with No. 8 Squadron of No. 1 Wing RNAS. The Royal Flying Corps quickly ordered the Scout to replace the 1½ Strutter and it entered combat service with No. 54 Squadron in December 1916.

The Pup was extremely effective at the battles of Ypres, Cambrai and Messines, where it proved to be superior to the Albatros and Halberstadt scouts of the time. At the Battle of Arras in spring 1917, it was used largely against observation balloons but also scored many victories over enemy aircraft. Lightweight and fast, the Pup was able to hold its altitude well and was fully aerobatic up to 15,000 ft (4572 m). Even by the standards of the time, however, the Pup was underpowered with only an 80-hp (59.9-kW) engine. It was built for light weight from spruce with fabric covering and was armed with a single Vickers machine-gun. The rear decking was not built up, being

The Sopwith Pup was almost delicate in appearance. The level rear decking was one feature that distinguished it from the later Camel. (Philip Jarrett collection)

Seen here attracting much attention, this Standard Motors-built Pup survived the war to become G-EAVX on the British civil register. (Philip Jarrett collection)

parallel to the fuselage longerons. Pilots loved the Pup and it is regarded as one of the most enjoyable flying machines ever built.

Although most so-called 'naval' Pups flew from airfields on land, an RNAS Pup flown from a platform on the cruiser HMS *Yarmouth* by Flight Sub-Lieutenant B.A. Smart destroyed the naval Zeppelin *L23* in August 1917. That same month, a Pup became the first aircraft to land on a ship at sea when Lieutenant-Commander Dunning landed aboard the converted cruiser HMS *Furious*. Sadly, he was drowned in a crash following his third landing. Experiments with Pups and 1½ Strutters on *Furious* helped develop a workable arrestment system and other features later standardised on aircraft-carriers.

Owing to the rapid technical progress of the time, the Pup was essentially obsolete by the spring of 1917, but it established the basic configuration of the more famous Camel. Pup production ended in the autumn of 1918 with over 1,800 examples built. Only 216 saw service in France and about 80 in the Middle East. Seventy-three remained in the UK for home defence and the rest were used for training purposes. The home defence Pups were mainly fitted with the more powerful 100-hp (74.6 kW) Gnome Monosoupape engine, giving greatly improved performance.

Specification: Sopwith Pup

Type: single-seat biplane fighter
Powerplant: one 80-hp (59.9-kW) Le Rhône 9-C 9-cylinder rotary piston
Dimensions: span 26 ft 6 in (8.08 m); length 19 ft 4in (5.89 m); height 9 ft 5 in (2.87 m); wing area 254 sq ft (23.6 m²)
Weights: empty 787 lb (357 kg); loaded 1,225 lb (556 kg)
Performance: max. speed 111 mph (179 km/h); climb to 5,000 ft (1525 m) in 5 minutes 20 seconds; service ceiling 17,500 ft (5334 m); endurance 3 hours
Armament: one 0.303-in (7.7-mm) Vickers machine-gun

SPAD S.VII to S.XIII

The French company SPAD (originally Société Provisoire des Aéroplanes Deperdussin, later Société Pour Aviation et ses Dérivés) built a variety of fighters designed by Louis Béchereau. Early designs were two-seaters with a tractor propeller but a gunner's position mounted ahead of the engine. By late 1915, Béchereau had turned to more conventional designs and produced the SH.1, which was first flown in April 1916. A version with a greater wing area was ordered by the Aviation Militaire as the Spa.VII (or **S.VII**) in May, soon after its first flight.

The S.VII was a single-seat biplane with a synchronised fixed Vickers gun. The wings were of equal span and area, with the lower wing mounted slightly ahead of the upper wing. Power came from a 150-hp (111.9-kW) Hispano-Suiza 8Aa V-8 engine with a distinctive circular radiator and long exhaust pipes. The development of this powerplant in Spain proved crucial to both the SPAD series and the British S.E.5. Later model S.VIIs had a 180-hp (134.2-kW) Hispano.

Georges Guynemer of Escadrille N.3 'Les Cigognes' (Storks) was an early recipient of the S.VII. René Fonck, later to become France's leading ace with 75 kills, began his career with S.VII-equipped Spa 103.

Seven firms in France, two in Britain and one in Russia built a total of about 5,820 S.VIIs. After the war, examples served with a number of European and South American air forces.

Georges Guynemer, France's leading ace, requested

This Spad S.XIII was operated by the US Air Service from March 1918. This one was equipped with a camera for reconnaissance. (Philip Jarrett collection)

a fighter able to firing a 37-mm gun and Béchereau designed the **S.VIII**. This aircraft saw limited service, mainly due to the immense skill needed to hit anything with the single-shot Puteaux cannon.

The 200-hp (149.2-kW) Hispano-Suiza 8b of the S.XII was fitted to a new airframe, visually similar but structurally different to the S.VII, to produce the definitive **S.XIII**, which had twin Vickers and was bigger in all dimensions. It first flew on 4 April 1917. Problems with the geared 8b engine of the S.XIII (as opposed to the direct-drive 8Aa) led to the S.VII's retention in front-line service until the end of the war. Some S.XIIIs had 220-hp (164.1-kW) 8Bcs. The 'Spad 7' remained in French service up to 1928.

The 'Lafayette Escadrille' of American volunteers was superseded by the air squadrons of the American Expeditionary Force. As with the French, the Americans replaced their Nieuports with S.XIIIs, of which they accepted 893. Over 430 of these went to the US at the Armistice. The leading US ace, 'Eddie' Rickenbacker scored his 26 victories in the S.XIII.

A groundcrewman swings the propeller to help start the Hispano-Suiza motor of this Spad S.VII, seen in the markings of SPA.99. (Philip Jarrett collection)

Specification: SPAD S.XIII
Type: single-seat biplane fighter
Powerplant: one 220-hp (164.1-kW) Hispano-Suiza 8Bc 8-cylinder inline piston
Dimensions: span 27 ft 1 in (8.25 m); length 20 ft 6 in (6.25 m); height 8 ft 6.5 in (2.60 m); wing area 227.23 sq ft (21.11 m²)
Weights: empty 1,326 lb (601 kg); loaded 1,888 lb (856 kg)
Performance: max. speed 135 mph (218 km/h); climb to 6,560 ft (2000 m) in 4 minutes 40 seconds; service ceiling 21,820 ft (6650 m); endurance 1 hour 40 minutes
Armament: two Vickers 0.303-in (7.7-mm) machine-guns

Sopwith Triplane

United Kingdom
May 1916

Like the Pup, the Sopwith **Triplane** came about as the result of a naval requirement and again the designer was Herbert Smith. The triplane layout gave the widest possible field of vision for the pilot. Three wings allowed a narrower chord that in turn allowed a shorter fuselage. Distributing the wing area over three sets of wings with ailerons on each kept the wingspan short and gave an excellent roll rate. Concentrating the weight near the centre of gravity made the Triplane easy to handle. The three wings were evenly staggered back from the top. The Triplane's armament was a single Vickers gun synchronised to fire through the propeller arc, although a small batch of later aircraft built by Clayton & Shuttleworth had twin guns.

The prototype was built in just three months and flew on 28 May 1916. Another three months later it was despatched to the front for evaluation and flew a combat mission within an hour of arrival. At least two victories were scored in the prototype, a feat that may be unique in the annals of fighter aviation. By December 1916 the first unit, No. 1 Squadron RNAS, was fully equipped with Triplanes. This was one of four RNAS squadrons attached to the Royal Flying Corps. The RFC also ordered Triplanes, which were built by other contractors, but they were destined not to see action with the RFC. In a deal to alleviate an RFC fighter crisis, the RNAS swapped all its SPADs for the 266 Triplanes on order for the RFC. Less than half this number were actually to be completed.

Probably the most famous Triplane pilot was Flight

The Sopwith Triplane had a short front-line career, but its success led to a number of imitators. Armament was a single machine-gun. (Philip Jarrett collection)

Sub-Lieutenant Raymond Collishaw of No. 10 (Naval) Squadron. Leading 'Black Flight', comprised of fellow Canadians, Collishaw shot down 16 German aircraft, mostly single-seaters, in June 1917 alone. His score of 29 on Triplanes was part of a wartime total of 59. The five Black Flight pilots accounted for 87 kills from May to July, with only one Triplane pilot lost.

The appearance of the Sopwith Triplane led to a 'triplane frenzy' among manufacturers. At least 15 German and Austro-Hungarian companies built 'Tripes' in response, of which the Fokker Dr.I was the only real success.

The Triplane's front-line career was a brief one. The battle of Ypres was their swansong and they were replaced by Camels by November 1917. Late production models had a smaller tailplane, but otherwise there were few differences between aircraft. In August 1917 the Sopwith Camel began to replace the Triplane in France and the last major action it saw was the Battle of Ypres. A total of only about 150 Triplanes were completed and, given their combat record, it must be regarded as being among the best value for money per airframe of any fighter.

Triplanes saw all their service with the Royal Naval Air Service, notably with 'Black Flight' of No. 10 Squadron, whose 'Tripes' had black-painted fuselages. (TRH Pictures)

Specification: Sopwith Triplane
Type: single-seat triplane fighter
Powerplant: one 130-hp (96.9-kW) Clerget
Dimensions: span 26 ft 6 in (8.08 m); length 19 ft 6 in (5.94 m); height 10 ft 6 in (3.20 m); wing area 231 sq ft (21.46 m²)
Weights: empty 993 lb (450 kg); loaded 1,415 lb (642 kg)
Performance: max. speed 116 mph (187 km/h); climb to 6,500 ft (1980 m) in 6 minutes 20 seconds; service ceiling 20,000 ft (6096 m); endurance 2 hours 45 minutes
Armament: one 0.303-in (7.7-mm) Vickers machine-gun

Albatros biplane fighters

C hief Designer of the Albatros Werke, Dipl.-Ing Robert Thelen was largely responsible for the company's **D.I** and **D.II** fighters. Over 250 of these semi-monocoque wooden-fuselage fighters were built from August 1916, but by this time Thelen was developing a more advanced type that combined the fuselage and tail surfaces of the D.II with a wing influenced strongly by the French Nieuport 17, which had a smaller lower wing (or sesquiplane configuration). The upper wing had tapered ailerons, giving a swept-wing appearance. The 'V'-shaped wing struts were the main recognition feature of the new model for Allied pilots. The large spade-shaped tailplane had a relatively small elevator. The 160-hp (119-kW) Mercedes D.IIIa inline engine was exhausted through a pipe on the starboard side. The first aircraft in this configuration was flown in August 1916, and large-scale production began in January 1917. The aircraft's service entry was with Jasta 11, led by Manfred von Richthofen, and by April all of the first-line fighter squadrons on the Western Front were equipped with the **D.III**. The superiority of the new Albatros D.IIIs led to the so-called 'Bloody April' when the Jasta pilots regained air superiority, taking their toll on British aircraft in particular.

The V-strut configuration of the D.III was a source of structural weakness, however, and several broke up in the air when the lower wing twisted in a fast dive. Baron von Richthofen's first all-red D.III was nearly lost this way in January 1917. The design of a lightened,

Von Richthofen's 'Flying Circus' saw some of the most outlandish schemes ever applied to fighters. Here Leutnant Von Hippel poses with D.V 'Blitz' (lightning). (TRH Pictures)

aerodynamically refined version was already underway by the time the D.III entered service, and 200 were ordered in April 1917 as the **D.V**, which also featured a more powerful 180-hp (134-kW) engine. The same weaknesses were present as on the D.III and a number of D.Vs were also lost through structural failure. The response to this was to strengthen the airframe and to route the aileron cables up from the lower wing as on the D.III. Such machines were designated **D.Va**s and were delivered from October 1917. German ace Werner Voss did not live to see this, however, being shot down by the S.E.5a of Major James McCudden on 23 September.

A total of about 1,350 D.IIIs were built, as were over 2,000 D.Vs and D.Vas, making the series one of the most widely produced of the war. Over 1,500 DVs served on the Western Front. In the hands of the Turkish air arm, the latter was able to keep air superiority over Palestine, Syria and Mesopotamia until quite late in the war when the most modern British types arrived in the Middle East.

The Albatros D.III and its successors were some of the most attractive World War I fighters, although they were not wholly successful in service. (The Aviation Picture Library)

Specification: Albatros D.III
Type: single-seat biplane fighter
Powerplant: one 160-hp (119-kW) Mercedes D.IIIa inline piston
Dimensions: span 29 ft 8 in (9.05 m); length 24 ft (7.33 m); height 9 ft 9 in (2.98 m); wing area 220.67 sq ft (20.50 m²)
Weights: empty 1,457 lb (661 kg); max. take-off 1,953 lb (886 kg)
Performance: max. speed 109 mph (175 km/h); climb to 9,845 ft (3000 m) in 12 minutes 1 second; service ceiling 18,045 ft (5500 m); endurance 2 hours
Armament: two fixed synchronised 0.31-in (7.92-mm) LMG 08/15 machine-guns

Bristol F.2 Fighter

The British and Colonial Aeroplane Company, based in Bristol, England, and more commonly known simply as Bristol, replied to the RFC's requirement to replace the B.E.2c with a design by Frank Barnwell called the R.2A (R standing for reconnaissance). The Royal Aircraft Factory's entry was the R.E.8, which was adopted for service but proved less than successful. The R.2A, a two-seat biplane with the lower wing separated from the fuselage by struts, was revised into the R.2B with a Hispano-Suiza engine and then a 190-hp (141.7-kW) Rolls-Royce Falcon engine. Showing potential as a fighter, the R.2B was renamed the **F.2A** and the first true example flew on 9 September 1916.

After successful testing in October, the F.2A was approved for production and the RFC ordered 50 examples, the first of which reached No. 48 Squadron in December. In the squadron's first combat on 5 April 1917, four F.2As were lost to the guns of the 'Red Baron's Flying Circus', including that of Captain Leefe Robinson VC who became a prisoner of war. This disaster was blamed on poor tactics rather than faults with the design, and an improved version with an enlarged tailplane, modified lower wing and a revised centre fuselage for better view followed the initial batch as the **F.2B**.

The first 150 F.2Bs were delivered with the 220-hp (164.1-kW) Falcon II engine and the majority of the

The Bristol Fighter, with its choice of powerful engines, was the best two-seater of the war. The last F.2s in service were retired by New Zealand in 1938. (TRH Pictures)

4,747 eventually built had the 275-hp (205.1-kW) Falcon III. Other engine installations included the 200-hp (149.2-kW) Sunbeam Arab (153 built) and the 230-hp (171.6-kW) Siddeley Puma (18 built). Deliveries began in April 1917 and when it was realised that the F.2B's power allowed it to be flown aggressively like a single-seat scout, the initially unofficial name 'Fighter' began to have real currency. Nicknames applied by the satisfied crews included 'Biff' and 'Brisfit'.

The F.2B's armament consisted of one Vickers gun mounted forward of the front cockpit and single or twin Lewis guns in a Scarff ring for the observer. It could also carry light bombs on racks between the lower wing centre-section. The F.2B was retained in service for the army co-operation role and in fact production was reinstated as the **F.2B Fighter Mk II**. The designations **Fighter Mk III** and **Mk IV** related to strengthened aircraft delivered in 1926 and redelivered in 1928, respectively. They were used for colonial policing duties by the RAF until 1930.

Following its successful wartime use, production of the Bristol fighter continued into the 1920s. This is the first post-war built F2.B Fighter Mk II. (TRH Pictures)

Specification: Bristol F.2B Fighter
Type: two-seat biplane fighter/reconnais-sance aircraft
Powerplant: one 275-hp (205.1-kW) Rolls-Royce Falcon III 12-cylinder piston
Dimensions: span 39 ft 3 in (11.96 m); length 25 ft 10 in (7.87 m); height 9 ft 9 in (2.97 m); wing area 405.6 sq ft (37.68 m²)
Weights: empty 1,930 lb (875 kg); loaded 2,848 lb (1292 kg)
Performance: max. speed 123 mph (198 km/h); climb to 10,000 ft (3050 m) in 11 minutes 51 seconds; service ceiling 21,500 ft (6553 m); endurance 3 hours
Armament: two or three 0.303-in (7.7-mm) machine-guns

Royal Aircraft Factory S.E.5 and S.E.5a

United Kingdom
November 1916

After Geoffrey de Havilland left the Royal Aircraft Factory for Airco in 1914, 24-year old Henry Folland was appointed as chief designer. His first design was the S.E.4a, with the initials standing for Scouting Experimental. This appeared in late 1914 and was a rotary-engined biplane of attractive appearance, but only four were built. The **S.E.5** project began in early 1915 to take advantage of the new Hispano-Suiza engine that was then entering production. Both 150-hp (111.9-kW) and 200-hp (149.8-kW) versions were developed. The prototype S.E.5s with the 150-hp (111.9-kW) Hispano-Suiza 8Aa motor, which first flew in late November 1916, led to about 75 production aircraft, the first of which entered service with No. 56 Squadron in April 1917. The third, 200-hp (149.8-kW) prototype (first flight 4 December 1916), led to the definitive **S.E.5a**. Experience with the early S.E.5s led to changes to the airframe, including shorter wings with new tips, improved aileron controls and a smaller windscreen on the S.E.5a. Many of these modifications were suggested by Captain Albert Ball VC, then the commander of No. 56 Squadron.

The S.E.5a was a slab-sided equal-span biplane with pronounced wing stagger and dihedral. The radiator was on the front face of the fuselage, giving a boxy appearance to the nose. Long exhaust pipes ran back behind the cockpit. Armament consisted of a synchronised Lewis gun, and a Vickers gun mounted

The wartime censor has removed serials and unit identification from these S.E.5as preparing to set out on patrol from an airfield in France. (TRH Pictures)

on the upper centre-section firing outside the propeller arc.

The S.E.5a entered service, also with No. 56 Squadron, in June 1917. This squadron alone scored 401 'kills' with the S.E.5a, with its new leader, James McCudden VC, being a leading exponent with a total of 57 kills. Albert Ball scored 11 of his 44 victories in the S.E.5. Both these aces were killed in crashes of their respective machines. The US air service received many examples and by November 1918 over 20 British and American squadrons on the Western Front were equipped with S.E.5as.

The 200-hp (149.8-kW) Hispano-Suiza was produced in Britain as the Wolseley W.4B Adder and a derivative as the W.4A Viper. The aircraft itself was built by five companies as well as the R.A.F. works at Farnborough for a total production of over 5,200. Some were built in Australia, South Africa and Canada. US production was much less than the 1,000 originally planned. Fifty US-built machines were re-engined with the Wright-Hispano E engine as the **S.E.5e**.

This is the unusually painted S.E.5a flown by the Australian ace Roderic Dallas, who scored 32 victories before his death in action in June 1918. (Philip Jarrett collection)

Specification: RAF S.E.5a
Type: single-seat biplane fighter
Powerplant: one 200-hp (149.8-kW) Hispano-Suiza 8B V-8 piston
Dimensions: span 26 ft 7.5 in (8.11 m); length 20 ft 11 in (6.37 m); height 9 ft 6 in (2.87 m); wing area 245.8 sq ft (22.83 m²)
Weights: empty 1,531 lb (694 kg); loaded 2,048 lb (929 kg)
Performance: max. speed 126 mph (203 km/h); climb to 10,000 ft (3050 m) in 13 minutes 15 seconds; service ceiling 17,500 ft (5180 m); endurance 2 hours 15 minutes
Armament: one 0.303-in (7.7-mm) Vickers and one 0.303-in (7.7-mm) Lewis machine-gun

Sopwith F.1 Camel

Sopwith's replacement for its own successful Pup first flew at Brooklands Aerodrome on 16 December 1916 in the hands of Harry Hawker, powered by a 110-hp (82.1-kW) Clerget 9Z rotary. A variety of engines were tested on the prototypes before two types were selected, the 130-hp (97-kW) Clerget 9B and the 130-hp Le Rhône. The 150-hp (111.9-kW) Bentley BR.1 was also used, mostly by RNAS aircraft.

The Sopwith **1F.1** was similar in general appearance and construction methods to the Pup, the new fighter was a much more effective machine with double the armament and higher performance in all areas. Twin synchronised Vickers guns were mounted ahead of the pilot. Fairings by the gun breeches gave a humped appearance and the name 'Camel' stuck, even though it was entirely unofficial. Upper wing dihedral was eliminated to simplify production and doubled on the lower wing to compensate. The fuselage was deeper and more tapered than on the Pup. The wingspan was greater but length and height were reduced.

Naval orders included the **Camel 2F.1** variant, which had shorter wings and was usually powered by the 150-hp (111.9-kW) Bentley B.R.1 radial. It was operated from shore bases but also from lighters, cruisers and the new carriers HMS *Argus*, *Pegasus* and *Eagle*. After April 1918 these shipborne aircraft were (as were all British military aircraft) on Royal Air Force charge.

This 1F.1 Camel was the first to be fitted with a 180-hp Le Rhône rotary instead of the usual 130-hp Clerget. (Philip Jarrett collection)

The Camel was very difficult to fly in comparison with the Pup and the Triplane and many student pilots were killed in crashes caused by spins in the early part of their training. This was due to the concentration of mass (engine, guns, and pilot) in the first third of the fuselage. Gyroscopic effect of the rotary engine would cause rapid right turns with nose drop and gentler left turns with a climbing tendency. A poorly made right turn could easily develop into a spin, which was invariably fatal at low level. This could be exploited to get behind an opponent, making the Camel one of the greatest dogfighters of all time.

The Camel's combat debut was in June 1917 with No. 4 Squadron RNAS. The first RFC Camels arrived on the Western Front in July and were issued to No. 70 Squadron. In all, ten RFC squadrons were equipped with Le Rhône Camels and seven with Clerget Camels. In all, Camels built for the RFC destroyed 908 enemy aircraft and RNAS Camels a further 373, more than any other fighter of the war. Some were supplied to Belgian and American forces, but the type was retired quickly after the war's end.

Tricky to fly, but deadly in the right hands, the Camel was the best-known RFC fighter. This Camel has one Vickers gun (above wing) and one Lewis gun. (Aviation Picture Library)

> **Specification: Sopwith F.1 Camel**
> **Type:** single-seat biplane fighter
> **Powerplant:** one 130-hp (97-kW) Clerget 9B 9-cylinder rotary piston
> **Dimensions:** span 28 ft 0 in (8.53 m); length 18 ft 9 in (5.71 m); height 8 ft 6 in (2.59 m); wing area 231 sq ft (21.46 m²)
> **Weights:** empty 929 lb (421 kg); loaded 1,453 lb (659 kg)
> **Performance:** max. speed 115 mph (185 km/h); climb to 6,500 ft (1980 m) in 6 minutes; service ceiling 17,300 ft (5273 m); endurance 2 hours 30 minutes
> **Armament:** two 0.303-in (7.7-mm) Vickers machine-guns

Nieuport 28

France
June 1917

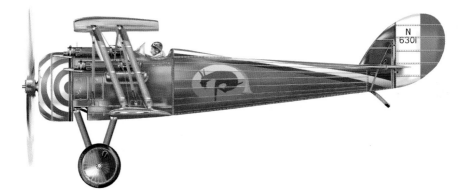

Following the successful Nieuport 17, the most significant models from this company were the almost identical Nie 23 and similar Nie 24 and 27, all of which were sesquiplanes with good agility but poor speed and climb performance compared with the enemy scouts and competing SPAD designs.

The prototype of the all-new **Nieuport 28** (Nie 28) was first flown on 14 June 1917 with a 160-hp (119.4-kW) Gnome 9N rotary engine. It had an upper wing with considerable dihedral that was mounted directly to the fuselage, but this was replaced on production aircraft with a raised wing with no dihedral. The lower wing was slightly smaller but not half size as on a sesquiplane. Ailerons were only fitted on the lower wing. The traditional Nieuport 'V' struts were dispensed with and more conventional parallel struts were used. The fuselage tapered notably to the rear, and the wings had rounded tips, giving an attractive and almost delicate appearance to the Nie 28. Armament consisted of two 0.303-in (7.7-mm) Vickers machine-guns firing over the cowl. The production model was designated **Nieuport 28C 1**.

Although the French and British rejected the Nie 28 in favour of SPAD fighters, the squadrons of the American Expeditionary Force were initially equipped with Nie 28C.1s, and in all, received 297 examples. Machine-guns were not supplied with the aircraft delivered to the Americans and had to be acquired from various sources. Major Raoul Lufbery led the first

The Nieuport 28 was used almost exclusively by the US Air Service. This Nie 28C 1 wears the colours of the third flight of the famous 94th Aero Squadron. (D.I. Windle)

(unarmed) combat patrol on 15 March 1918. Once enough guns were available for one per machine, Douglas Campbell became the first American ace on Nie 28s. Harold Hartney was another Nie 28 ace, with six kills. Lafayette Escadrille veteran Lufbery scored the last of his 17 kills before he was killed on 19 May 1918 by the gunner of a German two-seater aircraft.

Despite some successes, and popularity with their pilots, when the Nieuports were moved to a tougher sector of the front in July they suffered heavy losses and were soon exchanged for SPAD XIIIs. One problem was a tendency to shed wing fabric from the leading edge (and on occasion the entire upper wing) during aerobatics, another was a somewhat unreliable engine that occasionally caught fire. The French ordered the type grounded for a period until more flexible and less fracture-prone fuel lines were fitted.

The Swiss air arm was one of a number of foreign air forces to acquire the Nie 28 after the war, buying 14 for use as trainers, in which role they served as late as 1930.

Seen at an aerodrome close to Paris, this Nieuport 28 shows the slender fuselage, contrasting with the box-like shape of earlier Nieuport scouts. (TRH Pictures)

Specification: Nieuport 28
Type: single-seat biplane fighter
Powerplant: one 160-hp (119.4-kW) Gnome Monosoupape rotary piston
Dimensions: span 26 ft 9.25 in (8.16 m); length 21 ft 0 in (6.40 m); height 8 ft 2.5 in (2.50 m); wing area 172.23 sq ft (16.00 m²)
Weights: empty 961 lb (436 kg); loaded 1,539 lb (698 kg)
Performance: max. speed 123 mph (198 km/h); climb to 6,560 ft (2000 m) in 5 minutes 30 seconds; service ceiling 17,060 ft (5180 m); endurance 1 hour 30 minutes
Armament: two 0.303-in (7.7-mm) Vickers machine-guns

Fokker Dr.I Triplane

Like its Sopwith namesake, Fokker's Dr.I Triplane had a short career and was built in small numbers, but it gained fame with Richthofen's 'Flying Circus'. (Philip Jarrett)

Like the Nieuport 17, the Sopwith Triplane impressed the German High Command and they ordered all aircraft makers to produce a triplane (or *dreidecker*) design. Of all the designs that emerged, only two, the Pfalz Dr.I and the **Fokker Dr.I** entered production and only ten of the former were built. Anthony Fokker was reluctant to spend time on a triplane, but produced an aircraft based around the fuselage of an experimental biplane named the **V4**. To this was added three fabric-covered wings and an aerofoil-section wheel axle. The armament was two synchronised machine-guns and the engine was a 110-hp (82.1-kW) Le Rhône rotary. Two preproduction V4s were shipped to the front for evaluation in late August 1917 as the **F.I** and had increased wing area and interplane struts. They were handed to ace pilots Manfred von Richthofen (the 'Red Baron') and Werner Voss. Von Richthofen's machine, F.I 102/17, was soon painted overall red and in it he scored his sixtieth victory on 31 August.

Werner Voss was shot down and killed on 23 September 1917 after an epic dogfight and the Red Baron's F.I was lost with another pilot. Production Fokker Dr.Is (with a 110-hp (82.1-kW) Oberursel rotary, a German copy of the Le Rhône) entered service with JG 1 in October but were withdrawn from the front on

Early Dr.Is had a tendency to inflight failures. Leutnant Gontermann seen here was killed when his Triplane broke up on 30 October 1917. (TRH Pictures)

2 November after structural failures caused by moisture-weakened glued joints.

Deliveries of modified aircraft soon recommenced, although the Dr.I never totally replaced the Albatros and Pfalz fighters. In fact, only 320 production aircraft were built and peak strength in service never exceeded 170 aircraft. The Dr.I was very successful in the German spring offensive in 1918 and achieved lasting fame in the hands of von Richthofen, who scored 20 of his 80 kills in at least three different examples. Von Richthofen himself was shot down and killed in his red triplane on 21 April 1918 after a long low-level dogfight, either by Canadian pilot Roy Brown or by Australian machine-gunners. The remains of the Red Baron's Fokker triplane were displayed in Berlin after the war but destroyed by bombing in World War II. All Fokker triplanes seen flying or in museums today are modern replicas.

Although it was slower than its biplane contemporaries and difficult to land, the Dr.I had the best climb rate of any wartime fighter and a very good rate of roll. Nonetheless, it was not the greatest fighter by any means and had only a brief combat career. The association of the triplane with the Red Baron, however, has made it one of the most famous fighter aircraft types of all time.

Specification: Fokker Dr.I
Type: single-seat triplane fighter
Powerplant: one 110-hp (82.1-kW) Oberursel UR.II, 9-cylinder rotary piston
Dimensions: span 23 ft 7 in (7.19 m); length 18 ft 11 in (5.77 m); height 9 ft 8 in (2.9 m); wing area 200.9 sq ft (18.66 m²)
Weights: empty 895 lb (406 kg); loaded 1,292 lb (586 kg)
Performance: max. speed 115 mph (185 km/h); climb to 3,380 ft (1000 m) in 2 minutes 54 seconds; service ceiling 20,013 ft (6100 m); endurance 1 hour 30 minutes
Armament: two synchronised 0.31-in (7.92 mm) LMG 08/15 machine-guns

Fokker D.VII

The fighter competition for single-seat scouts held at Aldershof, Germany, in January 1918 saw Fokker's VII design the clear winner among the prototypes presented for evaluation by front-line pilots. Von Richthofen in particular was a big fan and urged its production, which was ordered immediately.

Like the Dr.I, the **D.VII** was built quickly using existing components (in this case the fuselage of the Dr.I) by Fokker, who would have preferred to develop new monoplanes. The actual design was mainly the work of the modest Reinhold Platz and the D.VII was first flown by Anthony Fokker in December 1917.

The D.VII featured cantilever wings without dihedral or anhedral and had no wire bracing. The straight wing appearance was an important recognition feature for Allied pilots. The powerplant was a six-cylinder water-cooled Mercedes with a car-type radiator. The small rudder was given a fixed tail fin for stability as on the Dr.I. Baron von Richthofen flew the first D.VII and made suggestions (mainly that the fuselage be lengthened) but was killed in his Dr.I before the new Fokker was fully operational with JG 1. The D.VII's real combat debut came at the end of May 1918 when it stunned the Allies with its speed and manoeuvrability.

Despite a tendency for its ammunition to explode (cured by better ventilation) and being slightly underpowered (cured by a 185-hp (138-kW) BMW engine), the D.VII was an instant success with the Jasta pilots. Among the aces to score highly on the

The Fokker D.VII was of advanced construction for its day with a steel tube frame and external rather than internal wire bracing. (TRH Pictures)

D.VII was Ernst Udet, the second-ranking German ace, and the D.VII is widely regarded as the best all-round fighter of World War I. Particularly praised was its high-altitude ability.

Production struggled to keep up with demand. Much to its chagrin, Albatros, Fokker's great rival, was ordered to turn over two plants to D.VII production and pay Fokker a royalty for the privilege. Albatros turned out 1,749 D.VIIs by the war's end and Fokker itself built 877. When the war ended, 775 D.VIIs were in use with the German Air Service. An article of the Armistice Agreement dealing with equipment to be handed to the Allies stipulated 'especially all first-line D.VII aircraft'.

The D.VII was in great demand for evaluation and even service use after the Armistice. Some went to the Netherlands, Soviet Union and Switzerland, while over 120 were shipped to the US, some being tested with a variety of engines. Some production carried on in the Netherlands post war, and the type was used in the East Indies into the 1920s.

Hermann Goering was more famous for his role in WWII German aviation, but he was a 22-victory ace in WWI. This was his D.VII. (Philip Jarrett collection)

Specification: Fokker D.VII
Type: single-seat biplane fighter
Powerplant: one 160-hp (119.4-kW) Mercedes D-III 6-cylinder inline piston
Dimensions: span 29 ft 2.3 in (8.90 m); length 22 ft 9.75 in (6.95 m); height 9 ft 0 in (2.75 m); wing area 217.44 sq ft (20.20 m²)
Weights: empty 1,508 lb (684 kg); loaded 2,006 lb (910 kg)
Performance: max. speed 115 mph (185 km/h); climb to 3,280 ft (1000 m) in 5 minutes 48 seconds; service ceiling 18,000 ft (5486 m); endurance 1 hour 30 minutes
Armament: two synchronised 0.31-in (7.92 mm) LMG 08/15 machine-guns

Curtiss Hawk biplanes

The progenitor of the famous Curtiss Hawk series was the **XPW-8** inline-engined (W stood for water-cooled) biplane fighter of 1923, itself inspired by earlier racing planes. Three prototypes were followed by a US Army Air Corps (USAAC) order for 25 **PW-8**s, which were delivered in 1924. One made the first dawn-to-dusk transcontinental US flight (with four stops) on 23 June 1924. The engine was a Curtiss D-12 (V-1150) V-12 and armament was two 0.30-in (7.62-mm) machine-guns, which fired through the propeller arc. The next order was for the **PW-8B** with a tunnel radiator and tapered wings, which entered service as the **P-1 Hawk**. The last five P-1s had the V-1400 engine and were designated the **P-2**. This was not a very satisfactory engine and the subsequent **P-1A** reverted to the D-12C and had some minor improvements. Deliveries totalled 23 new P-1As plus the P-2s that were converted back. The **P-12B** was ordered in August 1926 and had some shape revisions and the 435-hp (325-kW) D-12D engine. The **P-1C** was delivered from April 1929 and featured wheel brakes and the D-12E engine. The last P-1s were retired by the 17th Pursuit Squadron in 1930. A few P-1s were sold to Chile and a single example to Japan in 1927.

The P-1 was the production version of the XPW-8B. The 10 built were the first US fighters designated under the simpler P for Pursuit designation. (TRH Pictures)

The P-6E was the definitive Air Corps version of the Curtiss Hawk biplane series. This example served with the 17th Pursuit Squadron. (TRH Pictures)

The US Navy bought examples of the P-1 as the **F6C-1** (five, with floats and/or wheels) and the **F6C-2** (four, with tailhook). The Navy bought another 33 P-1As in 1927 as the **F6C-3**. There were 33 new **F6C-4**s that had the US Navy's favoured R-1340 Wasp engine, which made this version of the Hawk lighter and more manoeuvrable. They served with one squadron on the USS *Langley* until 1930 and with the US Marine Corps (USMC).

There were also a number of experimental versions with different engines and optimised for racing, at which the Army and Navy competed in the 20s and 30s. The new Curtiss Conqueror engine of 600-hp (448-kW) output was installed on a P-1, P-1A and P-2 in 1927 for racing and record purposes. This led to the **P-6** and **P-6A** service versions. Nine **P-6D**s were built with turbo superchargers and glycol cooling.

The definitive **P-6E** model was created by merging the related YP-20 and Y1P-22 test aircraft. The P-6E was more streamlined and faster than previous Hawks. Forty-five P-6Es were built and they served with the USAAC from 1932 to 1937. Eight P-6s went to the Netherlands East Indies and again one was sold to Japan (as the **Hawk I**). The last P-6E was completed as the **XP-23** with a metal fuselage and was the last biplane fighter ordered by the USAAC.

Specification: Curtiss P-6E Hawk
Type: single-seat biplane fighter
Powerplant: one 700-hp (522-kW) Curtiss V-1570C Conqueror V-12 piston
Dimensions: span 31 ft 6 in (9.60 m); length 25 ft 2 in (7.67 m); height 8 ft 7 in (2.62 m); wing area 252 sq ft (23.41 m²)
Weights: empty 2,699 lb (1224 kg); loaded 3,172 lb (1439 kg)
Performance: max. speed 193 mph (311 km/h); initial climb rate 2,480 ft (756 m) per minute; service ceiling 23,900 ft (7285 m); range 244 miles (393 km)
Armament: two 0.30-in (7.62-mm) machine-guns in wings

Bristol Bulldog

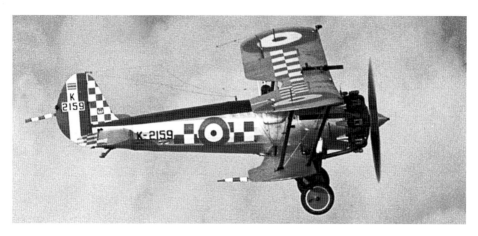

The classic **Bristol Bulldog** fighter began as a private venture and, like the Bristol F.2 Fighter, was designed by Frank Barnwell. A conventional sesquiplane, the Bulldog's structure was high-tensile steel strip covered by fabric. The prototype first flew on 17 May 1927 with a 440-hp (330-kW) Bristol Jupiter VII engine and was evaluated alongside the official contenders for the F.9/26 specification. Found to be superior to all but the Hawker Hawfinch, an example was ordered by the Air Ministry for a 'fly-off' evaluation. This was built as the **Type 105A Bulldog II** with a longer fuselage and a new fin.

The Bulldog II defeated the Hawfinch for an order for 25 production aircraft in August 1928. This was followed by a contract for 92 **Bulldog IIAs** with Jupiter VIIF engines. The armament was two 0.303-in (7.7-mm) machine-guns mounted on the fuselage sides. In all, 92 Mk IIs and 268 Mk IIAs were delivered to the RAF. Although the Bulldog was slower than the Hart light bomber, at £4,600 it was cheaper than the £5,400 Hawker Fury and so was bought in greater numbers.

Although possessing better handling than its predecessor the Sopwith Snipe, the Bulldog was not much faster, did not possess better climbing abilities and its armament was the same. However, the Bulldog did introduce a radio and oxygen supply for the first time in an RAF fighter. Owing to the conservative approach of the Air Ministry, which

A Bulldog IIA in the colourful blue and white chequered markings of No. 19 Squadron. Based at Duxford, No. 19 flew Bulldogs from 1931 to 1935. (The Aviation Picture Library)

issued over-cautious specifications, British fighter development progressed little in the 1920s.

The Bulldog entered service with No. 3 Squadron RAF in June 1929 and equipped ten front-line squadrons by 1932, forming the bulk of the RAF's fighter force. In 1937 the last Bulldogs were phased out, replaced by Gauntlets and Gladiators, and soon afterwards, Hurricanes and Spitfires.

Bristol had reasonable export success with the Bulldog II, selling small numbers to Latvia, Estonia, Sweden, Siam, Australia and Denmark. Two Bristols were evaluated by the US Navy. The **Bulldog IIIA** was powered by the 560-hp (417.6-kW) Bristol Mercury and had a deeper wing section, which contained the fuel tanks. Only two were built, but they led to the **Bulldog IVF** with a 645-hp (481-kW) Mercury VIS.2 in a long-chord cowl.

The Finns received 17 **Bulldog IVAs** and two ex-Swedish IIAs. These aircraft, armed with two Vickers Mk II guns, served in the front line until the spring of 1940 and thereafter in the advanced training role.

A production Bulldog IIA shows off its Jupiter engine and large fixed-pitch propeller. The two guns fired between the cylinder heads. (TRH Pictures)

Specification: Bulldog Mk IIA
Type: single-seat biplane fighter
Powerplant: one 440-hp (330-kW) Bristol Jupiter VIIF radial piston
Dimensions: span 33 ft 10 in (10.31 m); length 25 ft 0 in (7.62 m); height 9 ft 10 in (2.99 m); wing area 306.5 sq ft (28.47 m²)
Weights: empty 2,412 lb (1094 kg); loaded 3,530 lb (1601 kg)
Performance: max. speed 174 mph (280 km/h); climb to 20,000 ft (6096 m) in 14.5 minutes; service ceiling 29,300 ft (8930 m); range 350 miles (563 km/h)
Armament: two 0.303-in (7.7-mm) machine-guns

Boeing F4B/P-12

In 1928, Boeing built two privately funded fighter prototypes, the Model 83 and the Model 89, which were essentially the same but for their undercarriages, the former having a spreader bar between the wheels. Both were entirely conventional fabric-covered biplanes powered by the proven Pratt & Whitney Wasp radial. Their success lay in the use of slight refinements in materials and aerodynamics that eked the last bit of performance out of the available horsepower. Notable was the increased use of a lightweight aluminium structure rather than welded steel. Armament was the standard for the time – namely two 0.30-in (7.62-mm) machine-guns (with an alternative of one 0.50-in (12.7-mm) and one 0.30-in (7.62-mm) machine-gun) which were mounted in troughs in front of the cockpit. The propeller was variable pitch, but only adjustable on the ground.

The Models 83 and 89 were tested by the US Navy under the designation XF4B-1. The Navy soon ordered 27 **F4B-1** fighters (Boeing Model 99) and the US Army ordered ten as the **P-12** (Model 102). Both models were similar except for the arrester hook on the Navy version. The XP-12A led to the **P-12B** (90 ordered) with improved ailerons, a shorter undercarriage and bigger wheels. It was slightly heavier and had a slightly lower

The P-12C was the Air Corps equivalent of the Navy's F4B-2. Appearing in 1931, it was of fabric-covered duralumin tube structure. (Philip Jarrett collection)

The F4B-3 was the first of Boeing's biplanes to have a metal fuselage structure. It was used by the US Navy and Marines and Brazil. (Philip Jarrett collection)

performance. The Army ordered 131 of the slightly revised **P-12C** and the Navy took 44 similar **F4B-2**s. Both versions had ring cowlings, previous models having streamlined cylinder 'hats'. The **P-12D** had few differences other than to the ignition system but the **P-12E** had many changes, most notably a new semi-monocoque metal fuselage and a new tail with rounder tips. The **F4B-3** and **F4B-4** (with a larger fin and rudder) were the naval equivalents. Despite their similar external appearance, the P-12E and F4B-3/4 had different internal structure and instrumentation. The F4B-3 entered service in December 1931 and the -4 in July 1932. Twenty-three of the latter were exported to Brazil. The US Air Corps took delivery of 110 P-12Es and 25 **P-12F**s with the SR-1340E engine, which performed better at altitude. The last P-12F had an enclosed canopy.

The P-12 was the most numerically important of the US Air Corps' interwar fighters and served with front-line units until 1935 in the US, Hawaii and Panama. A number of P-12Es were given to the Navy in 1942 for use as **F4B-4A** target drones.

The Navy's own F4B-3s and F4B-4s served on the carriers USS *Langley* and *Saratoga* from 1931 until 1937. The Marines received 21 F4B-4s. In total, 546 of the P-12/F4B series were built.

Specification: Boeing P-12E
Type: single-seat biplane fighter
Powerplant: one 525-hp (391.7-kW) Pratt & Whitney R-1340-17 Wasp 9-cylinder radial engine
Dimensions: span 30 ft 0 in (9.14 m); length 20 ft 3 in (6.17 m); height 9 ft 0 in (2.74 m); wing area 227.5 sq ft (21.13 m²)
Weights: empty 1,999 lb (907 kg); loaded 2,690 lb (1220 kg)
Performance: max. speed 189 mph (304 km/h); climb to 10,000 ft (3050 m) in 5 minutes 48 seconds; service ceiling 31,400 ft (9571 m); range 585 miles (941 km)
Armament: two fixed 0.30-in (7.62-mm) Browning machine-guns

Hawker biplane fighters

The **Hawker Fury** fighter was one of a number of successful aircraft to stem from the Hart bomber of 1928, all based around the Rolls-Royce Kestrel V-12 engine. The Hart and its bomber and trainer derivatives could outperform most of the RAF's fighters of the day and so Hawker developed a single-seat fighter of the same basic configuration in competition with the similar-looking Fairey Firefly IIM. The prototype was flown in March 1929 and selected in 1930 as the Fury. Despite its looks, the Fury was smaller and structurally different to its progenitors. Of mixed metal, wood and fabric construction, the Fury had a tightly cowled engine with a radiator slung between the undercarriage legs.

The Fury was the RAF's first dedicated interceptor fighter. The Bristol Bulldog and other fighters were intended for long-standing patrols. As such, and due to its £700 greater cost, the Fury only equipped three 'elite' squadrons of the RAF (Nos. 1, 25 and 43). The **Fury Mk I** entered service in May 1931 with No. 43 Squadron at RAF Tangmere.

In order to increase the number of fighter squadrons in the RAF prior to the arrival of the new monoplanes, a batch of 99 Fury **Mk II**s were ordered and delivered in July 1936. These differed in having the more powerful Kestrel VI engine and were issued to Nos. 25, 41, 73 and 87 Squadrons. Like other RAF fighters of the era, the Furies were finished in a 'silver' scheme of polished metal and metallic doped fabric,

The classic Hawker Fury epitomised the RAF in the interwar years. Although sleek and agile, it was basically a refined World War I fighter. (TRH Pictures)

with colourful squadron markings. Those aircraft in service at the time of the Munich Crisis in 1938 were repainted in dark earth and green camouflage. The three remaining Fury squadrons were re-equipped with Hurricanes and Spitfires during 1939.

Small numbers of Furies (I and II) were exported. Recipients included South Africa (7 plus 24 surplus RAF aircraft), Portugal (3), Iran (24), Norway (1) and Spain (3). Yugoslavia received 16, and 40 were built there under licence. Some of these export versions, notably Iran's, had radial engines and other inline engines such as the Hispano-Suiza 12Xbr. The two-seat **Hart Fighter** was bought in small numbers and then adopted as the **Demon**, of which 232 were built from 1933 to 1938.

The related **Nimrod** for the Navy was strengthened to withstand catapult loads and had an arrester hook and flotation gear. The **Nimrod Mk I** had the 525-hp (391.5-kW) Kestrel IIMS and the **Nimrod Mk II** had the 650-hp (484.7-kW) Kestrel V. Forty-two Mk Is and 36 Mk IIs were built, serving until 1939.

The carrier-based Nimrod was substantially different to the Fury although sharing the same basic configuration and Kestrel engine. (The Aviation Picture Library)

Specification: Hawker Fury I
Type: single-seat biplane fighter
Powerplant: one 480-hp (358.1-kW) Rolls-Royce Kestrel IIS V-12 piston
Dimensions: span 30 ft 0 in (9.15 m); length 26 ft 3.75 in (8.00 m); height 9 ft 6 in (2.89 m); wing area 251.8 sq ft (23.40 m²)
Weights: empty 2,623 lb (1190 kg); loaded 3,490 lb (1583 kg)
Performance: max. speed 207 mph (333 km/h); initial climb rate 2,380 ft (725.4 m) per minute; service ceiling 26,999 ft (8230 m); range 305 miles (492 km)
Armament: two 0.303-in (7.7-mm) Vickers machine-guns

PZL P.7a to P.24

Zygmund Pulaski, chief designer of PZL (Panstwowe Zaklady Lotnicze – National Aero Factory) was the designer of a series of gull-wing parasol monoplanes from the P.1 of 1930 to the **P.7a** of 1932. The best of these, and the first to be ordered in numbers was the P.7a, of which 150 were built and which was still serving with three regiments at the time of the German invasion. The P.7 was of duralumin and steel construction with a parasol wing, and had a gull centre-section. This combined lower drag with good forward and upper view. The engine was the 520-hp (384.8-kW) Bristol Jupiter VII.F and the armament consisted of two 0.303-in (7.7-mm) Vickers 'E' machine-guns firing between the cylinders.

The availability of more powerful Bristol Mercury radial engines from Britain spurred the development of the **P.11**, although the prototype actually flew with a Jupiter in August 1931 while PZL awaited Mercury deliveries. Tragedy struck at this time when Pulaski was killed in the crash of the PZL-12H amphibian prototype, but his deputy Wsiewolod Jakimiuk took over development of the P.11. Flown at an international meeting in Istanbul, the P.11 beat the competition and attracted the attention of Romania, who ordered 70, which they built under licence with

In 1939 Poland had 20 squadrons of PZL fighters, mainly P.11a and c models. Although modern when introduced, they were no match for the Bf 109. (The Aviation Picture Library)

A line-up of PZL fighters of 113. Eskadrille at Okecie is headed by a P.11a. This unit was involved in the defence of Warsaw in September 1939. (Philip Jarrett collection)

the 640-hp (477-kW) IAR-K9 engine as the **P.11f** (company designation **P.11b**)

The initial service version was the **P.11a**, of which 50 were ordered for the Lotnictwo Wojskowe (Polish Air Force). The **P.11c** of 1934 had revised engine cowling contours for better visibility, new tail surfaces and provision for wing guns and a radio, neither of which were usually fitted. By 1936, 175 had been delivered with Mercury VS 2 and VS 12 engines.

The P.11c was the most modern fighter in the world when it appeared. When war broke out in September 1939 the P.11c equipped 12 squadrons of the Polish Air Force and fought against superior numbers of more modern German aircraft without the help of any early warning system and amidst a general breakdown of order. Despite all this, the P.11 pilots were credited with the destruction of 126 enemy aircraft against the loss of 114 of their own.

The **P.24** was a development of the P.11 with the ability to take a range of more powerful engines, such as the 900-hp (671-kW) IAR-K14-II, which was used on the **P.24E** for Romania. Other export versions were the **P.24F** for Turkey and the **P.24G** for Greece with the 970-hp (723-kW) Gnome-Le Rhône 14N. None were ordered by Poland itself.

Specification: PZL P.11c
Type: single-seat parasol wing fighter
Powerplant: one 645-hp (481-kW) PZL Mercury 9-cylinder radial piston
Dimensions: span 35 ft 2 in (10.72 m); length 24 ft 9 in (7.55 m); height 9 ft 4 in (2.85 m); wing area 192.7 sq ft (17.90 m²)
Weights: empty 2,524 lb (1145 kg); loaded 3,960 lb (1795 kg)
Performance: max. speed 242 mph (390 km/h); initial climb rate 2,625ft (800 m) per minute; service ceiling 36,090 ft (11000 m); range 503 miles (810 km)
Armament: four 0.303-in (7.7-mm) KM Wz 33 machine-guns; up to two 27-lb (12.25-kg) bombs

Grumman FF to F3F

Leroy Grumman's company initially built floats for US Navy amphibians and won its first aircraft contract in 1931 with the prototype of a two-seat fighter designated the **XFF-1**. It was unusual in that it featured an enclosed canopy and was the first US Navy fighter with a retractable undercarriage, which was housed in the lower fuselage. It was first flown in late 1931, and the Navy ordered 27 as the **FF-1** (Grumman model G-5). They served from 1933 to 1936 with VF-5B aboard the USS *Lexington*. The engine was the 700-hp (522.2-kW) Wright R-1820-78 Cyclone and armament consisted of one fixed and two flexible 0.30-in (7.62-mm) machine-guns. The Canadian Car and Foundry Company built 57 as the **Goblin I** for the RCAF (15), Nicaragua and Japan (one each) and Turkey (40, later given to the Spanish Republicans).

Impressed by the FF, the US Navy ordered a single-seat version as the **F2F** in November 1932. This was very similar apart from the cockpit, larger cowl and Pratt & Whitney R-1535-72 engine. The armament was two 0.30-in (7.62-mm) guns mounted on the forward fuselage. The **F2F-1** (G-8) flew on 18 October 1933 and had a metal fuselage and fabric-covered wings. Fifty-five F2F-1s were ordered for service aboard the USS *Lexington* and USS *Ranger*. The first were delivered in early 1935 and they served until September 1940.

The last F2F-1 was completed with longer wings and a longer fuselage, as the XF3F-1 in May 1935,

This rare contemporary colour view of an F3F-2 of Fighting Squadron Three (VF-3B) shows well the rotund appearance and retracted undercarriage of the type. (TRH Pictures)

improving the stability of the design. The production **F3F-1**, of which 54 were built, had the 650-hp (484.7-kW) R-1535-84 Twin Wasp engine and served aboard the USS *Saratoga* and USS *Ranger*.

The **F3F-2** (G-37) reverted to Wright power in the form of the 950-hp (708.7-kW) R-1820-22 engine, which necessitated a large cowl without the characteristic dimples of the Pratt & Whitney-powered F3Fs. The US Marine Corps was the main user of the 81 F3F-2s built, and others served as part of the *Enterprise* air group.

The final version of the 'Flying Barrel' was the **F3F-3**, of which 27 were built. They served mainly on the USS *Yorktown*. They finaly left front-line service with the Marine Corps in October 1941. The Grumman biplane fighters were an important stepping stone between the biplanes of the World War I era and the all-metal, retractable landing gear monoplanes of World War II.

This F2F-1 of VF-2 shows its shorter fuselage and wingspan compared to the later F3F. The undercarriage design was used on the F3F and F4F Wildcat. (The Aviation Picture Library)

Specification: Grumman F3F-3
Type: single-seat carrier-based biplane fighter
Powerplant: one 950-hp (708.7-kW) Wright R-1820-22 radial piston
Dimensions: span 32 ft 0 in (9.75 m); length 23 ft 2 in (7.04 m); height 9 ft 4 in (2.84 m); wing area 260.6 sq m (24.21 m²)
Weights: empty 3,285 lb (1490 kg); loaded 4,795 lb (2175 kg)
Performance: max. speed 256 mph (412 km/h); initial climb rate 2,750 ft (838 m) per minute; service ceiling 33,200 ft (10119 m); range 980 miles (1577 km)
Armament: two fixed 0.30-in (7.62-mm) machine-guns

Boeing P-26 'Peashooter'

The **Boeing P-26** arose out of a US Army Air Corps (USAAC) requirement for a monoplane fighter that would be faster than contemporary bombers. Boeing built three prototypes with its own money and retained ownership of the airframes while the government supplied and owned the engines and instruments.

The first **XP-936** (the government designation for this privately owned pursuit aircraft) flew on 20 March 1932. After evaluation, the Army bought the three prototypes as the **XP-26** and ordered 111 (later increased to 136) of an improved version as the **P-26A** (Model 266), which first flew on 10 January 1934.

The P-26 was an all-metal low-wing monoplane, the first to enter US service. Nonetheless it still had at least one foot in the past with its externally braced wing, fixed, spatted undercarriage and open cockpit. The engine was the tried and tested Pratt & Whitney Wasp with a Townend ring-type cowl. The propeller was a two-bladed variable pitch Hamilton Standard. Armament was two machine-guns mounted on the cockpit floor, firing between the engine cylinders.

The P-26A entered service with the USAAC in early 1934 and was issued to 17 pursuit squadrons in the US and Hawaii. Some were later transferred to the

Guatemala used a few P-26As as trainers as late as 1957. This one was recovered for display and restored by the Planes of Fame Museum at Chino. (Author)

The Boeing P-26 was the last production fighter designed and built by Boeing. It combined a modern monoplane layout with many biplane features. (Philip Jarrett collection)

(Panama) Canal Zone and the Philippines. The P-26 was regarded as something of a 'hot ship', although it was slower than the Martin B-10 bomber and had a lower ceiling than contemporary biplane fighters. The 'Peashooter', as it was unofficially known, was usually painted in bright blue with yellow wings and colourful unit markings. A prominent feature was the solid headrest, which was enlarged during production to provide better rollover protection for the pilot.

The last two P-26As were built as **P-26B**s with fuel-injected engines and wing flaps. The **P-26C** was basically the same as the P-26A owing to a shortage of the fuel-injected engines. Twenty-three were built and most were later converted to P-26Bs with the SR-1230-33 engine. In order to lower the 'high' landing speed of 73 mph (117 km/h), wing flaps were fitted during P-26B/C production and retrofitted to P-26As in service.

The P-26 was gone from regular squadron service by 7 December 1941, but a few were destroyed on the ground at Pearl Harbor. A few were in service with the Philippine Army Air Force and had some successes against more modern Japanese aircraft. The last P-26As in the Canal Zone were transferred to Guatemala in May 1943 and a few remained in use as trainers there as late as 1957.

Specification: Boeing P-26A
Type: single-seat monoplane fighter
Powerplant: one 600-hp (447-kW) P&W R-1340-27 Wasp 9-cylinder radial piston
Dimensions: span 27 ft 11.6 in (8.52 m); length 23 ft 7.25 in (7.19 m); height 10 ft 5 in (3.17 m); wing area 149.5 sq ft (13.89 m²)
Weights: empty 2,194 lb (995 kg); loaded 2,935 lb (1331 kg)
Performance: max. speed 211 mph (339 km/h); initial climb 2,360 ft (719 m) per minute; service ceiling 27,400 ft (8351 m); range 635 miles (1022 km)
Armament: one 0.50-in (12.7-mm) and one 0.30-in (7.62-mm) or two 0.30-in (7.62-mm) machine-guns, up to 200 lb (91 kg) bombs

Fiat CR.30 to CR.42 Falco

Like Polikarpov in the Soviet Union, Celestino Rosatelli of Italy was a strong believer in biplanes until well after their day had passed. As chief designer of Fiat Aeronautica, Rosatelli produced a series of agile biplanes for Mussolini's air force. Following the **CR.30** of 1932, he designed the similar **CR.32** which first flew on 28 April 1933. CR stood for Caccia (fighter) and Rosatelli after the designer. Entering service in March 1934, the CR.32 soon equipped three Stormi of the Regia Aeronautica, one of which was known for its spectacular formation aerobatic displays. The CR.32 had a 600-hp (447-kW) Fiat A.30 V-12 engine and was armed with two 0.303 (7.7-mm) SAFAT machine-guns in the forward fuselage. The improved **CR.32bis** also had 0.303 (7.7-mm) machine-guns in the wings. A number of these went to the Luftwaffe and then to Hungary. A total of 1,309 CR.32s were built, some of them licence-produced in Spain, where they were heavily used by the Nationalists. A few were exported to Paraguay and Venezuela. By the outbreak of World War II, there were 294 still in Italian service, mostly in North Africa, where they were reasonably effective. Before long, however, most CR.32s were relegated to night harassment duties.

Despite the obsolescence of the biplane, Fiat's follow up to the CR.32 was the **CR.42 Falco**, which was to be the last biplane fighter in production anywhere. The prototype first flew on 23 May 1938. As with Polikarpov's I-153 and I-16 fighters, the

The Fiat CR.30 had a distinctive chin radiator for its inline engine and a long exhaust pipe. It was followed by the similar CR.32. (The Aviation Picture Library)

company's last biplane (CR.42) came later than the company's first monoplane (G.50). Armament was two synchronised 0.50-in (12.7-mm) machine-guns. The **CR.42CN** night-fighter had underwing searchlights powered by a propeller-driven generator.

Production ended in 1943 with over 1,780 built, the highest number of any Italian fighter. Widely regarded as the peak of biplane development, the Falco served with several air forces, including that of Belgium who acquired them in 1939, and used them against Germany the following year. Sweden operated 72, some as target tugs. The Luftwaffe used over 100, mainly for night harassment.

The Regia Aeronautica itself used the CR.42 in its brief involvement in the Battle of Britain in late 1940 and against Malta from July 1940, where they fought against RAF Gladiators. There were several variants – the **CR.42CB** fighter-bomber, the **CR.42LW** night-attacker and the **CR.42AS**, with sand filters and bomb racks for desert fighting.

The Fiat CR.42 Falco was the last and one of the best biplane fighters ever produced. Some were exported. This is a Swedish example. (TRH Pictures)

Specification: Fiat CR.42
Type: single-seat biplane fighter
Powerplant: one 840-hp (626-kW) Fiat A74R 1C 14-cylinder radial piston
Dimensions: span 31 ft 10 in (9.70 m); length 27 ft 1.5 in (8.27 m); height 11 ft 9.5 in (3.59 m); wing area 241.12 sq ft (22.40 m²)
Weights: empty 3,765 lb (1708 lb); loaded 5,033 lb (2283 kg)
Performance: max. speed 267 mph (430 km/h); climb to 19,685 ft (6000 m) in 8 minutes 40 seconds; service ceiling 33,465 ft (10200 m); range 482 miles (775 km)
Armament: two 0.50-in (12.7-mm) SAFAT machine-guns

Polikarpov I-16

The **Polikarpov I-16** is unique in the annals of fighter aviation in that it was designed and built by prison inmates. Dimitri Grigorovich and Nikolai Polikarpov had designed the PO-2 biplane but by 1929 had not come up with the modern fighter Stalin had ordered in 1927, and were sent to prison 39 near Moscow. There they worked on a design for a monoplane fighter with an open cockpit and retractable undercarriage. The resulting Polikarpov I-16 first flew on 31 December 1933 with a 480-hp (358.1-kW) M-22 engine and combined a laminated wooden fuselage and fabric-covered metal wings and tail surfaces. The pre-series **I-16 Type 1** was followed by the **Type 4** with a longer-chord cowl. The **I-16 Type 5** introduced the licence-built 700-hp (522-kW) M-25 (Wright Cyclone) engine and had two 0.30-in (7.62-mm) machine-guns in the wings.

About 475 Type 5s were supplied to the Spanish Republicans and they proved successful against biplane opposition in the Spanish Civil War, where they gained the nickname *Rata* (rat). Other nicknames included *Mosca* (fly) and *Ishak* (little donkey). A small number of **Type 10**s were built in Spain. China received many I-16s and by 1939 they were used in action against the Japanese.

The I-16 was the most modern fighter of its day. This one fell into the hands of the Spanish Nationalists. Note the telescopic gun sight. (Philip Jarrett collection)

An I-16 Type 24 sporting a patriotic slogan. This version had two cannon in the wings and two machine-guns in the cowling. (D.I. Windle)

The **Type 12** and the **Type 17** had a pair of 20-mm ShVAK cannon in the wings and 750-hp (559.5-kW) M-25V engines. By 1939 the I-16 was becoming heavier and more power was needed. This came in the form of the 800-hp (596.8-kW) Shvetsov M-62 on the **Type 18** with four machine-guns and the 930-hp (693.8-kW) M-63 on the **Type 24**. The Type 24 had two 20-mm cannon in the wings and the **Type 27** had one 0.50-in (12.7-mm) machine-gun in the cowl and two 0.30-in (7.62-mm) machine-guns in the wings as well as the capability for underwing rockets.

The Soviet Air Force (VVS) fighter arm was largely equipped with I-16s and I-153 biplanes at the outbreak of the German–Soviet war in 1941. Several thousand aircraft were lost in the opening days and weeks of the German invasion but significant numbers of I-16s remained in service until 1943. The sturdy and manoeuvrable I-16 had two unusual roles, in (officially discouraged) ramming or *Taran* attacks and as a parasite fighter as part of the *Zveno* combination with the Tupolev TB-3 bomber.

Some 1,640 two-seat trainers, the **Type 4 UTI** and the **Type 15 UTI**, were built. A few I-16s remained in service as trainers in Spain until the 1950s.

Specification: I-16 Type 24
Type: single-seat monoplane fighter
Powerplant: one 930-hp (693.8-kW) Shvetsov 9-cylinder M-63 radial piston
Dimensions: span 29 ft 2 in (8.88 m); length 20 ft 1.3 in (6.1 m); height 7 ft 9.75 in (2.41 m); wing area 160.06 sq ft (14.87 m²)
Weights: empty 3,252 lb (1476 kg); loaded 4,215 lb (1912 kg)
Performance: max. speed 304 mph (489 km/h); climb to 16,405 ft (5000 m) in 5.8 minutes; service ceiling 29,500 ft (8998 m); range 500 miles (805 km);
Armament: four 0.30-in (7.62-mm) machine-guns

Arado 68

An Ar 68F of the 'Flying Group Doeberitz', a front title for a fighter unit that was in reality JG 132 'Richthofen', seen in 1935. Ar 68s were built until 1936. (Aerospace Publishing)

The Treaty of Versailles prevented the development and operation of combat aircraft in Germany after 1919, but German aircraft designers were not idle, creating a number of sport or touring planes that served to develop technology for future warplanes.

Arado's Walter Rethel designed a series of biplane trainers beginning with the SSD I floatplane of 1930. Twenty Ar 64 fighters were issued to training units and were succeeded by the Ar 65, of which 85 were produced. A dozen were given to Bulgaria.

In 1933–4 Rethel designed two prototypes, the Ar 67 with a 640-hp (479-kW) Rolls-Royce Kestrel and the **Ar 68** with a 750-hp (562-kW) BMW VId. The latter was chosen and flown as the **Ar 68A** in the late summer of 1934. Subsequent prototypes were the Jumo 210–powered **Ar 68B** on floats and the **Ar 68C** with a 240-hp (179-kW) Argus As 10c inverted V-8. The Ar 68 was a sesquiplane with forward stagger to the top wing, a structure of welded steel tubing with metal skinning around the nose and along the fuselage spine. The tail was all metal but the rest was fabric-covered. The lower wing had full-span metal landing flaps. The armament was two MG 17 machine-guns mounted along the top of the cowl. The first production version was the **Ar 68F-1**, which entered service in 1936 with I/JG 134.

The Ar 68 was just beaten by the Heinkel He 51 to be the first fighter of the rebuilt Luftwaffe. The two fighters had almost identical performance on paper but the Arado was much easier to fly and suffered fewer accidents in training. Ernst Udet flew an Ar 68F in trials against a Heinkel flown by one of the Luftwaffe's best pilots and outfought it time after time. Arado production was soon increased and the Jumo 210Ea supercharged inverted V-12 engine of 690-hp (515-kW) was made available, resulting in the Ar 68E. The Ar 68E had much better altitude performance than the Ar 68F.

The **Ar 68E** was the most numerous Luftwaffe fighter by 1938 when the Bf 109 became dominant. It was mainly used as a night-fighter and developed some of the tactics that would be used in the war, although there was no radar or radio control. Three Ar 68Es were sent to Spain for combat evaluation and used as night-fighters, flying mainly twilight patrols without success, and they were then used on day ground-attack missions.

In 1940 the Ar 68 left front-line service and was relegated to the training role, and was occasionally encountered by Allied fighters through the war.

The Arado 68F was the first production version. Under the guise of sport aviation, the Nazis built the core of the Luftwaffe in the mid-1930s. (Philip Jarrett collection)

Specification: Arado Ar 68E-1
Type: single-seat biplane fighter
Powerplant: one 690-hp (515-kW) Junkers Jumo 210Da piston
Dimensions: span 36 ft 0 in (11.0 m); length 31 ft 2 in (9.5 m); height 10 ft 10 in (3.3 m); wing area 293.86 sq ft (27.30 m²)
Weights: empty 4,057 lb (1840 kg); loaded 5,457 lb (2475 kg)
Performance: max. speed 192 mph (310 km/h); initial climb 2,480 ft (756 m) per minute; service ceiling 24,280 ft (7400 m); range 342 miles (550 km)
Armament: two 7.9-mm MG 17 machine-guns above engines and up to six 110-lb (50-kg) bombs

Gloster Gladiator

United Kingdom
September 1934

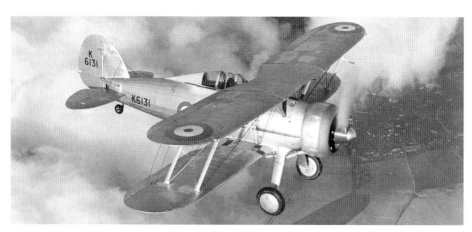

The **Gloster Gladiator** was designed by H.P. Folland as a private venture to improve on the performance of the Gauntlet. The **SS.37**, as the prototype was known, first flew in September 1934 and was offered to meet an Air Ministry specification calling for an interim biplane fighter to equip RAF squadrons until the new monoplane fighters then on the drawing board became available. The design was ordered as the **Gladiator Mk I** in July 1935, and first flew in June 1936. The Gladiator was an attractive radial-engined biplane with an enclosed, sliding canopy, hydraulic landing flaps and was armed with four guns, two in the fuselage and two under the wings. The structure was metal and wood with fabric and metal covering. Early examples had a two-bladed wooden Watts propeller, but later aircraft had a three-bladed metal Fairey-Reed propeller. A total of 378 Mk Is were built and they equipped a dozen home defence squadrons of the RAF.

The **Gladiator Mk II** was built for use in North Africa with electric starting, a desert survival kit and a sand filter. The engine was the 830-hp (619 kW) Mercury VIIIA. Mk II production totalled 270.

The first 38 **Sea Gladiators** for the Fleet Air Arm (FAA) were basically Mk IIs with naval equipment and an arrester hook. These were followed by 60 **Sea**

Finland's own ex-RAF Gladiators flew against the Soviet Union alongside the J8s of Swedish volunteer unit F19. One of the former is shown here. (TRH Pictures)

Although of obsolescent biplane configuration, the Gladiator introduced modern features such as flaps and a radio. This is the third production Mk I. (TRH Pictures)

Gladiator Mk Is with more fuel capacity and catapult equipment. Sea Gladiators had a small role in the Battle of Britain, flew from frozen lakes in the Norwegian campaign and were briefly the only air defence for the strategic island of Malta.

The Gladiator was widely exported before the war. Export models were designated by customer, such as **Gladiator (China)**, of which 36 were delivered in 1938. Other customers included Belgium (22), Ireland (4), Greece (2 plus 17 later transferred from the RAF), Latvia (26), Lithuania (14), Norway (12), Portugal (15) and Sweden (55). Although Sweden was neutral, a unit of volunteer pilots equipped with Gladiators and Harts (F19) fought with the Finnish Air Force against the Soviet Union in 1939–40. Others supplied from RAF stocks included 30 for Finland, 45 for Egypt, 14 for Iraq and 12 for South Africa. No. 3 Squadron, RAAF was equipped with Gladiators in the Western Desert, claiming over 20 Italian aircraft for three combat losses in late 1940 to early 1941.

As the last RAF biplane fighter, the Gladiator was obsolescent when delivered, but in secondary theatres was manoeuvrable and well-armed enough to provide effective fighter defence where it was needed.

Specification: Gloster Gladiator Mk I
Type: single-seat biplane fighter
Powerplant: one 840-hp (626-kW) Bristol Mercury IX 9-cylinder radial piston
Dimensions: span 32 ft 3 in (9.85 m); length 27 ft 5 in (8.38 m); height 10 ft 4 in (3.17 m); wing area; 323 sq ft (30.01 m²)
Weights: empty 3,450 lb (1565 kg); loaded 4,750 lb (2155 kg)
Performance: max. speed 253 mph (407 km/h); climb to 15,000 ft (4572 m) in 5 minutes 40 seconds; service ceiling 33,000 ft (10060 m); range 440 miles (708 km)
Armament: initially two 0.303-in (7.7-mm) Vickers and two 0. 303-in Lewis machine-guns, later four 0.303-in Browning guns

Mitsubishi A5M 'Claude'

T he Imperial Japanese Navy's (IJN) 1934 specification for a new single-seat fighter was met by a design by Mitsubishi's Jiro Horikoshi and colleagues. Compared with previous Japanese carrier aircraft, which were all biplanes, the **Mitsubishi Ka-14** prototype was a radical design, being an all-metal monoplane with an inverted gull wing. The pilot sat in an open cockpit with good vision behind the 550-hp (410-kW) Nakajima Kotobuki (Congratulation) 5 engine, which was a licence-produced development of the Bristol Jupiter. The prototype first flew on 4 February 1935 and was generally a success, although the gull wing was problematic, and was abandoned for the second prototype and subsequent aircraft. With a more powerful 585-hp (436-kW) Kotobuki engine, the Ka-14 was ordered by the IJN as the **A5M1** or Navy Type 96 Carrier Fighter Model 1. The army tested the A5M as the Ki-18, but regarded it as not manoeuvrable enough. Nonetheless, it was the first Japanese warplane with flush riveting and full-span flaps, and was faster and better climbing than the biplanes then in service. With a ventral auxiliary fuel tank, the range of the A5M increased from a creditable 460 miles (740 km) to an extraordinary 746 miles (1200 km). The **A5M-1a** had two 20-mm Oerlikon FF cannon but was not widely adopted.

Entering service in 1938, the **A5M2** was the IJN's chief fighter during the Sino-Japanese War, flying from both carriers and land bases. In one celebrated

The A5M2 was Japan's main carrier-based fighter by 1939, at the same time that the US and Royal navies were still equipped with biplanes. (TRH Pictures)

incident, a flight of A5Ms destroyed ten Soviet biplanes for no loss. The top IJN ace of World War II, Tetsuzo Iwamoto, scored the first 14 of his 80 kills at this time. The A5M equipped the air groups of the Akagi, Hosho, Kaga, Ryujo and Zuihu. The A5M2a had a 610-hp (455-kW) Kotobuki and an enclosed cockpit. The **A5M3** was an experimental version with a 610-hp (455-kW) Hispano-Suiza 12Xcrs engine as used on the French Dewoitine D.510. Only two were built. The last production version was the **A5M4** with a 710-hp (529-kW) Kotobuki 41. The **A5M4-K** was a two-seat trainer version, of which 103 were built.

By December 1941 the A5M4, which the Allies designated 'Claude', was the main naval fighter, despite the increasing number of A6M 'Zeros' in service. This was the swan song of its career, however, and it was no match for faster, more modern Allied fighters. Those still in service of the 1,094 produced by late 1944 were mostly expended in *kamikaze* attacks around Japan.

In 1939 the fighter squadrons aboard Japan's carriers were mainly equipped with A5M4s such as these seen aboard Soryu. (Aerospace Publishing)

Specification: Mitsubishi A5M4
Type: single-seat carrier-based monoplane fighter
Powerplant: one 710-hp (529-kW) Nakajima Kotobuki 41 9-cylinder radial piston
Dimensions: span 36 ft 1 in (11.00 m); length 24 ft 9.25 in (7.55 m); height 10 ft 6 in (3.20 in); wing area 191.6 sq ft (17.8 m³)
Weights: empty 2,681 lb (1216 kg); max. take-off 3,759 lb (1705 kg)
Performance: max. speed 273 mph (440 km/h); climb to 9850 ft (3000 m) in 3 minutes 35 seconds; service ceiling 32,150 ft (9800 m); range 746 miles (1200 km) with extra tank
Armament: two 0.303-in (7.7-mm) machine-guns and up to 122 lb (60 kg) of bombs

Messerschmitt Bf 109

Germany
May 1935

In early 1934 Willy Messerschmitt of the Bayerische Flugzeugwerke company was invited to design a fast 'single-seat courier' for a German Air Ministry (Reichsluftfahrtministerium – RLM) competition. As a starting point, Messerschmitt used the Bf 108 four-seat tourer but designed a new fuselage behind a Jumo 210 inverted-vee 12-cylinder engine.

When the prototype **Bf 109V1** flew on 28 May 1935 it embodied many advanced features for the first time in one fighter airframe, including a retractable undercarriage, an enclosed cockpit and a stressed-skin monocoque construction, thus setting the pattern for fighters for the next decade. Pending delivery of a 610-hp (454-kW) Junkers Jumo, the V1 initially had a 675-hp (503-kW) Rolls-Royce Kestrel engine.

A small number of early **Bf 109B**s, armed with three machine-guns, were rushed to Spain for combat evaluation where, from July 1937, the Luftwaffe developed its tactics and its pilots developed combat experience. The **Bf 109C**, also with a Jumo engine, and the **Bf 109D** with a 1,000-hp (746-kW) Daimler-Benz DB 600 soon followed, before the **Bf 109E** appeared in 1938. With the DB 601 of various models from 1,100-hp (821-kW) to 1,300-hp (969-kW) and armament of two machine-guns and up to three cannon, the 'Emil' was the version that fought from

The BF 109 (this is an F) was the mount of the top Luftwaffe aces. Erich Hartmann scored an incredible 352 victories in 109s. (TRH Pictures)

Switzerland was the main export user of the Bf 109E. They were used to protect the nation's neutrality from incursions by Allied and Axis aircraft alike. (The Aviation Picture Library)

the Blitzkrieg through the Battle of Britain where it achieved better than even results in combat with RAF Spitfires and Hurricanes.

The **Bf 109F**, which had a revised nose shape and other refinements, was regarded as the nicest to fly of all variants and was mainly used in the Mediterranean and North Africa from 1941. The engine-mounted 30-mm cannon, which had only appeared on some late Bf 109Es, was fitted to all Fs and subsequent Messerschmitt 109s (the company name after 1938). The **Bf 109G** series introduced the DB 605 engine rated at 1,475 hp (1100 kW). With water/methanol boost the rating increased to 1,800 hp (1342 kW). The final production version was the **Bf 109K**, which had a DB 605AS engine capable of 2,000 hp (1492 kW) with boost.

The Bf 109 was supplied to several nations including Switzerland, Finland, Hungary, Romania and Italy. After the war, Spain developed the Hispano **Ha-112 Buchon** based on the Bf 109G, with Hispano and later, Merlin engines and these served into the late 1960s. Czechoslovakia developed the **Avia S.199** with a Jumo 211F engine. Twenty-five of these were supplied to Israel and used in the War of Independence with some success despite their horrible handling characteristics.

Specification: Messerschmitt Bf 109G-6
Type: single-seat interceptor fighter
Powerplant: one 1,475-hp (1100-kW) Daimler-Benz DB-605A inverted V-12 piston
Dimensions: span 32 ft 6.5 in (9.92 m); length 29 ft 7 in (9.02 m); height 11 ft 2 in (3.40 m); wing area 172.8 sq ft (16.05 m²)
Weights: empty 5,952 lb (2700 kg); max. take-off 6,944 lb (3150 kg)
Performance: max. speed 387 mph (623 km/h); climb to 19,685 ft (6000 m) in 6.0 minutes; service ceiling 38,550 ft (11,750 m); range 450 miles (725 km)
Armament: two (7.92-mm MG 17 machine-guns and one 30-mm MK 108 cannon in nose, two 20-mm MG 151 underwing cannon

Hawker Hurricane

United Kingdom
November 1935

Built to essentially the same specification as the Spitfire and fitted with the same Merlin engine, the Hawker Hurricane was slower and less manoeuvrable, but was a more stable gun platform and was often available where and when Spitfires were not. Sydney Camm began design work in 1934 and the Hurricane prototype first flew on 6 November 1935. The Hurricane was of fabric-covered metal and wood construction with many similarities to the earlier Hawker biplanes. Armament was eight 0.303-in (7.7-mm) machine-guns and power came from a 1,030-hp (768-kW) Rolls-Royce Merlin II engine. The first aircraft had a two-bladed wooden propeller, but later versions had three-bladed metal units.

The **Hurricane Mk I** first saw action in the Battle of France and was the most numerous RAF fighter in the Battle of Britain, destroying more enemy aircraft than all other defences combined. Robert Stanford-Tuck was the RAF's top Hurricane ace with 29 kills.

Although quickly replaced on home defence duties after the Battle of Britain, the Hurricane was issued to units in the Mediterranean, North Africa and Far East, where it was often the best Allied fighter available. Hurricanes distinguished themselves in the defence of Malta, in North Africa and on the Burma front. The Hurricane was adapted as a successful night-fighter in several versions. The **Hurricane Mk II** had a Merlin XX with two-stage supercharger and spawned many sub-variants, differing mainly in their armament.

After the Battle of Britain, Hurricanes were mainly used in other theatres. This Mk IIA (with sand filter) was one of the first sent to the Middle East. (Author's collection)

The **Mk IIB** had 12 machine-guns and could carry light bombs, the **Mk IIC** had four 20-mm cannon. The **Mk IID**, with two underwing 40-mm Vickers 'S' cannon and two machine-guns, operated mainly in the Western Desert in the anti-armour role.

With its wide-track undercarriage and good endurance, the Hurricane made a better naval fighter than the Spitfire/Seafire. The first naval version was the **Sea Hurricane Mk I**, fired from a merchant ship's catapult on one-way trips as a convoy defender. The **Sea Hurricane IB** was a tail-hooked version for the smaller escort carriers. The **Sea Hurricane IIC** had the 1,280-hp (955-kW) Merlin XX and four cannon.

After two squadrons of RAF Hurricanes flew in northern Russia, the Soviet Union received around 3,000 examples. Hurricanes were also exported to Finland, India, Turkey, Ireland and Portugal. The Canadian Car and Foundry (CCF) built 1,451 Hurricanes, mainly **Mk X**s. They were used in Canada for training and by front-line RAF and RCAF squadrons.

Hurricanes differed little in appearance between models. This is the first production Hurricane. Note the two-bladed propeller. (TRH Pictures)

Specification: Hawker Hurricane Mk IIC
Type: single-seat fighter and fighter-bomber
Powerplant: one 1,280-hp (955 kW) Rolls-Royce Merlin XX V-12 piston
Dimensions: span 40 ft 0 in (12.19 m); length 32 ft 0 in (9.75 m); height 13 ft 1 in (3.99 m); wing area 257.5 sq ft (23.82 m²)
Weights: empty 5,800 lb (2631 kg); loaded 8,100 lb (3674 kg)
Performance: max. speed 336 mph (541 km/h); climb to 20,000 ft (6095 m) in 9 minutes 6 seconds; service ceiling 35,600 ft (10850 m); range 480 miles (740 km)
Armament: four 20-mm Hispano or Oerlikon cannon, two 500-lb (227-kg) bombs or eight 60-lb (27.2-kg) rocket projectiles

Fokker D.XXI

Although the most modern fighter available to the Dutch in 1940, the **Fokker D.XXI** was low-powered, slow and of outdated construction by the outbreak of war. More seriously, there were not enough of them. Fokker's E. Shatzki designed the D.XXI to a requirement for the Netherlands East Indies Air Force. The prototype D.XXI first flew on 27 February 1936 and had a fixed undercarriage, wooden wings and a fabric-covered welded aluminium tube fuselage. The forward fuselage was covered with aluminium panels. Armament was two 7.9-mm machine-guns in the wings and another pair firing between the cylinder banks.

The Finnish Air Force was desperately looking for modern fighters and ordered seven **D.XXI-2**s in November 1936, which were delivered a year later. Denmark bought two in 1937 and the Danish Naval Dockyard licence-built a further ten with the Mercury VI-S engine. The Danish **D.XXI-1**s were the best-armed versions with two 20-mm Madsen cannon in underwing blisters as well as two 7.9-mm Madsen machine-guns in the fuselage.

The Dutch themselves were actually the last to receive their own best fighter. A total of 36 were delivered in 1938 and 1939. In May 1940, 29 were in service with the 1st, 2nd and 5th Fighter Groups. In the three days of fighting that followed the German invasion of 10 May, Dutch D.XXI pilots claimed at least 13 kills, mainly against Bf 110s and Ju 88s before

The Dutch Air Force's D.XXIs were the last of the type to be delivered. There was little the few in service could do against the German onslaught of 1940. (TRH Pictures)

ammunition supplies ran out. Eight were lost in air combat and another 12 to bombing or other causes.

The first batch of Dutch-supplied Finnish D.XXIs were followed by 38 more licence-built **D.XXI-3** versions produced by the Finnish State Aircraft Factory at Tampere with the Mercury VII engine. These were delivered during 1938 and were followed in 1941 by 50 more locally modified to **D.XXI-4** standard to take the 825-hp (615-kW) Pratt & Whitney R-1535 Twin Wasp Junior engine and four 0.303-in (7.7-mm) machine-guns in the outer wings. The twin-row radial prevented the use of the fuselage guns. Performance with the R-1535 engine was poorer in all respects except in low-level speed, but Finland had purchased 80 of these powerplants as spares for other types and had no surplus Mercuries. The Finnish D.XXIs, which were usually operated on skis in the winter, were quite successful against Soviet fighters until more modern types arrived on both sides. The total production of all models was a modest 202.

Danish D.XXI-1s had cannon in underwing blisters and fuselage machine-guns. This was the first of 10 locally built examples. (The Aviation Picture Library)

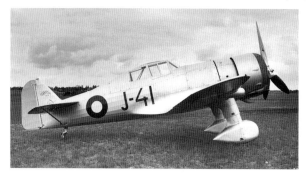

Specification: Fokker D.XXI

Type: single-seat monoplane fighter
Powerplant: one 830-hp (618-kW) Bristol Mercury VIII 9-cylinder radial piston
Dimensions: span 36 ft 1 in (11 m); length 26 ft 11 in (8.22 m); height 9 ft 8 in (2.94 m); wing area 174.38 sq ft (16.20 m²)
Weights: empty 3,180 lb (1442 kg); max. take-off 4,519 lb (2050 kg)
Performance: max. speed 286 mph (480 km/h); climb to 9,842 ft (3000 m) in 3 minutes 30 seconds; service ceiling 36,090 ft (11000 m); range 590 miles (950 km)
Armament: four 7.9-mm FN Browning machine-guns, two in fuselage and two in wings; armament varied on export aircraft

Supermarine Spitfire

United Kingdom
March 1936

Undoubtedly the most famous fighter of them all, the Supermarine Spitfire was built in over 20 distinct versions and in greater numbers than any other Allied warplane. The antecedents of the Spitfire were the Schneider Trophy-winning Supermarine seaplanes of the 1920s and 1930s designed by R.J. Mitchell. The Spitfire itself arose from a 1934 call for a monoplane fighter capable of 275 mph (443 km/h).

The prototype Spitfire first flew on 5 March 1936 with a 1,030-hp (768-kW) Rolls-Royce Merlin II. The initial production **Sptfire Mk I** entered service with the RAF in August 1938. The Spitfire was a low-wing monoplane with stressed-skin monocoque construction, a blown canopy and armament of eight machine-guns. Nineteen squadrons had Spitfires at the time of the Battle of Britain and the Spitfire was instrumental in Britain's survival.

Principal later versions included the cannon-armed **Mk V** (6,479 built). The 'interim' **Mk IX** was a combination of the Mk V airframe and the two-stage supercharged Merlin 60 series – 5,665 were built. Mk IXs with Packard-built Merlins were **Mk XVI**s, some with bubble canopies and 'low back' fuselages.

The **Mk VIII** actually followed the Mk IX and was widely used in Australia, New Guinea and the

The first Spitfire unit was No. 19 Squadron at RAF Duxford. This Mk I fought with the squadron in the Battle of Britain. (Philip Jarrett collection)

Mediterranean. The **Mk XII** was the first to have the new Rolls-Royce Griffon of 1,735 hp (1294 kW). Other 'Griffon Spits' included the **Mk XIV**, which was especially suited to combating V-1 flying bombs, and the **Mk XVIII**, capable of 442 mph (711 km/h). Some **Mk 22**s had a contra-rotating propeller.

Beginning with a few converted fighters, a series of high-altitude photoreconnaissance versions with pressurised cabins were developed, culminating in the **PR.XIX**, which served until 1954 in the Far East.

Later versions had almost nothing in common with the early versions except the name, having two and a half times the weight and almost twice the power, and being over 100 mph (160 km/h) faster. The last Mk 24s were retired from Royal Auxiliary Air Force service in Hong Kong in 1955.

The Fleet Air Arm operated 2,556 **Seafires**, which roughly paralleled Spitfire development from the **Seafire Mk I** of 1942 to the **Seafire FR.47**, which saw combat in Korea. Production versions had folding wings, cannon armament and catapult and arrester equipment. Exported Spitfires were used in various other conflicts including the Israeli War of Independence (on both sides), in the Greek Civil War and (French Seafires) in Indochina.

The Spitfire Mk XVI was produced in both 'high-back' and 'bubble-top' versions, as seen on this post-war example. (TRH Pictures)

Specification: Spitfire Mk IX
Type: single-seat interceptor fighter
Powerplant: one 1,290-hp (962-kW) Rolls-Royce Merlin 61 V-12 supercharged piston
Dimensions: span 36 ft 10 in (11.23 m); length 31 ft 1 in (9.47 m); height 12 ft 7.75 in (3.86 m); wing area 242 sq ft (22.48 m²)
Weights: empty 5,634 lb (2556 kg); loaded 9,500 lb (4309 kg)
Performance: max. speed 408 mph (657 km/h); initial climb rate 4,100 ft (2150 m) per minute; service ceiling 38,000 ft (11880 m); range 434 miles (700 km)
Armament: two 20-mm Hispano cannon and two 0.50-in (12.7-mm) Browning machine-guns in wings

Messerschmitt Bf 110

The late 1930s saw a vogue for twin-engined 'strategic' fighter designs such as the Bell Airacuda and the Fokker G.I. These were intended to escort bombers into enemy territory, carry out ground-attack missions and intercept bombers at long range. In 1934 the Luftwaffe issued a specification for a strategic fighter (or *Zerstörer* – destroyer) and Willy Messerschmitt set to work, designing a sleek aircraft with tandem seating, twin tails and twin Daimler-Benz DB 600A engines. The bombing requirement was ignored in favour of speed and range.

On 12 May 1936 the prototype **Bf 110V1** flew with DB 600As, but these unreliable motors were replaced by Jumo 210Das of 680 hp (507 kW) on the pre-production **Bf 110A-0**. Armament was four machine-guns in the nose and a defensive machine-gun in the rear cockpit. The initial production **Bf 110B** added two 20-mm cannon in the nose. When the DB 601A engine (1,100 hp/821 kW) was available, the **Bf 110C** followed.

In September 1939 there were 82 Bf 110Cs in service and one scored the first aerial victory of World War II when Leutnant Frank Neubert destroyed a P.11c over Poland on the first day of the German invasion. In the assault on the Low Countries the Bf 110s had further success, but in the Battle of Britain the Zerstörers were no match for the RAF's Spitfires and Hurricanes and had to be escorted by Bf 109s on

Bf 110Cs were effective until faced with modern fighters in the Battle of Britain. Its main advantage was its long-range capability. (TRH Pictures)

many occasions. The bombing capability had been restored with the Bf 110C and several effective precision raids were made during the battle, but afterwards the Bf 110 was relegated to less demanding theatres such as Sicily and to the fighter-bomber and convoy escort roles. Variants for these roles included the **Bf 110D**, **Bf 110E** and **Bf 110F**.

Owing to difficulties with its supposed successors, the Me 210 and 410, the potential of the Bf 110 as a night-fighter (tested with some Bf 110Cs) was fulfilled with the installation of centimetric airborne intercept (AI) radar on various sub-types of the **Bf 110G**. Many of these had a third crewman, a radar operator, in the centre cockpit. Aces such as Heinz-Wolfgang Schnaufer (121 kills, all at night) were able to use the stable, long-endurance, well-armed Bf 110 to devastating effect against RAF bombers.

In the last years of the war, Bf 110s were used against USAAF bomber formations, often with rocket armament. The Bf 110s were extremely vulnerable to the escorting Mustangs and Thunderbolts.

Although obsolescent, the Bf 110 was produced throughout the war, the last of about 6,050 being completed in March 1945. (TRH Pictures)

Specification: Messerschmitt Bf 110C-4
Type: twin-seat, twin-engine heavy fighter
Powerplant: two 1,100 (821-kW) Daimler-Benz DB 601A inline pistons
Dimensions: span 53 ft 4.75 in (16.27 m); length 41 ft 6.75 in (12.65 m); height 11 ft 6 in (3.50 m); wing area 413.3 sq ft (38.40 m²)
Weights: empty 11,464 lb (5200 kg); max. take-off 14,881 lb (6750 kg)
Performance: max. speed 349 mph (560 km/h); initial climb rate 2,165 ft (660 m) per minute; service ceiling 32,810 ft (10000 m); range 482 miles (772 km)
Armament: two 20-mm MG 151 cannon and four 0.31-in (7.92-mm) MG 17 nose guns, Twin 7.92-mm MG 81Zs in flexible mount

Polikarpov biplane fighters

Soviet Union
August 1936

Although almost all other nations had abandoned biplane fighters by the late 1930s, the dictates of Stalin meant that design work on biplanes continued in the Soviet Union even after monoplanes such as the I-16 were in service. Nikolai Polikarpov had built a series of compact sesquiplane fighters such as the **I-5**, the **I-15** and the **I-152** (or **I-15bis**). The I-15 featured a 'gulled' upper wing to provide better forward view in flight and gained the nickname *Chaika* (Gull) during service with the Spanish Republicans. The take-off and landing view was poor and the I-152 had its wing raised above the fuselage as well as having a revised structure. Over 2,400 were built by 1939. In 1937 work began on an improved version, the **I-153**, utilising the retractable undercarriage developed for the I-16 and returning to a gull-wing configuration. Test flying began in the summer of 1938. The engine on early aircraft was the 775-hp (578-kW) M-25V, but production was soon switched to the 850-hp (634.1-kW) Shvetsov M-62. The armament was four 0.30-in (7.62-mm) ShKAS machine-guns mounted in the wings. Later models could also carry four small bombs or six 3.23-in (82-mm) RS-82 rockets or drop tanks and were fitted with radios. A retractable ski undercarriage could be fitted in place of wheels.

Unlike Luftwaffe fighters, the I-153 was equally at home on skis and on wheels. The open cockpit made winter operations tough on the pilots. (TRH Pictures)

The I-153 'Chaika' was the last in a series of Polikarpov biplane fighters. Despite their obsolescence by 1941, Russian I-153s served throughout the war. (D.I. Windle)

There were few separately designated variants, but these included the **I-153P** with two 20-mm ShVAK cannon and two 0.30-in (7.62-mm) ShKAS machine-guns in the wings, and the **I-153DM** testbed with two DM-4 ramjet boosters.

The I-153 entered service in the spring of 1939 and first saw action against the Japanese in the undeclared war in the border area between Mongolia and Manchuria in July. Against the Ki-27 fighters of the Japanese Army, the I-153s had initial success, partly because they were mistaken for slower I-15s.

Production had totalled 3,427 when it ended in 1941. By the time of the German invasion of the Soviet Union in June 1941, the I-153 was the second most numerous fighter in the VVS. Two I-153 regiments were destroyed on the first day and others badly battered, but the defences rallied and made claims of 800 German aircraft by 5 July, most of them to Chaika units. By 1944 there were very few left except with naval units.

The Finns obtained some captured I-153s, but achieved little success with them against more modern Russian fighters. Like the I-16s, some I-153 fighter trainers lingered on in Spain until the 1950s.

Specification: Polikarpov I-153
Type: single-seat biplane fighter
Powerplant: one 850-hp (634.1-kW) Shvetsov M-62 9-cylinder radial piston
Dimensions: span 32 ft 9.5 in (10.00 m); length 19 ft 3 in (6.17 m); height 9 ft 2.25 in (2.80 m); wing area 238.31 sq ft (22.14 m²)
Weights: empty 3,201 lb (1452 kg); loaded 4,652 lb (2110 kg)
Performance: max. speed 280 mph (444 km/h); climb to 9,840 ft (3000 m) in 3 minutes; service ceiling 29,527 ft (8999.8 m); range 546 miles (830.4 km)
Armament: four 0.30-in (7.62-mm) ShKAS machine-guns, provision for 220 lb (99.8 kg) bombs or six 80-mm rockets

Fiat G.50 Freccia

The Regia Aeronautica issued a specification in 1935 for an all-metal monoplane fighter. Among the competing designs were the Macchi MC.200 and the first design by Giuseppe Gabrielli of Fiat, which was dubbed the **G.50**. The G.50 was an all-metal low wing monoplane with retractable undercarriage and an 840-hp (626-kW) Fiat radial engine. The armament was a frankly, inadequate, pair of 0.50-in (12.7-mm) machine-guns, at a time when contemporary fighters mounted four, six or eight machine-guns. At one point in the development the Air Ministry decided it only wanted one gun, but it was too late to change the design. The first 47 aircraft had a sliding canopy but all others had an open or only partially enclosed cockpit. An exception was the **G.50B** two-seat trainer, which had a long glazed canopy.

The prototype G.50 *Freccia* (Arrow) first flew at Turin on 26 February 1937. There were some initial stability problems, partly cured by modifying the upper fuselage contours and revising the tail. When the first 12 production models were finished, they were sent to Spain for combat trials with the Nationalists but saw limited action before the end of the war.

The G.50 entered Italian service with 22 Gruppo of 51 Stormo in the spring of 1939 and about 120 were

With its open cockpit and good agility, the G.50 was popular with pilots. Its low power and poor armament doomed it against serious opposition. (TRH Pictures)

Early Fiat G.50 Freccias fly over the Mediterranean. Later models had a raised spine to cure lateral stability problems. (TRH Pictures)

on hand by September.The Freccia had a less than glorious career, mainly in North Africa. It was outclassed by better-armed contemporary fighters, most of which sported 1,000-hp (745-kW) engines and were 100 mph (160 km/h) faster. In Greece, they were usually defeated by RAF Gladiators and perhaps fortunately, never met British fighters during the Regia Aeronautica's limited involvement in the Battle of Britain.

Although Croatia was given a small batch of G.50s, the only real export customer was Finland, which bought 35 in 1939 because they were the only fighters it could obtain immediately. The Finns used them in the Winter War against the Soviet Union, where they gained 13 victories. A further 88 were scored in the Continuation War. The top Finnish Fiat ace was Oiva Tuominen who scored 23 victories against the faster and better-climbing Polikarpovs. The only other important version was the **G.50bis**, of 1940, with more fuel capacity and enlarged tail surfaces with an extended tailcone. In addition to the 212 original G.50s, almost all built by Fiat subsidiary CMASA, 421 G.50bis and 90 G.50Bs were built. In Italian service, the G.50 faded out at the armistice, but some remained in use in Finland until 1947.

Specification: Fiat G.50
Type: single-seat monoplane fighter
Powerplant: one 840-hp (626-kW) Fiat A.74 RC.38 14-cylinder radial piston
Dimensions: span 35 ft 11.5 in (10.96 m); length 25 ft 6.75 in (7.79 m); height 9 ft 8.5 in (2.96 m); wing area 195.37 sq ft (18.15 m²)
Weights: empty 4,354 lb (1975 kg); max. take-off 5,324 lb (2415 kg)
Performance: max. speed 293 mph (472 km/h); climb to 19,685 ft (6000 m) in 7 minutes 30 seconds; service ceiling 32,265 ft (9835 m); range 416 miles (670 km)
Armament: two 0.50-in (12.7-mm) Breda SAFAT machine-guns

Dewoitine D.520

Emile Dewoitine designed a dozen parasol-wing fighters in the 1920s and 1930s and several low-winged monoplanes, of which the D.500 and D.510 were built in reasonable numbers. These fixed-undercarriage, open cockpit machines were followed by several prototypes with retractable gear and sliding canopies. Joining with designers Robert Costello and Jacques Henrat, Dewoitine's autonomous design bureau produced two prototypes of the **D.520** to an Armeé de l'Air requirement, the first of which flew on 2 October 1938. The D.520 was an all-metal monoplane powered by a supercharged Hispano-Suiza 12Y 45 engine rated at 935 hp (697 kW). The armament was powerful for the time, consisting of a 20-mm cannon firing through the propeller hub and four machine-guns in the wings.

The first production D.520 was not flown until 2 November 1939, only seven months before the German assault. Deliveries began in January 1940.

Contracts for D.520s went up and down as war approached. The last, issued on 21 April 1940, called for the production of 350 per month, for a total ordered of 2,250. By this time there was little the factories could do to prevent the inevitable and, although they fought well, the under-trained French pilots and their bases were eventually overwhelmed by the German blitzkrieg. Nevertheless, the 79 D.520s in service were credited with 108 'kills' versus 54 combat losses in the Battle of France.

The second prototype D.520 is seen on a test flight. A lack of urgency in the programme saw that few were in service by the outbreak of war. (TRH Pictures)

The Germans permitted production to continue in the south-east of France by Société Nationale de Constructions Aéronautiques Sud Est (SNCASE). The company turned out 349 and completed a further 129 for the Luftwaffe, who gave them to training units JG 103 and JG 105 and to the Italian Regia Aeronautica, who used 60 as front-line fighters. Bulgaria was the recipient of 96 captured French and Vichy D.520s and these fought against US Army Air Force (USAAF) bombers and their escorts in 1944, scoring 14 confirmed victories.

The top Dewoitine ace was Pierre Le Gloan of GC III/6 with 18 'kills' against German (four) Italian (seven) and British (seven) aircraft, the latter when flying with Vichy forces in Syria.

The Vichy Air Force had nine groups of D.520s. During the Operation Torch landings in November 1942, they fought many combats with Allied aircraft.

Post war, 13 D.520s were converted to two-seat trainers as the **D.520DC** (*double commande*). The last D.520 was retired in September 1953.

Production of D.520s continued under German supervision. This aircraft (No. 494) was rolled out in Vichy colours in March 1942. (TRH Pictures)

Specification: Dewoitine D.520
Type: single-seat monoplane fighter
Powerplant: one 935-hp (697-kW) Hispano-Suiza 12Y 45 12-cylinder inline piston
Dimensions: span 33 ft 5.5 in (10.20 m); length 28 ft 8.25 in (8.76 m); height 8 ft 5 in (2.57 m); wing area 171.7 sq ft (15.95 m²)
Weights: empty 4,685 lb (2125 kg); loaded 5,897 lb (2675 kg)
Performance: max. speed 332 mph (535 km/h); climb to 13,125 ft (4000 m) in 5 minutes 49 seconds; service ceiling 33,630 ft (10250 m); range 553 miles (890 km)
Armament: one 20-mm Hispano-Suiza 404 cannon in propeller hub, four 0.295-in (7.5-mm) MAC 1934 M39 machine-guns in wings

Curtiss P-40 Hawks

The potential of the Curtiss Hawk 75 (P-36) was limited by the power of compatible radial engines, so in July 1937 a P-36A was tested with a turbocharged version of the new Allison V-1710 V-12 engine as the XP-37. A revised, non-turbocharged installation with an underwing radiator was flown as the **XP-40** (Model 75P) on 14 October 1938. Following testing the radiator was moved to a chin position beneath the spinner. In April 1939 the US Army made an order for 524 **P-40**s with the 1,040-hp (746-kW) V-1710-33 and two nose-mounted machine-guns. From the firewall back, the P-40 was essentially the same as the earlier Hawk 75s but had increased, if not stunning, performance and better handling. Most importantly, the P-40 could be produced quickly, and orders for more and better versions followed one after another. Deliveries to the USAAC began in June 1940, but only 199 P-40s (no suffix) were built as such. France placed a large order for these as **Hawk 81A**s, but the 130 built were diverted to the UK as the **Tomahawk I**. British and Commonwealth air forces took all models of the P-40 during the war, their own first (P-40) aircraft as the **Tomahawk IIA**. The **P-40B** and **P-40C** were the most numerous US fighters in December 1941, but quickly replaced thereafter.

Commonwealth air forces made much use of the P-40 series. This is a Kittyhawk Mk III of No. 5 Squadron, SAAF seen at a landing ground in Italy. (TRH Pictures)

Early P-40s were shorter with a deeper chin than later models. This Tomahawk IIB served with an RAF unit in the Western Desert. (TRH Pictures)

The American Volunteer Group (the 'Flying Tigers') famously fought the Japanese in China from late 1941 with Hawk 81A-2s and later in **P-40E**s. The P-40E (**Kittyhawk I**) was the first with the 1,150-hp (857-kW) Allison V-1710-39, a lengthened fuselage and armament of six wing guns. In all, 3,820 P-40Es were built, followed by 1,300 **P-40K**s with the V-1710-73 engine, and 600 **P-40M**s with the V-1710-81.

There were two Merlin-engined versions, the **P-40F** (330 built) and **P-40L** (700 built), known as the **Kittyhawk II**, almost all of which went to the Commonwealth or USSR. The final and most numerous model was the **P-40N Warhawk**, known to the Commonwealth as the **Kittyhawk IV**. Both four- and six-gun versions were built for a total of 5,216, and they were supplied to the Soviet Union, the Netherlands East Indies, Brazil, Australia and New Zealand. In all, 13,739 P-40s were built in three factories (St Louis, Buffalo and Columbus, Ohio) up to December 1944. Although pleasant to fly, each version of the P-40 was obsolescent by the time it reached the front. Nevertheless, they made a valuable contribution in theatres from North Africa to the South Pacific, and as trainers until more modern types became available.

Specification: Curtiss P-40N
Type: single-seat fighter
Powerplant: one 1,360-hp (1015-kW) Allison V-1710-81 V-12 piston
Dimensions: span 37 ft 3.5 in (11.36 m); length 33 ft 4 in (10.14 m); height 12 ft 4 in (3.75 m); wing area 237 sq ft (22 m²)
Weights: empty 6,700 lb (3039 kg); loaded 11,400 lb (5058 kg)
Performance: max. speed 343 mph (552 km/h); climb to 20,000 ft (6706 m) in 8 minutes 48 seconds; service ceiling 30,000 ft (9144 m); range 750 miles (1207 km)
Armament: six 0.50-in (12.7-mm) Browning machine-guns in wings, up to 1,500 lb (680 kg) bombs

Nakajima Ki-43 Hayabusa 'Oscar'

In December 1937 the Imperial Japanese Army issued a specification for a fighter to replace the Nakajima Ki-27 'Nate' which had only just entered service. Despite this apparent urgency, the requirement was not driven by a desire to push the technological boundaries, calling for only a small increase in speed, which was easily accomplished by fitting the specified retractable landing gear. Hideo Itokawa and Yasumi Koyama of Nakajima took the best features of the Ki-27, designed a new fuselage with an enclosed cockpit and applied the new 990-hp (738-kW) Nakajima Ha-25 14-cylinder radial. Confident of continuing superiority over fighters in China, the Army ordered the new fighter as the **Ki-43 Hayabusa** (Peregrine Falcon) without a competitive evaluation soon after its first flight in January 1939.

The Hayabusa featured a relatively large wing with a slight degree of forward sweep to the leading edge and a slim stressed-skin metal fuselage. The armament was only a pair of 0.50-in (12.7-mm) Type 89 machine-guns in the cowl aimed with the help of a telescopic gunsight. From the eighth aircraft built, 'butterfly' flaps extended from the trailing edge of the inner wing sections for increased combat manoeuvrability. Despite being built with little but lightness and agility in mind, the Ki-43 was slightly less agile than the Ki-27, which remained the most numerous Army fighter until well into 1942.

The Hayabusa was quickly sent to Burma and

To save weight and resources, later Hayabusas were usually delivered unpainted, but gained various field colour schemes. (Philip Jarrett collection)

southern China where it became the main fighter adversary of the 'Flying Tigers', who were usually able to exploit its weaknesses, unlike most other Allied fighter units in the early war period. In 1942 the Ki-43 was given the reporting name 'Oscar'. Despite its small engine and puny armament, the 'Oscar' was a very effective fighter in the early war years, particularly against heavier and less manoeuvrable British fighters such as the Buffalo and Hurricane.

With no armour or self-sealing tanks, the early Hayabusa was very vulnerable to the guns of Allied fighters, which generally had three times the firepower, and up to twice the horsepower. Like the 'Zero', the Hayabusa was obsolescent by mid-1943, not least due to its two-pitch two-bladed propeller.

Versions included the **Ki-43-II** with some armour protection for the pilot, self-sealing fuel tanks, a three-bladed propeller and a more conventional reflector gun sight. The **Ki-43-III** had a 1,230-hp (918-kW) Ha-115-II and the **Ki-43-III-Otsu** had two 20-mm cannon but only a handful of these versions were completed.

Like the Zero-Sen, the Hayabusa was kept in production too long, the last of about 5,850 emerging in August 1945. (TRH Pictures)

Specification: Nakajima Ki-43-IIb
Type: single-seat fighter
Powerplant: one 1,150-hp (858-kW) Nakajima Ha-115 14-cylinder radial engine
Dimensions: span 35 ft 6.25 in (10.84 m); length 29 ft 3 in (8.92 m); height 10 ft 8.75 in (3.27 m); wing area 230.36 sq ft (21.4 m²)
Weights: empty 4,211 lb (1910 kg); max. take-off 6,450 lb (2925 kg)
Performance: max. speed 329 mph (530 km/h); climb to 16,405 ft (5000 m) in 5 minutes 48 seconds; service ceiling 36,750 ft (11200 m); range 1,095 miles (1760 km)
Armament: two 0.50-in (12.7-mm) Ho-103 machine-guns and up to two 250-kg (551-lb) bombs under wings

Lockheed P-38 Lightning

Lockheed's first military aircraft was designed to a 1936 specification for a high-altitude interceptor. Lockheed offered its Model 22, which was a radical design for a single-seat fighter with twin tailbooms and a central nacelle containing the pilot and armament. Following evaluation of this proposal, the US Army ordered a prototype as the **XP-38** in June 1937. When completed in December 1938, the XP-38 Lightning was powered by two 1,090-hp (812-kW) V-1710-11/15 engines with turbosuperchargers driving opposite-rotating three-bladed propellers. The XP-38 had no armament, but the intention was to concentrate it in the central nacelle without the need for synchronisation gear. The high-aspect ratio wings had Fowler flaps, which aided combat manoeuvring. Each boom had a fin and rudder, connected by a tailplane and elevator.

The XP-38 first flew at March Field, California, on 27 January 1939 but crashed on delivery to Wright Field on 11 February. Despite this, the Army ordered 13 **YP-38**s, which were tested by the 1st Pursuit Group in spring 1941. The **P-38D**, with self-sealing fuel tanks and a 23-mm Madsen cannon, and the **P-38E**, with a 20-mm cannon, appeared before the end of the year. The P-38E's reconnaissance counterpart

Britain placed large orders for P-38s without superchargers and then rejected them due to low performance. They were passed to the USAAF for training. (TRH Pictures)

With long range and two engines, the P-38 was ideally suited to the Pacific theatre. In Europe, early models such as this suffered from the cold conditions. (TRH Pictures)

was the **F-4**, which was equipped with four nose cameras.

The RAF was to receive 143 **Lightning I**s and 524 **Lightning II**s, many originally intended for France. Ordered without superchargers and with right-rotating props, they proved disappointing and never entered British service.

The P-38 was the fastest fighter of its day and with a full set of drop tanks the later variants could stay in the air for 12 hours. A total of 10,037 Lockheed Lightnings were built in numerous further versions, from the **P-38F** (recon **F-4A**), through the **P-38G** (**F-5A**), the **P-38H**, the **P-38J** (**F-5B**, **F-5C** and **F-5E**), which with 2,970 built was the most numerous version, to the **P-38L** (**F-5F** and **F-5G**). The most radical version was the **P-38M** night-fighter with AN/APS-6 radar and an operator in a new raised rear cockpit. It saw only a little combat at the end of the Pacific War but had better performance than the P-61.

Although less famous than the P-51 and P-47, the P-38 was the mount of the USA's two top aces, Richard Bong (40 kills) and Thomas McGuire (38 kills). Ace Rex Barber destroyed the 'Betty' transport carrying Japan's Admiral Yamamoto. Despite initial problems, the P-38 was also successful in Europe.

Specification: Lockheed P-38L Lightning
Type: single-seat twin-engined fighter-bomber
Powerplant: two 1,475-hp (1100-kW) Allison V-1710-111/113 V-12 pistons
Dimensions: span 53 ft 0 in (15.85 m); length 37 ft 10 in (11.52 m); height 9 ft 10 in (2.99 m); wing area 327.5 sq ft (30.42 m²)
Weights: empty 12,800 lb (5806 kg); max. take-off 21,600 lb (9798 kg)
Performance: max. speed 414 mph (666 km/h); climb to 20,000 ft (6095 m) in 7 minutes; service ceiling 44,000 ft (13410 m); range 450 miles (724 km)
Armament: one 20-mm cannon and four 0.50-in (12.7-mm machine-guns in nose

Grumman F4F Wildcat

United States
February 1939

During 1936, Grumman's Dick Hutton and Bill Schwendler designed an improved biplane fighter to replace the US Navy's F2F and F3F. The G.16 was longer but of shorter span with a canopy mounted further aft than the F3F, and had a 900-hp (671-kW) Wright engine. The USN ordered a prototype as the XF4F-1, which was projected to be only slightly faster than the F3F-3 and was abandoned before it flew. Many features of the G.16 were incorporated in the **XF4F-2** (Model G.18) which was a mid-wing monoplane fighter with many of the features of the F2F and F3F biplanes, notably the fuselage shape and undercarriage layout.

Like the F3F, the XF4F-2, which first flew on 2 September 1936, was of all-metal construction with an enclosed cockpit and a hand-cranked undercarriage that retracted into the fuselage. The engine was a 1,050-hp (783-kW) Pratt & Whitney R-1830-66 Twin Wasp, which made it slightly faster than the competing Brewster F2A but otherwise inferior, and no orders followed. A comprehensive rework produced the **XF4F-3** (G.36) with revised, squared-off flying surfaces and a supercharged R-1830-76 of 1,200-hp (895-kW) with a three-bladed propeller. In its new guise, the XF4F-3 was first flown on 12 February 1939 and 54 **F4F-3** Wildcats were ordered in August by the USN. The first was delivered to units serving on the USS *Ranger* and USS *Wasp* in December 1940. By now, the Fleet Air Arm had taken delivery

The F4F Wildcat was slightly inferior to the Zero-Sen in most respects, but still produced many aces in the Pacific theatre. (TRH Pictures)

of 81 F4F-3s, which had been intended for France, as the **Martlet I.**

On Christmas Day 1940, two Martlet Is shot down a Ju-88 over Scapa Flow, achieving the first FAA kill of the war. USMC F4F-3s fought valiantly against overwhelming odds in the defence of Wake Island. The **F4F-4** (**Martlet II**) with manually folding wings was the main USN fighter at the Battles of Coral Sea and Midway, where they held their own against the A6M Zero. The armament was increased from four to six 0.50-in (12.7-mm) machine-guns on this model, which was also built by the Eastern Aircraft division of General Motors as the **FM1**, allowing Grumman to concentrate on the F6F Hellcat. The Royal Navy accepted 300 as the **Martlet V**.

General Motors developed a new version particularly designed for the small escort carriers as the **FM2**, with a lightened structure and powered by a single-row, 1,350-hp (1007-kW) 9-cylinder Wright R-1820. FM-2s could be identified by their taller fin and large exhaust vent.

The principal early war version of the Wildcat was the F4F-3 without folding wings. Many served with the US Marine Corps from island bases. (TRH Pictures)

Specification: Grumman F4F-4 Wildcat
Type: single-seat carrier fighter
Powerplant: one 1,200-hp (895-kW) Pratt & Whitney R-1830-86 radial piston
Dimensions: span 38 ft 0 in (11.58 m); length 28 ft 9 in (8.76 m); height 11 ft 10 in (3.60 m); wing area 260.0 sq ft (24.15 m²)
Weights: empty 5,785 lb (2624 kg); max. take-off 7,952 (3607 kg)
Performance: max. speed 318 mph (512 km/h); initial climb rate 1,950 ft (594 m) per minute; service ceiling 34,900 ft (10640 m); range 770 miles (1240 km)
Armament: six 0.50-in (12.7-mm) Browning machine-guns in wings; FM-2 had four guns and provision for two 250-lb (113-kg) bombs

Yakovlev Yak-1 to Yak-9

Soviet Union
March 1939

The famous Yak series of fighters arose from a 1938 requirement for a 'frontal fighter' intended to operate close above the battlefield and with its best combat performance below 13,125 ft (4000 m). Alexsandr Yakovlev's design bureau came up with the **Yak-26**, a fighter of conventional appearance with an elliptical wooden wing, a chin radiator and a plywood and steel tube fuselage. The engine was a Klimov M-105 V-12 of 1,000-hp (746-kW). As the **I-26**, it flew in March 1939 and was easily the best of the prototypes offered for the frontal fighter requirement. Ordered into production with a few changes as the **Yak-1**, the first flew on 13 January 1940.

As was common with Russian fighters, the prototype's performance was superior to that of the production examples, built mainly by semi-skilled labour. Production Yak-1s were considerably heavier, needing a 1,250-hp (933-kW) M-105PF to compete with the Bf 109E. A few Yaks were at the front in June 1941, acquitting themselves well in the circumstances.

The Yak-1 branched into two distinct paths of development – a heavy fighter with maximum armament, range and protection, and a lightweight interceptor. The latter series began with the **Yak-1M**, which featured a cut-down rear fuselage and a three-

The French volunteer Normandie-Niemen Regiment were enthusiastic users of the Yak-3. Total Yak-3 production reached 4,848 examples. (TRH Pictures)

In all, there were over 37,000 Yak fighters, the vast majority of them Yak-9s. This one was flown by female ace Lilya Litvak. (The Aviation Picture Library)

part canopy. At 4,461 lb (2024 kg) empty the 'lightened' Yak was the lightest Allied monoplane fighter of the war, owing to its extensive use of wood.

Using many of the same principles, but a shortened wing, the **Yak-3** entered service in June 1944 and proved a formidable dogfighter at low level, if slightly underpowered. The strengthened, all-metal **Yak-3U** with the 1,650-hp (1230-kW) M-107A engine was the best performer of the series. It was well armed with a 23-mm VYa-23V cannon and two wing guns.

The heavy fighter series began as the two-seat **UTI-26** (later **Yak-7V**), which was seen as worthy of development into the **Yak-7B** fighter with the M-105P engine, which appeared in 1941. The **Yak-7DI** was the long-range version. It led to the definitive **Yak-9**, which entered combat in November 1942. Versions included the ultra-long range **Yak-9DD** and the **Yak-9B** fighter-bomber, which carried four vertically mounted 220-lb (100-kg) bombs in a bay behind the cockpit. The **Yak-9T** had a powerful 37-mm hub-firing anti-tank cannon for anti-shipping missions. Most 'second generation' **Yak-9U**s were M-107A powered and metal-clad. They were equal to the best German fighters. The post-war **Yak-9P** was exported to Eastern Europe and to China.

Specification: Yakovlev Yak-9D

Type: single-seat fighter
Powerplant: one 1,360-hp (1015-kW) Klimov M-105PF-3 V-12 piston
Dimensions: span 31 ft 11.5 in (9.74 m); length 28 ft 0.75 in (8.55 m); height 9ft 10 in (3.00 m); wing area 184.6 sq ft (17.15 m²)
Weights: empty 6,107 lb (2770 kg); loaded 6,790 lb (3080 kg)
Performance: max. speed 374 mph (602 km/h); climb to 16,405 ft (5000 m) in 6 minutes; service ceiling 34,500 ft (10500 m); range 840 miles (1340 km)
Armament: one 20-mm ShVAK cannon firing through propeller hub and two 0.50-in (12.7-mm) BS machine-guns in wings

Mitsubishi A6M Zero-Sen 'Zeke'

Japan
April 1939

In 1937 the IJN issued a specification for a long-range carrier fighter to replace the Mitsubishi A5M ('Claude') then just entering service. Nakajima found the requirements too stringent but Jiro Horikoshi of Mitsubishi designed a modern fighter optimised for range and manoeuvrability with a lightweight structure of a new aluminium alloy.

The first two prototypes were designated **A6M1** (first model of the sixth Mitsubishi fighter). The first flew on 1 April 1939 with an 875-hp (652-kW) Mitsubishi Zuisei 13 radial and was accepted as the **Type 0 Carrier Fighter** (*Rei shiki Kanjo sentoki* – usually contracted to Rei-Sen or Zero-Sen) in September.

The first production model was the **A6M2** (Navy Model 21) with a Nakajima Sakae engine of 950 hp (708 kW) and armament consisting of two 0.303-in (7.7-mm) machine-guns in the cowl and two 20-mm cannon in the wings. Most of the A6M2s had manually folding wingtips.

Due to woeful intelligence, the Zero-Sen was a complete surprise to the Western Allies in December 1941, despite having seen combat in China from July 1940, where it had devastated the opposing Russian and American-built fighters. Code-named **'Zeke'** by the Allies, the A6M literally ran rings around Allied fighters in 1941 and 1942. Most impressive was the Zero-Sen's range, which made it an outstanding bomber escort, able to stay and fight over the target. The Battles of Coral Sea and Midway cost Japan many

This A6M2 was the mount of Navy pilot Saburo Sakai, who scored around 60 kills in the Pacific war. A total of 10,449 A6Ms were built before the war's end. (TRH Pictures)

aircraft, but more importantly, experienced pilots who went down with their carriers.

The **A6M3-32** of 1941 had shorter wings with fixed tips and the 1,130-hp (842-kW) Sakae 21. It was superseded by the similar **A6M3-22** with folding tips. The **A6M5**, introduced in March 1944, featured 'jet' exhaust stacks, fixed tips and thicker-gauge skins to prevent wing failure in high-*g* pullouts. The **A6M5-ko** had even heavier skins and revised cannon.

Nakajima developed a floatplane version designated the **A6M2-N** (or 'Rufe' to the Allies). Although useful for patrolling island areas without airfields, it was no match for any Allied fighter opposition.

The **A6M6** addressed some of the type's weaknesses with its self-sealing fuel tanks and a water/methanol-boosted Sakae 31, but by now production standards fell and output was reduced by US bombing. By mid-1943, the A6M was obsolescent. Higher fuel consumption, heavier armament and thicker skins reduced the range and climb rate by over a third, although the speed increased.

The Zero-Sen or 'Zeke' was regarded as almost invincible until examples fell into Allied hands and could be studied in detail. (Author's collection)

Specification: Mitsubishi A6M5-ko
Type: single-seat carrier/land-based fighter
Powerplant: one 1,130-hp (842-kW) Nakajima Sakae 21 14-cylinder radial engine
Dimensions: span 36 ft 1.25 in (11.0 m); length 29 ft 11 in (9.12 m); height 11 ft 6 in (3.51 m); wing area 229.28 sq ft (21.30 m²)
Weights: empty 4,136 lb (1876 kg); loaded 6,025 lb (2733 kg)
Performance: max. speed 341 mph (565 km/h); initial climb rate 3,150 ft (960 m) per minute; service ceiling 37,500 ft (11500 m); range 1,200 miles (1920 km)
Armament: two 0.303-in (7.7-mm) Type 97 machine-guns, two 0.52-in (13.2-mm) machine-guns, two 20-mm Type 99 cannon in wings, one 1100-lb (499-kg) and/or two 132-lb (60-kg) bombs

Bell P-39 Airacobra/P-63 Kingcobra

United States
April 1939

The Bell **P-39 Airacobra** and **P-63 Kingcobra** were the only single-engined wartime piston-engined fighters with a tricycle (nose-gear) undercarriage. The P-39 arose from a 1936 US Army requirement for a modern single-seat fighter. Bell's Robert J. Woods and Harland M. Poyer designed the Bell Model 4 around the 37-mm T-9 cannon (a modified anti-tank weapon), which was mounted in the nose, firing through the propeller hub. The engine was mounted at the centre of gravity behind the cockpit and drove the three-bladed propeller via an extension shaft running under the pilot's seat. The engine on the **XP-39** prototype was the 1,150-hp (858-kW) Allison V-1710-17 with supercharger and this aircraft first flew on 6 April 1939. NACA testing saw the prototype revised and the supercharger deleted, a decision that was to hinder the Airacobra's altitude performance throughout its career.

The first production model (20 built) was the **P-39C** with no wing guns, unlike all later versions. The RAF was to receive 600 **P-400 Airacobra I**s, but only fielded one squadron and the majority were issued to the USAAF in the Pacific. The P-400 had a 20-mm cannon, as did some **P-39D**s. The P-39D was followed by the similar **P-39K, P-39L, P-39M** and **P-39N**, which

Although comparable in performance to the P-51D Mustang, the P-63 Kingcobra saw no front-line US service. A total of 3,303 were built. (TRH Pictures)

This is the XP-39 Airacobra, seen after its supercharger and its large intakes. It was followed by 9,558 production examples. (Via Robert F. Dorr)

varied mainly in engine variant and propeller.

The **P-39Q** was the most numerous model, with 4,905 built. The majority went to the USSR, where this version's most notable feature, 0.50-in (12.7-mm) guns in wing pods, was usually deleted. There were a number of **TP-39Q** and **RP-39Q** two-seaters. The Soviets received 5,578 P-39s and used them mainly as ground attackers. Nonetheless, many top aces flew Airacobras, notably Alexsandr Pokrykshin, who scored 48 of his 59 kills on P-39s.

By April 1944 the P-39 had left front-line US service in favour of the P-38, P-47 and P-51. Although manoeuvrable and well armed, the Airacobra was underpowered, short-ranged and had a reputation for tumbling around its centre of gravity.

In an effort to realise the full potential of the design, Bell developed the larger P-63 Kingcobra, optimised for close support work, which first flew on 26 April 1943. The engine was a supercharged V-1710-47 of 1,325-hp (987-kW). The USSR took the bulk (2,456) of **P-63A** and **P-63C** production, although France had 114 of the latter, using some until 1962. The US used some **RP-63**s as armoured gunnery trainers and in other non-combat roles.

Specification: Bell P-39N Airacobra
Type: single-seat fighter
Powerplant: one 1,200-hp (895-kW) Allison V-1710-85 V-12 piston
Dimensions: span 34 ft 0 in (10.36 m); length 30 ft 2 in (9.19 m); height 12 ft 5 in (3.78 m); wing area 213.0 sq ft (19.79 m²)
Weights: empty 5,657 lb (2566 kg); max. take-off 8,200 lb (3720 kg)
Performance: max. speed 399 mph (642 km/h); climb to 15,000 ft (4570 m) in 3 minutes 48 seconds; service ceiling 38,500 ft (11735 m); range 750 miles (1207 km)
Armament: one 37-mm cannon, two 0.50-in (12.7-mm) Browning machine-guns, four 0.30-in (7.62-mm) machine-guns in wings

Focke-Wulf Fw 190

Germany
June 1939

The only major combat aircraft type to enter large-scale service with the Luftwaffe after the outbreak of war, the **Focke-Wulf Fw 190** arose from a 1937 RLM request for a single-seat fighter. Kurt Tank of Focke-Wulf took up the challenge, creating a compact fighter around the most powerful engine available.

The **Fw 190V1** first flew on 1 June 1939, powered by a fan-cooled 1,550-hp (1155-kW) BMW 139 air-cooled radial with a three-bladed propeller and ducted spinner. The pre-production **Fw 190A-0** was fitted with the 1,600-hp (1192-kW) BMW 801 14-cylinder, versions of which equipped most subsequent models.

The first **Fw 190A-1**s entered service in mid-1941 and the first air combats took place over the Channel front in September 1941, completely surprising Allied intelligence who until then had no inkling of the new fighter's development. The early Fw 190s were superior to the Spitfire V, setting in train a seesaw of development that was to last through the war. The **Fw 190A-8** was the main early version with 1,334 built. Armament was two machine-guns and four cannon.

Factory conversion kits allowed the basic fighter to take on new roles from fighter-bomber to torpedo-bomber. Other roles were as single-seat radar-equipped night-fighters, armoured 'ram fighters' and two-seat conversion trainers. The **Fw 190F** was a dedicated fighter-bomber with provision for a 1,102-lb (500-kg) bomb under the fuselage and two 551-lb (250-kg) bombs under the wings. The F-2 sub-type introduced

The appearance of the Fw 190A in late 1941 was a shock to RAF pilots. About 19,500 Fw 190s were built by Focke-Wulf and five contractors. (TRH Pictures)

a new blown canopy.

With longer range and more load capacity than the Messerschmitt 109, the Fw 190 fighter-bombers were effective on 'tip-and-run' raids against targets on the south coast of England. On the Eastern Front, the Fw 190 Wurger (butcher bird) was favoured by the Schlachtgeschwaderen (literally 'slaughter wings'), using a wide variety of anti-personnel and anti-armour weapons. The **Fw 190G** ground-attack variant had more fuel and only two guns to give longer range.

The BMW 801 gave the Fw 190 excellent performance below 22,965 ft (7000 m), but high-altitude performance was lacking. Installing a V-12 Junkers Jumo 213A of up to 2,240 hp (1671 kW) produced the **Fw 190D** series of which the **Fw 190D-9** was the main production version. An annular radiator kept drag down and the 'Dora-9' had a ceiling of 39,370 ft (12000 m). About 100 **Ta 152C** high-altitude interceptors were delivered but they saw little combat. The ultimate version was the Ta 152H with wings extended to 47 ft 6.75 in (14.5 m). It was capable of over 470 mph (760 km/h) at 41,010 ft (12500 m). Only ten were completed.

The Ta 152 (Ta standing for Tank) with elongated wings was the ultimate Fw 190 derivative, capable of over 470 mph (760 km/h) at 41,010 ft (12500 m). (TRH Pictures)

Specification: Focke-Wulf Fw 190A-8
Type: single-seat fighter
Powerplant: one 2,100-hp (1567-kW) BMW 801D-2 14-cylinder radial piston
Dimensions: span 34 ft 5.5 in; length 29 ft 1.5 in; height 13 ft 0 in; wing area 196.98 sq ft (18.30 m²)
Weights: empty 6,989 lb (3170 kg); max. take-off 10,802 lb (4900 kg)
Performance: max. speed 408 mph (654 km/h); initial climb rate 2,362 ft (720 m) per minute; service ceiling 37,400 ft (11400 m); range 500 miles (805 km)
Armament: two 0.51-in (13-mm) MG 131 machine-guns in nose cowl, four 20-mm MG 151/20 cannon in wings

Bristol Beaufighter

The **Bristol Beaufighter** was the Royal Air Force's first purpose-designed night-fighter and was developed when the RAF needed a stop-gap heavy fighter. In the remarkably quick time of six months from concept to completion of the prototype, Bristol created the Type 156 Beaufighter, a powerful fighter with twin 1,400-hp (1044-kW) engines and a narrow fuselage, which housed the pilot at the front and the crewman in the mid-fuselage under a Perspex dome. Development was aided by using the general layout of the Beaufort torpedo-bomber and many parts from it, namely the wings, tail group and undercarriage.

The Type 156 prototype first flew on 17 July 1939, but turning it into an operational combat aircraft took a year longer and service entry of the **Beaufighter IF** occurred in September 1940. Radar soon followed and night-fighter Beaufighters destroyed two dozen German bombers before the blitzkrieg on London ended in May 1941. The most famous crew were John 'Cat's-Eyes' Cunningham and C.F. Rawnsley.

Coastal Command took a version without wing guns as the Mk IC, many of which were used in the Middle East. The **Beaufighter IIF** had 1,250-hp (933-kW) Merlin XXs and equipped 19 RAF and 12 FAA squadrons. Some **Beaufighter VIFs** had a 'thimble'

A Beaufighter IF fighter taxies in at Malta in 1943. The fuselage and wing gun ports are covered with doped fabric patches. (TRH Pictures)

radome for AI VI, VII or VIII radar and late examples had pronounced tailplane dihedral for better stability. The USAAF operated a few as night-fighters in the Mediterranean. About 1,830 Mk VIs were built, some as **Mk VIC 'Torbeaus'** modified to carry a torpedo.

Although pushing the definition of 'fighter' somewhat, the **Beaufighter TF X** was developed as a long-range strike fighter, armed with rockets, torpedoes or bombs as well as cannon and machine-guns. Used mainly by Coastal Command, the TF X wreaked havoc on German shipping in Norway and against enemy patrol aircraft. A total of 2,205 Mk Xs were built out of 5,564 British-built 'Beaus'. The Australian Department of Aircraft Production (DAP) produced 364 **Mk 21**s, based on the TF X, from 1944. They were equally successful against Japanese shipping around New Guinea and were distinguished by a prominent hump in front of the windscreen.

In post-war years, the RAF operated the Beaufighter in the target towing and other support roles until 1960. Most were Mk Xs converted to **TT.10** configuration. There were a few exports; to the Dominican Republic, Israel (acquired surreptitiously) and Portugal.

Beaufighters served with most RAF commands. This Mk IF was with No. 252 Squadron of Coastal Command in early 1941. (TRH Pictures)

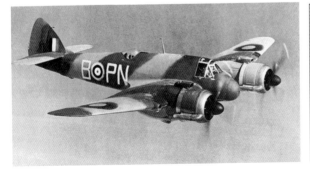

Specification: Beaufighter Mk VIF
Type: two-seat, twin-engined night-fighter
Powerplant: two 1,670-hp (1246-kW) Bristol Hercules VI or XVI radial pistons
Dimensions: span 57 ft 10 in (17.63 m); length 41 ft 8 in (12.70 m); height 15 ft 10 in (4.82 m); wing area 5030 sq ft (46.73 m²)
Weights: empty 14,600 lb (6623 kg); max. take-off 21,600 lb (9798 kg)
Performance: max. speed 333 mph (536 km/h); climb to 15,000 ft (4570 m) in 7 minutes 48 seconds; service ceiling 26,500 ft (8075 m); range 1,480 miles (2382 km)
Armament: four 20-mm Hispano cannon in nose, two 0.303-in (7.7-mm) machine-guns in port wing and four in starboard wing

Junkers 88 fighters

Luftwaffe Ju 88s destroyed more Allied night-bombers than all other fighters combined. This is a Ju 88G with Lichtenstein radar. (TRH Pictures)

The best of the German medium bombers, the Junkers 88 was built for speed and bomb load to a design by hired American engineers W H Evers and Alfred Gassner. Studies into a heavy fighter (Zerstörer) development of the Ju 88 began even before the bomber version entered service. During prototype trials in late 1939, the **Ju 88V7** (the second pre-production aircraft) was fitted with a solid nose containing three 0.31-in (7.92-mm) machine-guns and a 20-mm FF/M cannon, and was evaluated as a day-fighter.

The Ju 88C-2 was converted from bomber airframes on the production line to a solid-nose fighter variant with three machine-guns and two cannon. Engines were the 1,200-hp (895-kW) Jumo 211B-1, and the C-2 entered service as a day-fighter in early 1940. One use was as a long-range patrol fighter over the Bay of Biscay.

There were numerous variants and sub-variants. The **Ju 88C-4** was the first production fighter model, with two extra cannon in a ventral gondola. The **Ju 88C-6** was a more heavily armoured day-fighter. The **Ju 88C-6Bb** was the first radar-equipped night-fighter variant, with Lichtenstein radar.

The next variant produced was the **Ju 88R**, equivalent to the C-6 but with BMW 801 radials. The **Ju 88P** was a heavily-armed ground-attack fighter. The **Ju 88G** had a larger fin with a squarer outline, similar to that on the Ju 188 bomber and BMW engines. These powerplants were in demand for

Focke-Wulf Fw 190s and thus Jumo engines were more common. The **Ju 388J** was a lengthened, long-span derivative with four seats in a pressure cabin. Only a few prototypes were completed.

The Ju 88 night-fighters were equipped with many novel electronic countermeasures devices. Two of the most important were known as Flensburg, which homed in on emissions from Monica tail warning radar in RAF bombers, and Naxos, which tracked H2S navigation radar. Unbeknownst to the RAF, their bombers were guiding night-fighters to themselves. On 13 July 1944 a **Ju 88G-1** of 7/NJG 2 landed at RAF Woodbridge due to a navigation error, handing the secrets of Flensburg and Naxos to the British, who immediately stopped use of Monica and modified H2S, thus saving many bombers. The Luftwaffe derived one of their best airborne radars, named Berlin, from captured H2S sets. Unlike other German AI radars it used a dish, rather than a dipole antenna and had a thimble nosecone. Only ten installations were complete by the war's end.

About 3,200 of 10,774 Ju 88s built were fighters.

The Ju 88P-2 was armed with a huge 'bathtub' fairing containing twin 37-mm cannon in the belly. The P-1 variant sported a 75-mm anti-tank gun. (TRH Pictures)

Specification: Ju 88C-6
Type: three crew twin-engined night-fighter
Powerplant: two 1,340-hp (999 kW) Junkers Jumo 211J-1/2 inverted V-12s
Dimensions: span 65 ft 1 in (20.08 m); length 47 ft 1.3 in (14.36 m); height 16 ft 7.5 in (5.07 m); wing area 586.65 sq ft (54.5 m²)
Weights: empty 19,973 lb (9060 kg); loaded 27,225 lb (12349 kg)
Performance: max. speed 309 mph (494 km/h); climb to 19,685 ft (6000 m) in 12 minutes 42 seconds; service ceiling 32,480 ft (9900 m); range 1,230 miles (1979 km/h)
Armament: four 0.31-in (13-mm) MG 17 machine-guns and six MG 151/20 cannon, two in vertical mountings

Hawker Typhoon and Tempest

Even as the Spitfire and Hurricane were undergoing flight trials, the RAF issued a specification for its replacement, a four-cannon day-fighter. Hawker's Sydney Camm replied with two similar designs, the Tornado with the 24-cylinder X-configuration Rolls-Royce Vulture engine of 1,760 hp (1313 kW) and the **Typhoon** with the 24-cylinder, 2,200-hp (1641-kW) flat-H Napier Sabre. The Tornado first flew on 6 October 1939 and the Typhoon on 24 February 1940. Both versions suffered protracted engine troubles, but the Typhoon proved more promising and was ordered in early 1941 as the **Typhoon IA** with twelve 0.303-in (7.7-mm) machine-guns and the **Typhoon IB** with four 20-mm cannon. Because Hawker was busy developing the Hurricane, Gloster was given the contract for the Typhoon IA and Hawker built the IB. Only 105 of the former were built, but Gloster was to produce the great bulk of the eventual 3,330 Typhoons delivered.

The Typhoon was a very large all-metal fighter with a prominent chin radiator and noticeable dihedral on the outer wings. Early models had a framed canopy with a 'car door' for entry and a three-bladed propeller. Later aircraft had a bubble canopy and a four-bladed prop. Service began in September 1941 but there were

A Typhoon IB of No. 198 Squadron RAF gets airborne from Martragny, France, in July 1944 armed with eight rocket projectiles. (TRH Pictures)

many teething problems such as exhaust gas in the cockpit and tail failures. The Typhoon later proved a potent low-level fighter and in the ground-attack role, equipped with a battery of rockets or bombs, it wreaked havoc on enemy armour and ground transport in the Normandy campaign. At Falaise, 175 tanks were destroyed in one day.

As early as March 1940, Hawker was studying an improved 'Typhoon II' with better speed and altitude performance. A new, thin laminar flow wing was mated with an enlarged tail and a new undercarriage to produce the **Tempest**. The armament was similar to that of the Typhoon but with short-barrelled cannon. The production **Tempest V** with a Sabre Mk IV first flew on 21 June 1943.

Entering service in January 1944, Tempest units destroyed 20 Me 262s and many other Luftwaffe aircraft. Production amounted to 1,149 Napier-powered Tempests, including 142 **Tempest VI**s with the 2,340-hp (1746-kW) Sabre VA.

The Mk VI served in the RAF until 1949. The **Tempest II** was another post-war version, powered by the 2,520-hp (1880-kW) Bristol Centaurus. Of the 452 built, India received 89 and Pakistan 24.

The Tempest V could be distinguished from the late-model Typhoon by its larger fin and lack of protruding cannon barrels. (TRH Pictures)

Specification: Hawker Tempest Mk V
Type: single-seat fighter-bomber
Powerplant: one 2,260-hp (1686-kW) Napier Sabre VA H-24 piston
Dimensions: span 41 ft 0 in (12.49 m); length 33 ft 8 in (10.26 m); height 16 ft 1 in (4.90 m); wing area 302 sq ft (28.05 m²)
Weights: empty 9,250 lb (4196 kg); max. loaded 13,640 lb (6187 kg)
Performance: max. speed 435 mph (700 km/h); initial climb rate 4,700 ft (1433 m) per minute; service ceiling 37,000 ft (11280 m); range 740 miles (1191 km)
Armament: four 20-mm Hispano cannon, up to eight rockets and 2,000 lb (907 kg) of bombs

Lavochkin fighters

The LaGG/La fighter series developed by Semyon Lavochkin ranged from the disappointing inline-engined fighters of 1941 to the radial-engined mount of the greatest Allied ace of World War II, and to evolved versions that served in Korea.

The first of the line was the **LaGG-1** (standing for designers Lavochkin, Gorbunov and Gudkov), which first flew on 30 March 1940 as the **I-22** with a 1,100-hp (820-kW) Klimov M-105P V-12 engine. This mounted a 23-mm cannon firing through the prop hub and two 0.50-in (12.7-mm) machine-guns on top. The construction was a novel type of plastic-impregnated wood, giving rise to the nickname 'varnished guaranteed coffin', also a play on words in Russian from the initials 'LaGG'. The LaGG-1 proved inadequate in most respects, but the political situation prevented rectification before production began.

When given the chance, Lavochkin revised the design as the **I-301**, which became the **LaGG-3**. Changes included lighter armament (one 20-mm cannon and two 0.30-in (7.62-mm) machine-guns), wing slats and the 1,250-hp (940-kW) Klimov M-105PF engine. This was better, but still inferior to the Polikarpov I-16. The LaGG-3 was the mount of several naval aces and 6,528 were built up to summer 1942.

In late 1941 Lavochkin decided (or was ordered) to adapt the LaGG-3 to take a 1,330-hp (996-kW) M-82 radial. This was no easy job as the M-82 was 18 in (45.7 cm) wider than the LaGG's fuselage. Two 20-mm

The La-7 was the ultimate wartime development of the Lavochkin fighters. This example served with a Guards regiment in the winter of 1944/5. (Philip Jarrett collection)

ShVAK cannon above the cowl replaced the hub cannon on the **LaG-5** (Gorbunov having left), which first flew in January 1942. After a troubled debut in August, improved versions emerged, notably the **La-5FN** with a boosted engine giving 1,700 hp (1273 kW). These were available in large numbers (9,920 were built) for the Battle of Kursk in July 1943, where they were found equal, in the right hands, to contemporary Luftwaffe fighters.

The strengthened **La-7** flew in June 1943 with metal versus wooden spars and (usually) three cannon – two on the left wing and one on the right. Production amounted to 5,753. Top Allied ace of the war Ivan Kozhedub, scored 62 kills, including one Me 262, all on La-5s and La-7s.

In 1944 an improved all-metal derivative appeared with the Ash-82FN (formerly M-82FN) and armed with four 23-mm NS-23 cannon. Production of 1,630 **La-9**s began in 1947. The final model was the long-range three-cannon **La-11**, of 1947. Many of the 1,182 built went to China and North Korea.

The LaGG-3 was the main inline-engined Lavochkin fighter. Despite its modern looks, it compared poorly with the Bf 109 and even older Soviet biplanes. (TRH Pictures)

Specification: Lavochkin La-5FN
Type: single-seat fighter
Powerplant: one 1,700-hp (1273-kW) Shvetsov M-82FN 14-cylinder radial
Dimensions: span 32 ft 2 in (9.8 m); length 28 ft 2.5 in (8.46 m); height 8 ft 4 in (2.54 m); wing area 188.37 sq ft (17.50 m²)
Weights: empty 6,173 kg (2800 kg); loaded 7,407 lb (3360 kg)
Performance: max. speed 403 mph (648 km/h); climb to 16,405 ft (5000 m) in 5 minutes 12 seconds; service ceiling 31,166 ft (9,500 m); range 475 miles (765 km)
Armament: two 20-mm ShVAK cannon above engine, provision for up to 330 lb (150 kg) of light bombs

Mikoyan-Gurevich MiG-3

Soviet Union
April 1940

The first fighters of the legendary MiG design bureau (or OKB – experimental construction bureau) were high-powered inline-engined interceptors. Unlike later designs, they were less than completely successful and were overshadowed by the products of other bureaux.

The line began with a 1939 specification for a general-purpose fighter to compete with the Messerschmitt Bf 109. One of the ten proposals was from Nikolai Polikarpov who suggested an aircraft powered by the new 1,400-hp (1049-kW) Mikulin AM-37 supercharged V-12 engine. Polikarpov was directed to concentrate on the I-180 (a refined I-16), and the job of developing the new Mikulin-powered fighter, as the I-200, was given to Artem I. Mikoyan and his deputy Mikhail Y. Gurevich. Development of the AM-37 was abandoned, but work continued on the basis of the 1,350-hp (1007-kW) AM-35A. Around this they designed a sleek fighter of mixed wood and metal construction, which flew as the **I-61** on 5 April 1940. After cooling problems were cured, the I-61 was ordered as the **MiG-1** (from the designers' initials) in late May. Entry into service began in April 1941.

The MiG-1 gained a reputation as something of a 'hot ship', especially compared with the preceding

As better fighters came along, MiG-3s were relegated to Moscow defence and reconnaissance. These twelve IAP MiGs were based near Moscow in early 1942. (Philip Jarrett)

Despite its racy looks, the MiG-3 was not particularly fast or manoeuvrable. Pilot visibility was poor on the ground. (TRH Pictures)

biplanes, and accidents were many. The length of the engine caused poor directional stability and manoeuvrability was generally poor. Only about 100 were completed.

Even as the MiG-1 was under test, Mikoyan and Gurevich were working on an improved derivative. The first **MiG-3** flew in February 1941 with a simpler, stronger structure and a lower rear fuselage. Deliveries began at the same time as the MiG-1.

The MiG-3 was put into production too quickly and suffered from many faults owing to low manufacturing standards. Compared to the prototype, the production MiG-3 was heavier, with a centre of gravity too far aft, but was less of a handful and had refinements such as armour and radio. At the time of the German invasion in June 1941, there were 1,289 MiG-3s in service. In the first days of war, a number were expended in desperate *taran* ramming attacks. In fact, the first such victim was a Ju 88 credited to a MiG-3 pilot on the first day of the German invasion.

One of the best MiG pilots was Alexsandr Pokryshkin. Although he destroyed most of his 59 kills on P-39s to become the second-ranking Allied ace, he was also successful on the MiG-3.

Specification: MiG-3
Type: single-seat fighter
Powerplant: one 1,350-hp (1007-kW) Mikulin AM-35A V-12 inline piston
Dimensions: span 33 ft 9.5 in (10.30 m); length 26 ft 9 in (8.15 m); height 8ft 9 in (2.67 m); wing area 187.7 sq ft (17.44 m²)
Weights: empty 5,996 lb (2720 kg); loaded 7,694 lb (3490 kg)
Performance: max. speed 398 mph (640 km/h); initial climb rate 3,935 ft (1200 m) per minute; service ceiling 39,370 ft (12000 m); range 777 miles (1250 km)
Armament: one 0.50-in (12.7-mm) Beresin BS, two 0.30-in (7.62-mm) ShKAS and two 12.7-mm underwing machine-guns

Chance-Vought F4U Corsair

United States
May 1940

Built to a 1938 US Navy (USN) requirement for a single-seat shipboard fighter, the Vought **F4U Corsair** was designed by Rex Beisel and his team around the huge new Pratt & Whitney R-2800 Double Wasp radial engine driving a large three-bladed propeller. To keep the propeller clear of the ground, the Corsair had an inverted gull wing, which contained six machine-guns and had fabric-covered outer panels. The **XF4U-1**'s first flight was on 29 May 1940.

The original 'birdcage' canopy **F4U-1** failed its carrier suitability trials in September 1942 owing to the poor forward view on landing and tendency for the undercarriage to bounce, so entered combat with land-based USMC units on Guadalcanal, followed by the **F4U-1A** and **F4U-1D**. The most famous USMC unit was VMF-214 'Blacksheep', led by Gregory 'Pappy' Boyington, who was the top F4U ace, with 24 kills. USN Corsairs later went to sea and were credited with a kill ratio of 11 to one against Japanese aircraft.

The growing demand for Corsairs saw production undertaken by three manufacturers. Vought built 5,559 F4U-1s and subtypes, Goodyear produced 2,010 **FG-1**s and Brewster 735 **F3A-1**s. Goodyear later developed the **F2G** with the 3,000-hp (2238-kW) R-4360 and a bubble canopy, but only 18 were built.

Royal Navy Corsairs had 'clipped' wings to enable them to fit in the lower hangars of British carriers. Ninety-five Corsair Is (F4U-1s) and 510 Corsair IIs (F4U-1As and -Ds) were acquired, along with

A Goodyear-built FG-1D shows off the distinctive inverted gull wing of the Corsair. This kept the propeller clear of the ground. (TRH Pictures)

Goodyear-built **Corsair III**s and Brewster **Corsair IV**s for a total of 2,012. They were the best Fleet Air Arm fighters of the war and saw limited combat in Europe before participating in the final assault on Japan.

The Royal New Zealand Air Force (RNZAF) received 424 F4U-1As, F4U-1Ds and FG-1Ds, which were used in the Pacific in 1944 and 1945 and in the occupation of Japan. The **F4U-4** flew in April 1944 with a 2,450-hp (1828-kW) water-injected R-2800-18W. It had a four-bladed propeller, revised intakes, rocket stubs, four 20-mm cannon and metal-covered outer wings.

After the war, production of the F4U-4 continued and the **F4U-5** was introduced. Both saw extensive service in Korea. The latter had a 'squashed' cowl shape and saw most action in its **F4U-5N** night-fighter form. Final versions were the **AU-1** for ground-attack and the **F4U-7** for the French Navy, which saw action in Suez and Indochina.

The last of 12,571 Corsairs was completed in 1952, the last piston-engined fighter to be accepted by US forces.

The F4U-1A with a blown canopy replaced the original 'birdcage' F4U-1. With teething troubles over, the Corsair became the most successful USN fighter. (TRH Pictures)

Specification: Vought F4U-5 Corsair
Type: single-seat carrier/land-based fighter
Powerplant: one 2,850-hp (1828-kW) R-2800-32W 18-cylinder radial piston
Dimensions: span 40 ft 11.75 in (12.48 m); length 34 ft 6.5 in (10.53 m); height 14 ft 9.25 in (4.49 m); wing area 314 sq ft (29.17 m²)
Weights: empty 9,683 lb (4392 kg); max. take-off 14,610 lb (6627 kg)
Performance: max. speed 470 mph (756 km/h); initial climb 3,780 ft (1152 m) per minute; service ceiling 44,000 ft (13410 m); range 1,120 miles (1802 km)
Armament: four 20-mm cannon, up to 5,200-lb (2359-kg) bomb load

Macchi MC.202/MC.205 Veltro

Italy
August 1940

The Macchi MC.200's potential was limited by its low-powered radial engine, but in early1940 designer Mario Castoldi was able to obtain a Daimler-Benz DB 601 A-1 inline engine as used on the Bf 109E and fit it to a modified MC.200 airframe. The resulting **MC.202 Folgore** (Thunderbolt) was an instant success and was ordered soon after its initial flight on 10 August 1940.

After some initial production models with German-built engines, production switched to engines licence-built by Alfa Romeo as the RA.1000 Monsone (Monsoon). The increased power and the improved streamlining of the MC.202 with its enclosed cockpit and built-up rear fuselage gave the Folgore a 60-mph (100-km/h) greater top speed and 8,500 feet (2600 m) more altitude than the otherwise similar MC.200.

Built alongside the MC.200 in three factories, the MC.202 entered service in the spring of 1941 with 17 Gruppo and was quickly despatched to the Libyan front. In combat the Folgore was not quite a match for the fighters it was meeting by 1941, and attrition and poor spare parts supply led to a situation where only about 20 machines were available to meet the Allied invasion of Sicily. Folgore production was limited by the supply of engines, with a final total of about 1,500

The MC.202 was the best Italian fighter available in quantity during the war, but was underarmed, and underpowered compared to Allied fighters. (TRH Pictures)

Showing off its sleek lines, this MC.202 was captured in North Africa by British forces and given RAF markings for evaluation flights. (TRH Pictures)

built, 392 by Macchi itself. Variants included the MC.202AS tropical version and the **MC.202CB** fighter-bomber. To remedy the Folgore's lack of firepower, the last batch was equipped with a pair of German MG 151 cannon in the outer wings to supplement the cowl-mounted machine-guns and replace two rifle-calibre wing guns.

Fitted with a 1,475-hp (1100-kW) 605A engine, a series MC.202 became the prototype **MC.205V Veltro** (Greyhound), which first flew on 19 April 1942 and was quickly ordered into production. Due to difficulties in obtaining more engines, which were later produced by Fiat as the RA.1050 Typhoon, the Veltro's service entry was delayed until mid-1943, by which time it was unable to influence events. What combat it saw was mainly in the bomber escort and fighter-bomber roles. Only 177 were built before the armistice, but production was reinstated for the Italian Socialist Republic Air Force, ending at a total of 265. A few ended up in Luftwaffe hands, equipping one unit. After the war, a batch of 42 was built from parts and supplied to Egypt but most were destroyed on the ground in the Israeli War of Independence.

Specification: MC.205V
Type: single-seat fighter
Powerplant: one 1,475-hp (1100-kW) Fiat RA.1050 RC.58 inverted V-12 piston
Dimensions: span 34 ft 8.5 in (10.58 m); length 29 ft 0.5 in (8.58 m); height 9 ft 11.5 in (3.04 m); wing area 180.84 sq ft (16.80 m²)
Weights: empty 5,691 lb (2581 kg); max. take-off 7,514 lb (3408 kg)
Performance: max. speed 399 mph (642 km/h); climb rate unknown; service ceiling 37,090 ft (16,370 m); range 646 miles (1040 km)
Armament: two 0.50-in (12.7-mm) machine-guns in fuselage, two 0.303-in (7.7-mm) guns in wings or two MG 151 20-mm cannon in underwing pods

50

Republic P-47 Thunderbolt

United States
May 1941

Alexander Kartveli of the Seversky Aircraft Corporation designed the Seversky P-35, which the US Army had bought in small numbers in 1936, mainly to make up for delays in Curtiss Hawk production. Kartveli then improved on the design with a fully retracting undercarriage and other improvements under the designation XP-41. The company was renamed the Republic Aviation Corporation in 1938 and a revised XP-41 was offered for a new Army competition and accepted as the P-43 Lancer with the 1,200-hp (894-kW) R-1830 radial. Over 200 were built, of which 51 were delivered to China.

An enlarged derivative, powered by a turbosupercharged Pratt & Whitney R-2800 Twin Wasp was ordered as the **XP-47B Thunderbolt** in September 1940 after two earlier XP-47 proposals were discarded. The same month, the Army ordered 171 **P-47B**s and 602 **P-47C**s. This was eight months before the XP-47B's first flight on 6 May 1941. Accidents to the two XPs led to modifications, including metal control surfaces and a sliding canopy. Production P-47Bs had the 2,000-hp (1491-kW) R-2800 and eight machine-guns in the wings.

The P-47B entered service with the 56th Fighter Group in mid-1942. In early 1943 the first groups joined the 8th Air Force in Europe, where they were able to escort bombers well into Germany when fitted with external fuel tanks. After D-Day, the P-47 was particularly effective in the tank-busting and ground-

This P-47C is typical of early 'razorback' Thunderbolts used by 8th Air Force fighter squadrons in Europe from 1942. (TRH Pictures)

attack role. Francis Gabreski and Robert S. Johnson both scored 28 kills to be among the top five US aces of the war. In all, the P-47 scored well over 3,000 aerial victories and destroyed as many enemy aircraft on the ground.

A total of 12,602 **P-47D**s were built, in both 'razorback' and 'bubbletop' versions. Most had the 2,300-hp (1716-kW) R-2800-59).The RAF had 830 razorback **Thunderbolt I**s and bubbletop **Thunderbolt II**s, most of which were used in Burma and India. **The P-47M** was a lightweight version with six guns intended to combat V-1 flying bombs.

The **P-47N** had clipped wings with internal fuel tanks and an increased gross weight. It was designed for the Pacific theatre where it could escort B-29s from the Marianas Islands to Japan. Both Brazil and Mexico operated P-47s in combat in World War II, the former in Italy and the latter in the Philippines.

Total P-47 production was 15,660, more than any other US fighter. Post war, the P-47 had a long career with the Air National Guard and in Latin America.

Built for long-range missions in the Pacific, the P-47N with its clipped wings was the last production model. Over 15,300 Thunderbolts were built. (TRH Pictures)

Specification: P-47D-25 Thunderbolt
Type: single-seat long-range fighter
Powerplant: one 2,300-hp (1716-kW) P&W R-2800-59 18-cylinder radial piston
Dimensions: span 40 ft 9.5 in (12.43 m); length 36 ft 1.75 in (11.01 m); height 14 ft 2 in (4.32 m); wing area 300.0 sq ft (27.87 m²)
Weights: empty 10,000 lb (4536 kg); max. take-off 19,400 lb (8800 kg)
Performance: max. speed 428 mph (689 km/h); climb to 20,000 ft (6095 m) in 9 minutes; service ceiling 42,000 ft (12800 m); range 1,260 miles (2028 km)
Armament: eight 0.50-in (12.7-mm) Browning machine-guns in wings and up to two 1,000-lb (454-kg) bombs

Kawasaki Ki-45-KAI Toryu 'Nick'

A Japanese Army requirement for a twin-seat long-range fighter was issued in December 1937. Feeling the requirement was poorly defined, Mitsubishi and Nakajima did not offer designs, but Kawasaki was keen to build a modern design and Isamu Imashi set to work on the Ki-38. This was halted at the mock-up stage (owing to arguments over the requirement) and Imashi was replaced by Takeo Doi, who revised the design to produce the **Ki-45** . The first of three prototypes flew in January 1939. With two 820-hp (611-kW) Nakajima Ha-20-Otsu engines, the Ki-45 was slow and unmanoeuvrable and the project was suspended while the whole strategic fighter concept was redefined.

In May 1941 the much revised **Ki-45-KAI** was flown with 1,000-hp (745-kW) Ha-25 engines and ordered in November as the Army Type 2 Two-Seat Fighter Model A and named Toryu (dragon-slayer). The Toryu was a well-proportioned aircraft with separate cockpits for the pilot and gunner, who had a flexible machine-gun for self-defence. The main armament was two 20-mm cannon and two 0.31-in (7.92-mm) machine-guns in the nose.

The original production version, the **Ki-45-KAI-Ko** was usually used for ground-attack, as was the **Ki-45-**

This Ki-45 KAI was wrecked in an Allied air raid before the landings on the Wake Islands off northern New Guinea in May 1944. (TRH Pictures)

In the bomber interception role, the Toryu was armed with oblique-firing cannon between the cockpits. The total production was 1,198 Ki-45-KAIs. (Philip Jarrett collection)

KAI-Otsu, although they could hold their own against Allied single-seat fighters. When Otsus were used against B-24 bombers in New Guinea and found to be very effective, a production night-fighter was ordered as the **Ki-45-KAI-Hei.** The intended centimetric radar was not forthcoming and the nose remained empty on the 477 examples built. The Ki-45-KAI-Hei is often said to have destroyed eight B-29s on its first combat sortie in April 1944; in fact none were recorded as lost to twin-engined fighters on that day. Nonetheless this, the Japanese Army's only night-fighter, was to prove very successful in the defence against night B-29 raids, even though it was armed with only two upwards-firing cannon and had no radar. Captain Isamu Kashiide of the 4th Sentai claimed 26 B-29s over Japan although his actual score is probably seven.

The Toryu, known to the Allies as 'Nick', was also used in strikes against US Navy vessels, and is said to have made one of the first (if unofficial) *kamikaze* attacks, against a submarine chaser off New Guinea. An anti-shipping version was built with one 37-mm and two 20-mm cannon as the **Kai-45-KAI-Tei.** It had more powerful Ha-102 1,080-hp (805-kW) engines.

Specification: Kawasaki Ki-45-KAIc
Type: twin engined, two-seat night-fighter
Powerplant: two 1,080-hp (805-kW) Mitsubishi Ha-102 14-cylinder radial pistons
Dimensions: span 49 ft 4.5 in (15.05 m); length 36 ft 1 in (11 m); height 12 ft 1.5 in (15.05 m); wing area 344.46 sq ft (32 m²)
Weights: empty 8,818 lb (4000 kg); max. take-off 12,125 lb (5500 kg)
Performance: max. speed 339 mph (545 km/h); climb to 16,405 ft (5000 m) in 6 minutes 20 seconds; service ceiling 35,200 ft (10370 m); range 344.44 sq ft (32.0 m²)
Armament: two 0.50-in (12.7-mm) machine-guns in oblique mount, one 20-mm cannon and two 12.7-mm machine-guns in nose

De Havilland Mosquito fighters

United Kingdom
May 1941

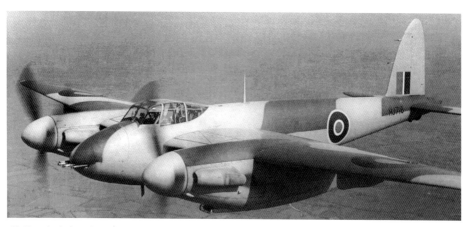

Although designed as an unarmed high-speed day-bomber, the **de Havilland Mosquito** branched into two distinct paths including a successful series of night-fighters and fighter-bombers.

Of mostly wooden construction, the early Mosquitoes were powered by two 1,230-hp (918-hp) Rolls-Royce Merlin 21 engines. The first batch of 50 Mosquito bombers included one prototype fighter version known as the **F II**, which had four cannon mounted under the fuselage and four machine-guns firing through the nosecone in place of the bomb-aimer's position. The first Mk II flew on 15 May 1941. Limited numbers of F IIs served as day-fighters, but the main use was as **NF II** night-fighters with radar in place of machine-guns.

The first Mosquito fighter squadron was No. 151 (equipped with NF IIs), which formed in 1942. In late May, the first of nearly 600 enemy aircraft were destroyed by 'Mossie' night-fighters in the home defence role. Later they were used in the bomber support role as escorts to the 'heavies' operating at night over Germany.

The main fighter variant was the **FB VI**, of which over 2,300 were built from mid-1942. These could carry bombs internally and externally and were used on some famous precision attacks such as that on the Amiens prison. The Mosquito fighter-bomber squadrons of the Tactical Air Force's 85 Group destroyed 299 enemy aircraft and 623 V-1s from

The main fighter version of the Mosquito was the FB VI, used mainly in the fighter-bomber role. It served as the basis for most export models. (Aviation Picture Library)

March 1944 to May 1945. The FB.VI was built under licence in Australia as the **FB 40** (178 built) and in Canada as the FB.26 (339). The **FB XVIII** was a specialised anti-shipping version with a 6-lb (57-mm) Mollins gun and known as the 'Tsetse' Mosquito. Improved night-fighter versions with centimetric radar in thimble radomes included the **NF XIII** and **NF 30**, the latter being one of the best wartime night-fighters.

Around 1,000 Mosquitoes were supplied to friendly nations after World War II, mostly fighters. Israel acquired a variety of fighter, trainer and PR 'Mossies' from 1948 until 1955, including FB VIs and NF 30s. Many of these were among the 100 previously operated by France. French Mosquitoes operated in Indochina and Morocco until 1953. Sweden designated its **NF XIX** Mosquitoes as the **J30**, retiring the last in 1955. The Czech Air Force had 19 **B-36**s (or Mosquito FB.VIs).

Of the 7,781 Mosquitoes (built, 6,710 during the war), approximately 4,280 were fighter variants.

The first operational Mosquito fighter version was the NF II with 'bow and arrow' radar antenna and armament of four 20-mm cannon in the belly. (TRH Pictures)

Specification: DH Mosquito FB VI
Type: two-seat twin-engined fighter-bomber
Powerplant: two 1,635-hp (1220-kW) Rolls-Royce Merlin 25 V-12 pistons
Dimensions: span 54 ft 2 in (16.51 m); length 30 ft 10.75 in (12.47 m); height 15 ft 3 in (4.65 m); wing area 450 sq ft (41.81 m²)
Weights: empty 14,300 lb (6489 kg); max. take-off 20,000 lb (9072 kg)
Performance: max. speed 356 mph (573 km/h); climb to 15,000 ft (4570 m) in 6 minutes 45 seconds; service ceiling 40,000 ft (13410 m); range 1,860 miles (2990 m)
Armament: four 20-mm Hispano cannon and four 0.303-in (7.7-mm) machine-guns up to 1,000-lb (464-kg) of bombs or eight rockets

Kawasaki Ki-61 Hien 'Tony'/Ki-100

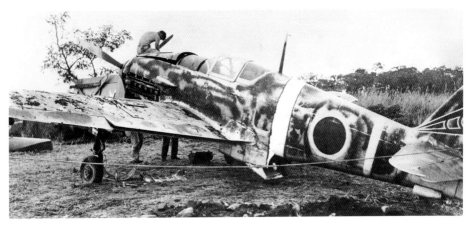

The Ki-61 was the only significant inline-engined Japanese fighter. This was the first example to fall into Allied hands, on the island of New Britain. (TRH Pictures)

Kawasaki acquired a licence for the Daimler-Benz DB.601A 12-cylinder inverted-vee engine in April 1940. This was the powerplant used in the Messerschmitt Bf 109E, which had already demonstrated its superiority over Poland and at the end of the Spanish Civil War. The first Japanese-built version, designated Ha-40, was available in mid-1940, by which time Kawasaki had developed two potential airframes, the Ki-60 and the slightly larger **K-61**. Both were designed by Takeo Doi and Shin Owada, but the K-61, first flown in December 1941, was much more stable and was chosen as the Army Type Fighter Model I, also known as the **Ki-61-I-ko Hien** (Swallow). The Hien was the only production Japanese fighter with an inline water-cooled engine. It had the effective armament of two 0.50-in (12.7-mm) machine-guns in the nose and two 0.303-in (7.7-mm) (Ki-61-Ia) or 0.50-in (12.7-mm) guns (Ki-61-Ib) in the wings. Featuring armour protection for the pilot and self-sealing tanks, the Ki-61 was considerably more durable than the Ki-43 Hayabusa.

The Allies first encountered the Ki-61 over New Guinea in July 1943. The unusual profile of the Hien led many US and Commonwealth pilots to claim that they had fought Messerschmitt 109s or Macchi 202s. The top ace on the Hien was Shogo Takeuchi of the 68th Sentai, who scored over 30 victories in the New Guinea theatre. Against the P-39 and P-40, the Ki-61 was undeniably superior, but as new USAAF fighters such as the P-38 and P-47 appeared in late 1943, the tide turned. A relative few (388) were rearmed with imported 20-mm Mauser MG 151 cannons as the **Ki-61-Ia** and **-Ib**.

The **Ki-61-I-KAIc** was a slightly longer and stronger version, designed for easier maintenance. Equipped with Type Ho-5 20-mm cannon, the -Ic was the main production version. In all 2,654 Hiens were built.

In the homeland defence role the Ki-61 served with seven sentais. It was more effective against carrier-based aircraft than the high-flying B-29s and their P-51 escorts. The shortage of engines caused by US bombing led to the **Ki-100**, which married 275 uncompleted Ki-61-II airframes with the new 1,500-hp (1119-kW) Ha-112 radial. First flown in February 1945, the Ki-100 was a great success and one of the most effective B-29 destroyers. A further 99 were built new as the **Ki-100-Ib** with a cut-down rear fuselage and teardrop rear canopy.

The Ki-100 was one of the best Japanese fighters of the war. This early model was converted from a Ki-61 and served with the 1st Chutaii, 59th Sentai. (Philip Jarrett)

Specification: Kawasaki Ki-61-Ic Hien
Type: single-seat fighter
Powerplant: one 1,175-hp (876-kW) Kawasaki Ha-40 inverted V-12 piston
Dimensions: span 39 ft 4.25 in (12.00 m); length 29 ft 4.25 in (8.95 m); height 12 ft 1.75 in (3.70 m); wing area 215.29 sq ft (20.00 m²)
Weights: empty 5,798 lb (2360 kg); max. take-off 7,650 lb (3470 kg)
Performance: max. speed 348 mph (560 km/h); climb to 16,400 ft (4999 m) in 5 minutes 31 seconds; service ceiling 32,810 ft (10000 m); range 1,181 miles (1900 km)
Armament: two 0.50-in (12.7-mm) machine-guns, in fuselage, two 20-mm Ho-5 cannon in wings, up to two 551-lb (250-kg) bombs

Mitsubishi J2M Raiden 'Jack'

Mitsubishi's Jiro Horikoshi convinced the IJN that they needed a land-based interceptor as early as October 1938, although no specification was issued until September 1939 owing to work on the A6M Zero-Sen. The official specification emphasised speed at altitude, climb rate and short take-off and landing distances, but not manoeuvrability. The same armament as the A6M was specified, but unlike the Zero-Sen, pilot armour was to be included.

The engine chosen was a supercharged 1,185-hp (883-kW) Mitsubishi Ha-32 Kasei (Mars) 13 14-cylinder twin-row radial with a three-bladed propeller on an extension shaft. This allowed the cowl to be tapered towards the front for reduced drag. Cooling was aided by an engine-driven fan as on the Focke-Wulf 190. The laminar-flow wing was very small with a low aspect ratio with combat flaps to aid manoeuvrability.

The first of three **J2M1** prototypes was flown on 20 March 1942 and exhibited a number of unsatisfactory characteristics, including poor forward visibility from its shallow, curved windscreen and lower climb and speed performance than specified. The fourth aircraft was modified as the **J2M2** with a deeper windscreen and a 1,820-hp (1357-kW) Kasei 23a engine with water/methanol injection. A shorter propeller shaft (driving a four-bladed propeller) allowed the nose to be shortened, further improving visibility. Soon after the J2M2's first flight in October 1942, the IJN ordered it

These J2Ms were pictured at Atsugi Airfield near Tokyo on 28 August 1945. Propellers and engine parts were removed to prevent unauthorised flights. (Philip Jarrett collection)

into production as the **J2M2 Raiden** ('Thunderbolt') Interceptor Model 1. The Allies code-named it 'Jack'. Production was slow due to engine problems and the first unit was not fully equipped until December 1943. Structural problems, including a number of in-flight break-ups meant that only 155 J2M2s were built before production switched to the **J2M3** Raiden Model 21 with beefed-up wings with four cannon, and no fuselage machine-guns. Late J2M2s and all J2M3s featured an oil cooler intake under the chin. The J2M3 had a mixed armament of two 20-mm Type 99 cannon plus two fast-firing Type 99-II cannon in the wings and no fuselage guns.

The high-altitude **J2M4** Raiden Model 34 with a turbocharger was developed, but this proved a failure and only two were built. The final production variant was the **J2M5** Raiden Model 33, combining the basic J2M4 airframe with an 1,820-hp (1357-kW) Kasei 26a with a mechanical supercharger. Engine shortages meant that only 34 J2M5s were completed.

This 'Jack' was taken to the USA after the war and evaluated by the US Navy. It was subsequently restored for the Planes of Fame Museum. (TRH Pictures)

Specification: Mitsubishi J2M3 Raiden
Type: single-seat interceptor fighter
Powerplant: one 1,800-hp (1343-kW) Mitsubishi MK4R-A Kasei 23a 14-cylinder radial piston
Dimensions: span 35 ft 5.25 in (10.8 m); length 31 ft 9.75 in (9.70 m); height 12 ft 6 in (3.81 m); wing area 215.82 sq ft (20.05 m²)
Weights: empty 5,489 lb (2490 kg); loaded 7,584 lb (3440 kg)
Performance: max. speed 363 mph (584 km/h); initial climb rate 3,610 (1100 m) per minute; service ceiling 38,385 ft (11000 m); range 1,580 miles (2520 km)
Armament: two 20-mm Type 99 cannon and two 20-mm Type 99-II cannon in the wings

Gloster Meteor

Frank Whittle spent many frustrating years in the 1930s developing his gas turbine engine and trying to encourage official interest in his work. In 1939 he joined with Gloster Aircraft's chief designer to develop an airframe for his powerplant, and the Air Ministry contracted Gloster to produce a prototype. The single-engine Gloster E.28/39 first flew in May 1941, by which time a further contract, for 500 twin-jet fighters, had been issued and other manufacturers were designing jet engines. The first **F.9/40** development aircraft flew on 5 March 1942, powered by two axial-flow de Havilland H1 Halford engines that gave 2,300-lb (10.23-kN) thrust.

Production **Meteor F.I**s, using Whittle's own centrifugal-flow W.2B engines, built by Rolls-Royce as the Welland, entered service with No. 616 Squadron RAF in July 1944. They quickly destroyed a dozen V-1s. In December 1944 the **Mk III** powered by the Rolls-Royce Derwent arrived and some aircraft were sent to the continent, where they mostly flew ground-attack missions, scoring no aerial victories. Meteor IIIs were used in aerial refuelling, ejection seat and carrier landing trials and with numerous jet and turboprop engines. The **F.4** had long-chord nacelles and a strengthened airframe and was exported to Argentina, the Netherlands, Belgium, Egypt and Denmark. The **T.7** trainer had a heavily framed tandem cockpit and 640 were built for the RAF and many for export.

The principal fighter version was the **F.8** with 3,500-

The F.8 was the definitive fighter version of the Meteor. By September 1960 when this RAF example was seen, the type was mainly in second-line service. (TRH Pictures)

lb (15.6-kN) thrust Derwent 8 engines, a longer fuselage, ejection seats and a new, taller tail. It was also widely exported. In Korea, the RAAF's F.8s were outperformed by the MiG-15, but scored a number of kills against them. They were mainly used for ground attack with rockets and bombs. Israel also received F.8s and they downed several Vampires in 1956. The **FR.9** and **PR.10** were reconnaissance versions with a camera nose and no armament.

Armstrong Whitworth built many Meteors under licence and developed the **NF.11**, **NF.12**, **NF.13** and **NF.14** night-fighters. The armament remained four 20-mm cannon, now mounted in the wings to leave room for the AI 21 nose radar. None had ejection seats. These variants differed mainly in length and canopy detail. Egypt, Syria and Israel received NF.13s. The total number of Meteors built was 3,875.

After the last Meteors left front-line RAF service in 1960, many remained in use as drones, target tugs and as squadron 'hacks'. Martin-Baker still operates two as ejection-seat testbeds.

Armstrong Whitworth built the dedicated radar-equipped night-fighter versions such as this NF.14, which served with No. 85 Squadron RAF. (TRH Pictures)

Specification: Gloster Meteor F.8
Type: single-seat twin-engined jet fighter
Powerplant: two 3,500-lb (15.6-kN) Rolls-Royce Derwent 8 turbojets
Dimensions: span 37 ft 2 in (11.32 m); length 44 ft 7 in (13.59 m); height 13 ft 0 in (3.96 m); wing area 350 sq ft (32.51 m²)
Weights: empty 10,684 lb (4846 kg); loaded 15,700 lb (7122 kg)
Performance: max. speed 598 mph (962 km/h); initial climb 7,000 ft (2134 m) per minute; service ceiling 40,000 ft (12190 m); range 980 miles (1588 km)
Armament: four 20-mm Hispano cannon, up to two 1,000-lb (454-kg) bombs and 8 HVAR rockets

Messerschmitt Me 163 Komet

An Me 163B-1a Komet seen on its take-off trolley at Bad Zwischenahn, the base of the first rocket fighter unit, JG 400. (Philip Jarrett collection)

Experiments with rocket-powered aircraft had begun in Germany well before World War II, with Dr Alexander Lippisch being one of the main proponents of this form of propulsion and the designer of several tailless gliders. Joining Messerschmitt in 1939, Lippisch and his team married an 882-lb (3.92-kN) thrust Walter rocket motor to his DFS 194 glider to produce the **Me 163A**. After satisfactory gliding tests, the first two of six **Me 163V1** prototypes were taken to Peenemunde on the Baltic coast for powered trials in mid-1941. With a new Walter engine producing 1,683 lb thrust (7.49 kN), and towed to height by a Messerschmitt Bf 110, the Me 163V1 demonstrated speeds up to 550 mph (885 km/h) and higher. To take advantage of the new Walter 109-509A motor with 3,750-lb (16.68-kN) thrust, the airframe was redesigned as the larger **Me 163B Komet** fighter, which first flew in April 1942.

The Me 163B was a compact design with a large moderately swept wing and no horizontal tail. Fuel was a volatile combination of hydrogen peroxide and phosphate called T-Stoff and an aqueous solution of calcium permanganate with a catalyst of hydrazine hydrate solution in methanol called C-Stoff. These fuels mixed in the combustion chamber, but would

An Me 163B makes a 'Sharpstart' or alert take-off. The wheeled trolley was jettisoned after take-off and the Komet landed on a skid. (Aerospace Publishing)

explode violently if the mixture was wrong. They would also dissolve anything organic, including the pilots, who had to wear a special protective suit.

Ordered into production as a point defence interceptor, deliveries of pre-production models to JG 400 began in May 1944 and combat operations began in late July. Although the arrival of the rocket fighters surprised the Allies, they are only credited with nine 'kills' in their brief combat career. Fuel efficiency was poorer than expected, giving only four minutes' running at full power or about 25-miles (40-km) radius from base. Other tactical problems included high closing speeds combined with a slow-firing gun and vulnerability when landing as a glider (both to enemy fighters and explosion of residual fuel on landing). Allied bombing in September 1944 stopped the flow of the specialised fuel and severely hampered operations. A total of about 400 Komets were built, but far fewer saw squadron service, let alone combat.

The Japanese were sent an Me 163B in order to begin licensed production, but the ship carrying it was sunk en route. Using only the handbook, they designed the similar but larger **J8M1**. Few were built and none saw action.

Specification: Me 163B Komet
Type: single-seat rocket-powered fighter
Powerplant: one 3,750 lb (16.68 kN) thrust Walter HWK 109-509A-2 rocket
Dimensions: span 30 ft 7 in (9.32 m); length 19 ft 2 in (5.84 m); height 9 ft 1 in (2.77 m); wing area 199.114 sq ft (18.50 m²)
Weights: empty 4,200 lb (1905 kg); max. loaded 9,061 lb (4110 kg)
Performance: max. speed 596 mph (960 km/h); climb to 39,700 ft (12,100 m) in 3 minutes 30 seconds; service ceiling 39,700 ft (12100 m); powered endurance 7 minutes 30 seconds
Armament: two 20-mm MG 151 cannon or two 30-mm MK 108 cannon in wing roots

Northrop P-61 Black Widow

Following observation of the night 'blitz' over London in 1940, the US Army requested that Northrop offer proposals for a radar-equipped night-fighter for US and British needs. John Northrop and Walter Cerney designed a bomber-sized aircraft (just smaller than a B-25) with a pair of 2,000-hp (1492-kW) Pratt & Whitney R-2800-65 18-cylinder radials. It was heavier than a B-25J and three times as heavy as a P-51. Of twin-boom configuration, the P-61's wings had long double-slotted flaps and both ailerons and spoilers for lateral control. The armament comprised four 20-mm cannon under the fuselage and a streamlined, remotely controlled turret atop the fuselage with four 0.50-in (12.7-mm) machine-guns. This was controlled by a gunner situated in a raised cockpit behind the pilot. The turret guns could also be fired by the radar operator who sat in a glazed compartment at the rear of the central nacelle. The nose contained an SCR-520 (AI-10) radar behind a frosted Plexiglas cover.

The **XP-61 Black Widow** first flew on 21 May 1942, by which time 13 **YP-61**s were in production, the first of which took to the air in August 1943. The **P-61A** entered service in Europe in March 1944 and in the Pacific in July. The production radar was the Western Electric SCR-720. Problems with the General Electric top turret meant that it was only fitted to the first 37 Black Widows.

The P-61A was used on anti-V-1 patrols in England as well as night intruder missions over Europe. In the

Not all Black Widows were black. This early model P-61A was finished in olive drab and grey, as were many examples sent to Europe. (TRH Pictures)

Pacific it was used to defend the B-29 bases on Saipan and on night intruder raids against Japanese airfields. In China the P-61 was used against Japanese intruders and then went on the offensive against enemy bases and ground transportation. There was relatively little night opposition by the time the P-61 entered service and only two pilots became P-61 aces in Europe and one in the Pacific. Turret problems were solved during **P-61B** production and 250 of the 400 built were so equipped.

The **P-61C** had larger engines, new superchargers and paddle-bladed propellers. Only 41 of a planned 500 were completed. The P-61C was used in the occupation of Japan and the Philippines and served until May 1950 with operational units.

The **F-15A Reporter** was a dedicated reconnaissance version based on the P-61C. The prototype flew in October 1945 and only 38 were built, serving in Japan and the Philippines in the early post-war years. Total production of the Black Widow and Reporter was 742 airframes.

P-61B 'Lady in the Dark' of the 548th NFS on Ie Shima was one of the most famous Black Widows and was credited with the last kill of World War II. (TRH Pictures)

Specification: Northrop P-61B
Type: three-seat, twin-engined night-fighter
Powerplant: two 2,000-hp (1492-kW) P&W R-2800-65 18-cylinder radial pistons
Dimensions: span 66 ft 0 in (20.12 m); length 49 ft 7 in (15.11 m); height 14 ft 8 in (4.46 m); wing area 664.0 sq ft (61.69 m²)
Weights: empty 22,000 lb (6095 kg); max. take-off 38,000 lb (17240 kg)
Performance: max. speed 366 mph (589 km/h); climb to 20,000 ft (6095 m) in 12 minutes; service ceiling 33,100 ft (10090 m); range 1,590 miles (2559 km)
Armament: four 20-mm cannon under nose, four 0.50-in (12.7-mm) Browning machine-guns in dorsal turret

Kawanishi N1K 'George'

Japan
May 1942

The Kawanishi company was known for its floatplanes and flying boats and in 1940 was tasked with the design of an offensive floatplane fighter to defend islands without airfields or where they were under construction. The IJN's interim solution was for Nakajima to develop the 'Rufe' floatplane version of the A6M Zero-Sen, but Kawanishi's **N1K1 Kyofu** (Mighty Wind) which first flew on 6 May 1942 was a larger, much more modern aircraft with much better armament.

The first prototype had a 1,460-hp (1088-kW) Mitsubishi Mk4D Kasei 14-cylinder radial engine driving a contra-rotating propeller. This proved troublesome and was replaced with a conventional three-bladed unit driven through an extension shaft. Apart from its large main float and wingtip stabilising floats, the Kyofu (Allied code-name 'Rex') was of conventional appearance with a mid-mounted wing and domed canopy with all-round vision.

Deliveries began in the spring of 1943, too late for the Guadalcanal campaign. Early aircraft were powered by a 1,460-hp (1088-kW) MK4C Kasei 13, and later models by a 1,530-hp (1141-kW) MK4E Kasei 15. The armament was two 0.303-in (7.7-mm) machine-guns in the nose and two 20-mm wing cannon.

The N1K1 Kyofu (or 'Rex') was, perhaps uniquely, the basis of a superb land-based fighter. It was quite successful as a floatplane fighter. (Philip Jarrett collection)

The N1K1-J had a mid-set wing as on the Kyofu floatplane. It was followed by the much better N1K2J or 'low-wing George'. (Philip Jarrett collection)

Only 97 N1K1s were built, but they claimed 29 Allied aircraft over Borneo, including B-24s, with Hidenori Matsunaga scoring five. Late in the war one unit was based on Lake Biwa on Honshu in the interceptor role. As early as December 1941, Kawanishi was studying a land-based version of the Kyofu and went ahead with it as a private venture when the IJN showed little interest. During 1942 the IJN changed its mind and ordered a prototype, which first flew in July 1943 with the 1,820-hp (1357-kW) Nakajima Homare 11. Production was authorised in late 1943 as the **N1K1-J Shiden** (Violet Lightning), which the Allies dubbed 'George' when they first encountered it over the Philippines in October 1944.

With four cannon (two in pods), two machine-guns and automatic combat flaps, the Shiden was equal or superior to the F6F Hellcat, let down only by the unreliable engine and poor brakes. The airframe was almost completely revised in the **N1K2-J Shiden-Kai** with a low-mounted wing, four cannon within the wing and a 1,900-hp (1484-kW) Homare 21. This definitive model first flew on 31 December 1943 and 354 were built.

Specification: Kawanishi N1K1-J
Type: single-seat fighter
Powerplant: one 1,990-hp (1485-kW) Nakajima NK9H Homare 21 radial piston
Dimensions: span 39 ft 4.25 in (12.00 m); length 29 ft 1.75 in (8.89 m); height 13 ft 3 in (4.06 m); wing area 252.95 sq ft (23.50 m²)
Weights: empty 6,387 lb (2897 kg); max. take-off 9,526 lb (4321 kg)
Performance: max. speed 363 mph (584 km/h); climb to 19,685 ft (6000 m) in 7 minutes 48 seconds; service ceiling 41,010 ft (12500 m); range 890 miles (1432 km)
Armament: two 0.303-in (7.7-mm) Type 97 machine-guns in nose and four wing-mounted Type 99 cannon

Messerschmitt Me 262

The first jet fighter to see operational service, the **Messerschmitt 262** began as a 1938 proposal by designer Waldemar Voigt for a turbine-engined research aircraft using two BMW 003 turbojets. The Messerschmitt Me 262 was a sleek aircraft with two engines slung under a moderately swept wing, a triangular section fuselage and a blown canopy. Delays with the BMW powerplant meant that the **Me 262 V1** prototype flew with a Jumo 210G piston engine in the nose on 18 April 1941.

On 19 July 1942, Flugkapitän Fritz Wendel took the Me 262 V3 aloft for the first time under jet power. With its conventional tailwheel undercarriage, the V3 proved almost impossible to rotate into the take-off position, so the design was revised with a nosewheel, which gave a level ground attitude. Production was ordered in May 1943, shortly after Adolf Galland made a flight in the fourth prototype.

The **Me 262A-1** Schwalbe (Swallow) entered service with test unit Erprobungskommando 262 in April 1944 with which it scored its first kill, a Mosquito, on 26 July. In May 1944 Hitler ordered that all Me 262s be completed as fighter-bombers, a decision which slowed production until it was rescinded in September. In the end, about 30 per cent

An unpainted Me 262 shows off its futuristic lines. The wing was swept to maintain centre of gravity, rather than to reduce compressibility effects. (TRH Pictures)

of Me 262s were dedicated Sturmvogel (Stormbird) bombers. In the fighter role, the Me 262 was rarely available in large enough numbers to make a difference. On its best day, JG 7 brought down 14 bombers and two fighters for four losses. The high closing speeds and the slow rate of fire of the powerful MK 108 cannons made head-on attacks difficult, so tactics switched to rear attacks on bombers.

High-temperature metals were in short supply, contributing to an engine life of about 25 hours, with an overhaul required every 10 hours. The Me 262 was difficult for escort fighters to catch at altitude, but vulnerable when it was flying slowly for take-off and landing and many were ambushed by P-51s near their home airfields.

Based on the two-seat **Me 262B-1a** conversion trainer, the **Me 262B-1a/U1** night-fighter with Neptun V radar entered service in limited numbers.

Of the 1,443 Me 262s built, only about 300 saw combat. When production facilities in Czechoslovakia were captured by the Soviets, a further 17 were completed as the **Avia S.92** and two as the two-seat **CS.92**, serving until 1950.

A small number of Avia S.92s were built in Czechoslovakia after the war using Me 262 parts left over by the Germans. (TRH Pictures)

Specification: Me 262A-1a
Type: single-seat twin-engined jet fighter
Powerplant: two 1,984-lb (8.83-kN) thrust Junkers Jumo 109-004B turbojets
Dimensions: span 41 ft 0 in (12.50 m); length 34 ft 9.5 in (10.61 m); height 12 ft 6.25 in (3.83 m); wing area 233.3 sq ft (21.68 m²)
Weights: empty 8,818 lb (4000 kg); max. take-off 14,936 lb (6775 kg)
Performance: max. speed 541 mph (870 km/h); initial climb rate 3,937 ft (1200 m) per minute; service ceiling 36,090 ft (11000 m); range 525 miles (845 km)
Armament four 30-mm MK 108 cannon in nose, 24 R4M rockets

North American P-51 Mustang

United States
October 1942

Widely regarded as the greatest fighter of World War II, the North American P-51 Mustang arose from a British requirement for a fighter. The British Air Purchasing Commission approached North American Aviation (NAA) in April 1940 with a view to the company producing P-40s for the RAF. Company President James 'Dutch' Kindelberger said that they could produce a much better fighter. A team including Raymond Rice, Edgar Schmued, and Ed Horkey designed, built and flew a prototype fighter in 117 days under the model number **NA-73X**. The British ordered 320 as the **Mustang I** on 29 May 1940, even though the prototype did not fly until 26 October 1942. The NA-73X was of all-metal, stressed-skin construction with laminar flow wings and hydraulic flaps, and was powered by a non-turbocharged Allison V-1710 V-12 engine giving 1,150-hp (857-kW), with a neat radiator in a 'doghouse' under the centre-section.

The USAAC evaluated two airframes as the **XP-51** at Wright Field in May 1941. Despite superior performance to other types then under test (XP-38, XP-39 and XP-47), they were slow to order any Mustangs, but finally signed for 310 P-51s and 500 **A-36A Apache** (or Invader) ground-attack versions in early 1942. They also requisitioned 57 aircraft destined for Britain as **F-6A** photoreconnaissance platforms. The RAF's Mustang Is were mainly used for low-level reconnaissance with two F.24 cameras.

The Mustang was widely exported after the war. This P-51D served with No. 2 Territorial Air Force Squadron of the RNZAF in the 1950s. (Author's collection)

Disappointed with the high-altitude performance of the Mustang I, the British tested the new Rolls-Royce Merlin 60 in ten airframes as the **Mustang X**, and NAA quickly designed a better installation for a Packard-built equivalent as the **P-51B (Mustang III)**.

In August 1942, the first 400 were ordered by the (now) United States Army Air Force (USAAF). Aircraft built at NAA's new Dallas factory were the **P-51C** and the reconnaissance version was the **F-6C**. The most important Mustang was the **P-51D**, introduced in 1944 with a 1,450-hp (1080-kW) V-1650-3, a four-bladed propeller and a 'bubble' canopy. Although slower than the B/C, the D could reach Berlin from England and was superior to all contemporary Axis piston-engined fighters. Over half of the 8th Air Force's 'kills' were scored by Mustangs, which were credited with over 5,000 aerial victories in all theatres. The last major version was the 'lightweight' **P-51H**, used mainly by the Air National Guard (ANG).

In all, 15,705 Mustangs were built, including 200 by Australia's Commonwealth Aircraft Corporation (CAC).

The P-51 was designed for the British with an Allison engine. This is one of the first Mustang Is for the RAF, seen in November 1941. (TRH Pictures)

Specification: P-51D Mustang
Type: single-engine fighter
Powerplant: one 1,450-hp (1080-kW) Rolls-Royce V-1650-3 Merlin V-12 piston
Dimensions: span 37 ft 0 in (11.28 m); length 32 ft 3 in (9.83 m); height 13 ft 8 in (4.16 m); wing area 233 sq ft (21.65 m²);
Weights: empty 7,635 lb (3466 kg); max. loaded 12,100 lb (5493 kg)
Performance: max. speed 437 mph (703 km/h); climb to 20,000 ft (6095 m) in 7 minutes 20 seconds; ceiling 41,900 ft (12771 m); range 1,650 miles (2655 km)
Armament: six 0.50-in (12.7-mm) machine-guns, up to 2,000 lb (908 kg) of bombs

Grumman F6F Hellcat

United States
October 1942

An F6F-3 in the colours of the USS Shangri-La (CV-38) Air Group in 1944. The main visual difference between this and later versions was the windscreen shape. (TRH Pictures)

In 1938 the XF4F-2 airframe, predecessor of the Wildcat, was to be modified with the 2000-hp (1492-kW) R-2600 radial, but it was soon realised that this was impractical, not least because the necessarily larger propeller would not clear the ground. A complete redesign was begun but this was put on hold as development of the Wildcat progressed. In 1940 Leroy Grumman and Bill Schwendler began anew with a design based around the 2,000-hp (1492-kW) Pratt & Whitney Double Wasp to replace the Wildcat in USN service.

The **XF6F-1** (Model G.50) first flew on 3 October 1942 and was broadly similar to the F4F, but was much larger (with the largest wing area of any US single-seat fighter) and its undercarriage retracted into the rearwards-folding wing.

Deliveries of the production **F6F-3** started in early 1943 and the F6F first saw combat on the Marcus Island raid of 31 August 1943. The first real battle with the 'Zero' took place in mid-September during which land-based F6Fs shot down five A6Ms for no losses. The Royal Navy received 252 F6F-3s as **Hellcat I**s.

The USN and USMC operated **F6F-3E** and **F6F-3N** night-fighters with APS-4 and APS-6 radar respectively, in a pod under the starboard wing. The

Surplus Hellcats were converted to F6F-3K drones and F6F-5D drone controllers. These were used to study nuclear bomb tests in the late 1940s. (Via Robert F. Dorr)

227 F6F-3Ns had a flat windscreen, which doubled as a gunsight.

The only significant major variant was the **F6F-5**, which incorporated all the changes introduced in F6F-3 production as well as the flat windscreen of the night-fighters. Other changes included increased armour, a closer-fitting cowl and revised ailerons. The engine was the same 2,000-hp (1492-kW) R-2800-10W with water injection as on late F6F-3s. Later -5s had two hardpoints able to carry a 1,000-lb (454-kg) bomb or a Tiny Tim rocket. Six 5-inch (127-mm) HVAR rockets could be mounted on the outer wings. There were 1,434 radar-equipped **F6F-5N** night-fighters. The FAA called their 930 F6F-5s the **Wildcat II**.

The Hellcat scored three-quarters of all USN air-to-air victories in the war, a total of 4,947 for carrier-based F6Fs. The USN's top ace (and the third-ranking American ace) was Hellcat pilot David McCampbell with 34 kills. In all, 307 American pilots became aces on the F6F. The total F6F production was 12,275 up to November 1945. A few radio-controlled F6Fs were used as guided bombs in the Korean War. The French Aéronavale received 179 F6F-5s and F6F-5Ns and they were used in action in Indochina up to 1954.

Specification: Grumman F6F-5 Hellcat
Type: single-seat carrier-based fighter
Powerplant: one 2,000-hp (1492-kW) P&W R-2800-10W 18-cylinder radial piston.
Dimensions: span 42 ft 10 in (13.05 m); length 33 ft 7 in (10.23 m); height 13 ft 1 in (3.99 m); wing area 334.0 sq ft (31.03 m²)
Weights: empty 9,238 lb (4190 kg); max. take-off 15,413 lb (6991 kg)
Performance: max. speed 380 mph (612 km/h); initial climb rate 2,980 ft (908 m) per minute; service ceiling 37,300 ft (11370 m); range 945 miles (1529 km)
Armament: six 0.50-in (12.7-mm) Browning machine-guns in wings and up to two 1,000-lb (454-kg) bombs

Heinkel He 219 'Uhu'

In 1940 Heinkel made a proposal for a twin-engined heavy fighter that could be adopted for torpedo-bombing or used as a medium bomber. After initial reluctance, the RLM called for the design to be adapted to a night-fighter to counter the increasingly heavy RAF bombing raids. In early 1942, bombing destroyed the newly completed production drawings, which delayed completion of the prototype. The Heinkel **He 219 V1** first flew on 15 November 1942 and was fitted with Daimler-Benz DB 603 inverted V-12 engines with annular radiators that gave the appearance of radials.

The He 219 was a very large aircraft for a fighter with the cockpit at the extreme front, well ahead of the main armament, which was in a ventral pack under the centre-section. The long fuselage ended at a twin-finned tailplane. The He 219 stood on a stalky tricycle undercarriage with twin mainwheels. The nose mounted a Lichtenstein radar array and the cockpit had a catapult ejection system, the first fitted to a combat aircraft. It soon gained the nickname *Uhu* (Owl).

The RLM was indifferent to the He 219, preferring the Ta 154 'Moskito', but Ernst Heinkel made sure that some **He 219A-0** prototypes were sent to 1/NJG 11 in Holland for combat evaluation. On the Uhu's first operational sortie, on 11 June 1943, Major Werner Streib shot down five four-engined bombers with the

One of the best night-fighters of the war, the He 219 was hampered by political infighting. This, the sixth prototype, was captured by British forces. (Philip Jarrett collection)

He 219 V9, although he crashed on landing. The unit went on to destroy a further 20 RAF bombers over the next 10 days.

The first production version was the **He 219A-2**, which was also the most numerous model with 137 built. Later examples had the twin 30-mm MK 108 cannon *Schrage Musik* ('oblique music' or jazz) installation firing upwards from behind the cockpit fitted as standard to the **He 219A-5**. This was employed by flying beneath bombers and firing into their unprotected bellies. Various field modification kits created versions with more power and increased range. The He 219A-5/R4 had a stepped cockpit with a third crewman and a flexible 0.51-in (13-mm) MG 151 machine-gun. The He 219A-6 was a stripped-down version with only four 20-mm cannon and 1,750-hp (1305-kW) DB 603L engines (capable of up to 2,100-hp (1566-kW) with methanol/nitrous oxide injection) and intended as a 'Mosquito swatter'. The last production model was the **He 219A-7** with DB 603G engines and the armament of the A-2.

The seventh prototype 'Uhu' wound up in American hands. A total of 288 of these specialised aircraft were built, but only one unit was ever equipped. (Philip Jarrett collection)

Specification: Heinkel 219A-7/R1 *Uhu*
Type: two-seat, twin-engined night-fighter
Powerplant: two 1,800-hp (1343 kW) Daimler-Benz DB 603E inverted V-12 pistons
Dimensions: span 60 ft 8.5 in (18.50 m); length 50 ft 11.75 in (15.54 m); height 13 ft 5.5 in (4.10 m); wing area 479.0 sq ft (44.50 m²)
Weights: empty 24,691 lb (11200 kg); max. take-off 33,730 lb (15300 kg)
Performance: max. speed 416 mph (670 km/h); initial climb rate 1,805 (550 m) per minute; service ceiling 41,665 ft (12700 m); range 1,243 miles (2000 km)
Armament: six 30-mm MK 108 cannon and two 20-mm MG 151/20 cannon

Nakajima Ki-84 Hayate 'Frank'

Japan
April 1943

An attempt to combine the manoeuvrability of the Ki-43 Hayabusa and the climbing ability of the Ki-44 Shoki interceptor led to the Nakajima **Ki-84 Hayate** (Gale) development, which began soon after the Pearl Harbor attack in December 1941. Unlike the Ki-43, the need to outperform all current and projected US fighters was stressed and so a large engine and heavy armament (at least for an Army fighter) of two heavy machine-guns and two cannon were specified. The engine was the new NK9A Homare 18-cylinder twin-row radial with direct fuel injection developed for the Imperial Navy, which gave 1,800 hp (1341 kW).

As with most Japanese fighters, the wing of the Hayate was integral with the centre fuselage to reduce structural weight. Like the Ki-43, the Ki-84 featured 'butterfly' combat flaps and a three-part canopy, but was much sturdier than the Ki-43 and featured an armoured windscreen and pilot's seat. The armour was usually too light to offer much protection against American heavy-machine-guns and cannon.

The first production examples rolled out in April 1944 but delays in engine production slowed the rate of deliveries and only 1,670 were built in 1944 out of a total of 2,565 ordered for that year. The total production was 3,514, the majority by Nakajima,

The 'Frank' was built around a powerful engine and could be considered as a redesign of the 'Oscar', also having a telescopic gunsight. (Aerospace Publishing)

The Hayate was one of Japan's best wartime fighters. Production was limited by material shortages caused by Allied bombing. This is a Ki-84-I-ko. (Philip Jarrett collection)

although 98 were built by subcontractors. The Ki-84 first saw combat in August 1944 in China where Yukiyoshi Wakamatsu became the leading ace, with 15 'kills' in the type. Seeing action on all fronts, and known to the Allies as 'Frank', the Ki-84 was increasingly allocated to homeland defence.

Variants included the **Ki-84-I-ko** with a four-bladed propeller and the **Ki-84-II** with wooden wingtips and rear fuselage. This entered production, unlike the Ki-106, with a completely wooden structure in order to save precious alloys and the largely steel Ki-113.

Unlike the Ki-43, the Ki-84 was strong, fast in level flight and well armed, and was equally manoeuvrable. Post-war tests with a captured Ki-84-I proved that it was superior in most respects to the latest Mustang (P-51H) and Thunderbolt (P-47N) variants.

The Hayate was, however, beset with numerous faults, including an engine that would often lose power at high altitudes, brake failures and hydraulic problems. Weak landing gear legs caused the loss of numerous Ki-84s. These problems were the result of the collapse of industry due to the American bombing of factories and naval destruction of shipping.

Specification: Nakajima Ki-84-Ia Hayate
Type: single-seat fighter-bomber
Powerplant: one 1,900-hp (1416-kW) Nakajima Ha-45 Model 11 18-cylinder radial
Dimensions: span 36 ft 10.5 in (11.24 m); length 32 ft 6.5 in (9.92 m); height 11 ft 1.25 in (3.38 m); wing area 226.05 ft (21.00 m²)
Weights: empty 5,864 lb (2660 kg); max. take-off 8,576 lb (3890 kg)
Performance: max. speed 392 mph (631 km/h); climb to 26,240 ft (7998m) in 11 minutes 40 seconds; service ceiling 34,350 ft (10,500 m); range 1,347 miles (2168 km)
Armament: two 0.50-in (12.7-mm) Type 1 machine-guns, two wing-mounted 20-mm Ho-5 cannon, up to 1,102 lb (500-kg) bombs

Grumman F8F Bearcat

United States
August 1944

The Pratt & Whitney R-2800 Double Wasp had proved successful in the F6F Hellcat and F7F Tigercat and in 1943 Grumman began design work to mate it to the smallest and lightest of airframes to produce one of the fastest and best-climbing piston fighters of World War II. The chief designer on the Grumman Model 58 was Bill Schwendler, and he and his team created a compact fighter with a raised bubble canopy, a four-bladed propeller and a wide-track undercarriage that gave much better ground handling than the Wildcat. The outer wings folded vertically upwards rather than backwards as on the F4F, F6F and TBF and it was found that 50 Bearcats could fit in the deck space occupied by 36 Hellcats. The armament was light, consisting of four machine-guns in the wings.

Two **XF8F-1** prototypes were ordered in November 1943 and the maiden flight was on 31 August 1944. Production of the **F8F-1 Bearcat** began six months later to fulfil orders totalling 2,033. After testing of a development batch of 23 XF8F-1s, the first production Bearcats were delivered to VF-19 in May 1945.

The vast majority of orders were cancelled when the war ended and planned production by General Motors (as the F3M-1) was abandoned. Production resumed after the war and deliveries continued until 1949. One batch of 100 was completed as the **F8F-1B** with four 20-mm cannon. The Bearcat could also carry 5-in (127-mm) HVAR rockets or a pair of Tiny Tim

The Bearcat was ready slightly too late for wartime service. This F8F-1 was assigned to the USS Boxer (CV-21) in 1947. (Philip Jarrett collection)

rockets or a 1,600-lb (726-kg) bomb. The **F8F-1N** night-fighter had cannon and APS-19 radar.

The improved **F8F-2** of 1948 had a revised cowling, a taller fin and other changes. A dozen were built as **F8F-2N**s and 60 as **F8F-2P** reconnaissance models with only two cannon. The final production figure was 1,263.

The 'Blue Angels' demonstration team used F8F-1s from 1946 to 1949. The Bearcat left the front-line USN and USMC squadrons in 1952 but served a little longer with the reserves.

France's Armée de l'Air was supplied with 140 F8F-1s and -1Bs. They were used in the ground-attack and reconnaissance roles in Indochina right up to the fall of Dien Bien Phu in 1954. Twenty-eight French Bearcats were passed to the South Vietnamese Air Force (VNAF) and formed the first combat unit of that air arm. The Thai Air Force was given 29 ex-French F8Fs, which served as late as 1963.

After a short front-line service career, most F8Fs were issued to the Naval Reserve. Reserve squadrons at that time wore an orange fuselage band. (TRH Pictures)

Specification: Grumman F8F-2 Bearcat
Type: single-seat carrier-borne fighter
Powerplant: one 2,750-hp (2049-kW) (with boost) Pratt & Whitney R-2800-30W 18-cylinder radial piston
Dimensions: span 35 ft 6 in (10.85 m); length 28 ft 3 in (8.61 m); height 13 ft 8 in (4.17 m); wing area 244 sq ft (22.67 m²)
Weights: empty 7,650 lb (3470 kg); max. take-off 13,460 lb (6105 kg)
Performance: max. speed 446 mph (719 km/h); initial climb 4,465 ft (1361 m) per minute; service ceiling 38,700 ft (11796 m); range 1,105 miles (1778 km)
Armament: four 0.50-in (12.7-mm) machine-guns in wings

Dornier Do 335 Pfeil

The **Dornier 335 Pfeil** (Arrow) was one of the most unusual fighters of all time, powered by engines fore and aft, one pulling and one pushing. (It was also called the 'Anteater' because of its shape.) This configuration had been patented by Dornier in 1937. Dornier's P.59 bomber project with this arrangement was cancelled in 1940 but Dornier continued work, submitting an improved design in response to a 1942 requirement for a high-speed bomber. This design was accepted as the Do 335 and, after some false starts, work began late that year. Willy Messerschmitt had persuaded Hitler that priority should be given to the Me 262, although the Dornier would have made a better bomber with a greater load.

The **Do 335 V1** first flew on 26 October 1943. It had two 1,750-hp (1304-kW) Daimler-Benz DB 603 engines, one driving a pusher and the other a tractor propeller, the latter aft of the cruciform tail. There were many novel features including a reversible-pitch forward propeller to shorten the landing run, leading edge de-icing, a tunnel radiator for the rear engine and a crew ejection system. This comprised a compressed air ejection seat and explosive bolts that sheared the upper vertical fin to provide clearance for the ejecting

This view of the Do 335 V9 shows the cruciform tail surfaces and the pusher propeller for the rear Daimler-Benz DB 603 engine. (TRH Pictures)

pilot. There were 14 prototypes, most of which trialled the configuration of projected variants such as the **Do 335B** heavy fighter with wing-mounted cannon and the **Do 335A-6** two-seat night-fighter. Two **Do 335A-12** two-seat conversion trainers were delivered.

An operational test unit, Erprobungskommando 335, was set up in December 1944 and may have flown some night interdiction missions before the end of the war with some of the 11 **Do 335A-1** production aircraft which were delivered. These were armed with one MK 103 cannon firing through the propeller hub and two 15-mm MG 151/15 cannon mounted atop the forward cowl, and had hardpoints for two external bombs or drop tanks. The Do 335 was faster than any Allied fighter, but it is not thought to have encountered any in combat.

Owing to official indecision and Allied bombing, only 37 Pfeils were built, including the prototypes, but Dornier had plans for many derivatives. These included the **Do 435** side-by-side two-seat night-fighter, the **Do 535** with a rear-mounted jet and the **Do 635** reconnaissance version, which would have mated two Do 335 fuselages side by side.

The Do 335 was one of the most extraordinary looking aircraft of the war. German pilots nicknamed it the 'Anteater' for its long nose. (TRH Pictures)

Specification: Dornier Do 335A-1
Type: single-seat twin-engined fighter-bomber
Powerplant: two 1,750-hp (1304-kW)
Dimensions: span 45 ft 3.25 in (13.80 m); length 45 ft 5.25 in (13.85 m); height 16 ft 4.75 in (5.00 m); wing area 414.42 sq ft (38.50 m²)
Weights: empty 16,314 lb (7400 kg); max. take-off 21,164 lb (9600 kg)
Performance: max. speed 478 mph (770 km/h); initial climb 4,600 ft (1508 m) per minute; service ceiling 37,400 ft (11400 m); range 857 miles (1380 km)
Armament: one 30-mm MK 103 and two 15-mm MG 151 cannon, plus one 1,102-lb (500-kg) or two 551-lb (250-kg) bombs internally and two 551-lb bombs externally

Grumman F7F Tigercat

In early 1941 Grumman started on the design of a new twin-engined carrier fighter for use on the new, larger 'Midway' class carriers. The contract for two prototypes was issued in June 1941, at the same time as the XF6F-1 order. As a result, development of the new fighter was purposely delayed. Detail design began in mid-1942 and the first of two **XF7F-1 Tigercats** first flew on 3 November 1943. Before this, the USMC had already ordered 500 for use as close-support fighters for island landings. In the end, the USMC was to operate almost all operational F7Fs. Carrier-suitability trials were not a total success and again all but a few Tigercats were land-based.

As well as being the first US twin-engined carrier fighter, the Tigercat had several other innovations such as a tricycle undercarriage and nose-mounted radar. The two 2,100-hp (1565-kW) Pratt & Whitney R-2800 Double Wasps were slung under the large wing, which folded inwards and upwards with an APS-6 radar in a pod. The nose contained four machine-guns. Four cannon were mounted in the wing roots.

The first of 34 **F7F-1**s were delivered in April 1944, these were the only single-seat production Tigercats, deliveries then switching to the two-seat F7F-2N that could accommodate a radar operator in a flush cockpit behind the pilot. There were 30 of this model and 189 **F7F-3**s with more fuel capacity and a slightly larger fin with a straight leading edge. The **F7F-3P** reconnaissance version flew some missions with the USMC before the

The Tigercat was just too late to see active combat in World War II. The F7F-1, seen here, was the initial single-seat production model. (TRH Pictures)

end of the war, but other fighter and night-fighter units arrived on Okinawa just as the war ended.

Most of the contracts were cancelled at the war's end, but 100, mostly **F7F-3N**s, were built after September 1945. The F7F-3N night-fighter had an extended nose containing an APS-19 radar.

The last new models were 13 **F7F-4N**s, built until November 1946. These were the only ones fitted with arrester hooks for carrier operation and flew with two squadrons from 'Essex' carriers.

F7F-3s were used as night interdictors and to designate targets for B-29 raids in the early part of the Korean War. In the night-fighter role for which it was designed, the Tigercat met little opposition and was only credited with three North Korean biplanes operating in the night harassment role. Interdiction missions were often flown with eight rockets under the wings and a centreline napalm tank. Tigercats were phased out of front-line service in 1952 but the **F7F-2D** (converted-2N) was used to control drone aircraft for a few more years. This version had an F8F canopy over the rear cockpit to give the drone control operator better visibility.

The Tigercat saw limited combat with the US Marine Corps in Korea, mainly in the night escort and interdiction role. This is an F7F-3N. (Author's collection)

Specification: Grumman F7F-3 Tigercat
Type: twin-engined carrier-borne fighter
Powerplant: two 2,100-hp (1565-kW) P&W R-2800-34W 18-cylinder radial pistons
Dimensions: span 51 ft 6 in (15.70 m); length 45 ft 5 in (13.85 m); height 16 ft 7 in (5.05 m); wing area 455 sq ft (42.27 m²)
Weights: empty 16,270 lb (7380 kg); max. loaded 25,720 lb (11667 kg)
Performance: max. speed 435 mph (700 km/h); initial climb 4,530 ft (1381 m) per minute; service ceiling 40,700 ft (12405 m); range 1,200 miles (1931 km)
Armament: four 20-mm cannons in wing roots, four 0.50-in (12.7-mm) machine-guns in nose and up to 2,000 lb (907 kg) bombs

Lockheed P-80 Shooting Star

Clarence L. 'Kelly' Johnson's team proposed a jet fighter as early as 1939, but official indifference and the lack of a suitable engine meant that the L-133 proposal was stillborn. In 1943, however, the US government returned to Lockheed with an order for a jet prototype based around a British de Havilland Goblin engine of 3,000 lb (13.34 kN) thrust. Lockheed's **XP-80** prototype (named *Lulu Belle*) was ready in only 143 days and flew at Muroc Dry Lake, California, on 8 January 1944. Lulu Belle looked little different from the thousands of aircraft to follow, having a tricycle undercarriage, unswept wings (later with rounded tips) and lateral intakes on the forward fuselage. Four 0.50-in (12.7-mm) machine-guns were fitted in the nose. Two **YP-80A**s were sent to England and two to Italy for operational evaluation just before the European war ended, and they saw no combat. The first major production version was the **P-80A** (redesignated **F-80A** in 1947). The P-80A had provision for fuel tanks or bombs at the wingtips and numerous minor changes, including dive brakes.

The first US jet fighter group was formed at March Field in November 1945 with P-80As, of which 524 were built. Reconnaissance versions were produced under the designations **F-14A**,

The F-94 was based on the F-80 but shared few components. Only the F-94C with mid-wing rocket pods was named Starfire. (TRH Pictures)

The F-80C was the first jet to serve with the Air National Guard, joining the 196th Fighter Squadron, California ANG in June 1948. (The Aviation Picture Library)

FP-80A and **RF-80A** with differing camera noses.

The **F-80C** was the first production US warplane with an ejection seat, and this version also had the armament increased to six machine-guns and strengthened to take bombs or rockets on mid-wing pylons. Late models had the J-33-A-35 engine of 5,400 lb (22.02 kN) thrust. The F-80C was the main version used by the Americans in Korea and on 8 November 1951, Lt Russell J. Brown shot down a MiG-15 for the first ever success in a jet-versus-jet combat. Other victories were scored against piston-engined aircraft but generally the F-80s were mostly used for ground attack and reconnaissance.

The **TP-80C**, a converted P-80C, led to the successful **T-33** trainer, some of which saw service as fighters. The TP-80C was converted into the longer, radar-equipped **YF-94** in 1949.

The **F-94A** entered service in May 1950 and was followed by the **F-94B** with an afterburning J33-A-33 and twin gun pods in the wings. This version had limited success in Korea. The **F-94C Starfire** was the definitive home defence version, with armament of 24 2.75-in (70-mm) rockets in the nose and in wing pods. In all, 894 F-94s were built.

Specification: Lockheed P-80C
Type: single-seat fighter
Powerplant: one 5,400 lb (22.02 kN) thrust Allison J-33-A-23 turbojet
Dimensions: span 39 ft 9 in (12.12 m); length 34 ft 5 in (10.49 m); height 11 ft 3 in (3.43 m); wing area 237.6 sq ft (22.07 m²)
Weights: empty 8,420 lb (3810 kg); max. take-off 16,856 lb (7646 kg)
Performance: max. speed 594 mph (956 km); climb 5,000 ft (1524 m) per minute; service ceiling 46,800 ft (14265 m); range 825 miles (1328 km)
Armament: six 0.50-in (12.7-mm) Browning M3 machine-guns, two 1,000-lb (454-kg) bombs and eight HVAR rockets

Hawker Sea Fury

United Kingdom
September 1944

Designed as a smaller and lighter version of the Tempest, the Hawker Fury/Sea Fury began as a requirement for a land-based interceptor in 1943, later merged with a naval requirement.

Six prototypes were built, the first flying on 1 September 1944, and they tested several different engines including the inline Sabre and Griffon. Three were navalised to varying degrees, the last one of which had folding wings, an arrester hook and a Bristol Centaurus XV radial with a five-bladed propeller. In April 1944 200 **Fury F I**s and 200 **Sea Fury F 10**s were ordered. In 1945, all the land-based aircraft and half the Sea Fury orders were cancelled, but the first of 50 F 10s was flown on 7 September 1946 and entered service with the Fleet Air Arm in spring 1947. The design proved a great success, and repeat orders and exports brought total production to 615 aircraft. The Sea Fury **FB 10** was the first ground-attack variant, with rocket and bomb armament and was followed by the **FB 11** with a longer hook and provision for rocket-assisted take-off.

Production Sea Furies had the 2,480-hp (1849-kW) Centaurus 18 and were similar in appearance to the Tempest II, but there was only 30 per cent commonality between the two types. The Fury had a redesigned tail, raised cockpit and shorter wings, and was of all-monocoque construction. Armament was four 20-mm Hispano cannon in the wings.

Royal Navy Sea Furies served in Korea from

The Netherlands Navy was one of several export customers for the Sea Fury. This is an FB 51, of which 25 were built by Fokker. (TRH Pictures)

October 1950 aboard the carriers HMS *Theseus*, *Ocean* and *Glory*, mainly in the ground-attack role. On 9 August 1952, Peter Carmichael of No. 802 Squadron shot down a MiG-15. The **T 20** was the two-seat trainer variant of which 60 were built.

Australia's 57 FB 11s served with six units and flew from HMAS *Sydney* and the loaned HMAS *Vengeance*. They saw combat in Korea and were in front-line service from 1948 to 1958. The Royal Canadian Navy took 74 FB 11s, with the first batch arriving in May 1948 and the last in November 1953. They only served on HMCS *Magnificent* and were replaced by F2H Banshees by 1956. The Netherlands took 12 **FB 50**s and 25 **FB 51**s, the latter built by Fokker, for service on Hr.Ms *Karel Doorman*. Iraq took 55 of a land-based version known as the 'Baghdad' Fury. Other users of land-based Furies, included Burma (18 aircraft), Pakistan (87 **FB 60**s) and Cuba, whose 15 FB 11s and two T 20s saw action over the Bay of Pigs in 1961.

Iraq's 'Baghdad' Furies omitted naval equipment such as wing folding and arrester hooks. Many were recovered by collectors in the 1970s. (TRH Pictures)

Specification: Hawker Sea Fury FB 11
Type: single-seat carrier-based fighter
Powerplant: one 2,480 hp (1849 kW) thrust 18-cylinder Bristol Centaurus radial piston
Dimensions: span 38 ft 4.75 in (11.70 m); length 36 ft 8 in (10.57 m); height 15 ft 10.5 in (4.84 m); wing area 280 sq ft (26.01 m²)
Weights: empty 9,420 lb (4191 kg); max. take-off 12,500 lb (5670 kg)
Performance: max. speed 435 mph (700 km/h); climb 4320 ft (1320 m) per minute; service ceiling 34,500 ft (10455 m); range 680 miles (1094 km)
Armament: four Hispano 20-mm Mk 5 cannon, two 1,000-lb (454-kg) bombs, napalm tanks or eight rockets

North American F-86 Sabre

United States
October 1947

Norton American had designed the straight-winged FJ-1 Fury for the US Navy and was working on a similar prototype for the US Air Force as the **XP-86** when the results of German swept-wing research were made available in mid-1945. The XP-86 was redesigned with a 35-degree swept wing before its first flight on 1 October 1947 and proved an immediate success. It is now believed that test pilot George Welch went supersonic in the XP-86 before 'Chuck' Yeager did in the Bell X-1.

The **F-86A Sabre** was the first production model and entered service in February 1949 with the 94th Fighter Squadron. The armament was six machine-guns in the nose and the engine was the General Electric J47-GE-13 of 5,200 lb (23.13 kN) thrust. The **F-86E** of 1950 had a 'flying' tail and provision for light bombs or drop tanks under the wings. Both versions and the **F-86F** fighter-bomber were heavily used in Korea, as were various **RF-86** reconnaissance models. All 39 UN jet aces of the Korean War flew Sabres. A total of 792 MiG-15s were credited to Sabres for 76 losses in air combat, even though the MiG was roughly equal on paper to the Sabre.

As well as about 6,200 Sabres built in the US up to 1956, several foreign companies assembled and

The F-86D 'Sabre Dog' had nose radar, a sophisticated fire control system and a tray of 24 'Mighty Mouse' rockets under the nose in place of guns. (TRH Pictures)

Japan was one of the largest Sabre operators. This F-86F is seen in the markings of the JASDF's 'Blue Impulse' aerobatic team. (TRH Pictures)

developed Sabre versions. Mitsubishi built 300 F-86Fs for the JASDF, the last of which left service in 1982. Canadair built over 1,800 Sabres. Many of these were **Sabre Mk 5**s and **Mk 6**s with the 6,000 lb (26.68 kN) thrust Avro Orenda engine and large numbers were supplied to NATO countries. Australia's CAC built 112 **CA-27** Sabres with the Rolls-Royce Avon 26 of 7,500 lb (33.38 kN) thrust and two 30-mm Aden cannon.

The Sabre was exported to or otherwise acquired by: Argentina, Bangladesh, Bolivia, Burma, Colombia, Denmark, Ethiopia, France, Greece, Honduras, Indonesia, Iran, Peru, Italy, Malaysia, the Netherlands, Norway, Peru, the Philippines, Portugal, Saudi Arabia, South Africa, South Korea, Spain, Taiwan, Thailand, Tunisia, Turkey, the United Kingdom, Venezuela, West Germany and Yugoslavia. Sidewinder-armed Taiwanese F-86Fs scored the first ever victories with air-to-air missiles against Chinese MiGs in 1958.

The **F-86D** ('Dog Sabre') had a radar nose and rocket armament. The engine was a 7,500 lb (33.38 kN) thrust J47-GE-17. The **F-86K** was the export version with two cannon. The 'lightweight' **F-86H** ('Hog Sabre') with a deeper fuselage was optimised for the nuclear strike role.

Specification: NAA F-86E Sabre

Type: single-seat fighter
Powerplant: one 5,200 lb (23.13 kN) thrust J47-GE-13 turbojet
Dimensions: span 38 ft 11in (11.85 m); length 44 ft 1 in (13.43 m); height 15 ft 8 in (4.77 m); wing area 306 sq ft (28.43 m²)
Weights: empty 10,845 lb (4919 kg); loaded 17,806 lb (8077 kg)
Performance: max. speed 697 mph (1093 km/h); initial climb 7,250 ft (2210 m) per minute; service ceiling 45,000 ft (13716 m) plus; range 1,000 miles (3048 km)
Armament: six 0.50-in (12.7-mm) machine-guns; up to two 1,000-lb (454-kg) bombs or 16 rockets

Grumman F9F Panther

United States
November 1947

The original design of Grumman's **XF9F-1 Panther** (Model G.59) began in 1946, based around no fewer than four 1,500-lb (6.6 kN) thrust Westinghouse J30 engines. As these left no room for fuel, attention turned to the Rolls-Royce Nene, which gave up to 5,700 lb (22.24 kN) thrust. As a back-up, the Allison J33-A-8 (4,600 lb thrust/20.45 kN) was developed.

The first **XF9F-2** flew on 29 November 1947 with a Nene engine. Other prototypes had the Allison J33 or a Pratt & Whitney J42, which was a licence-built Nene. The Nene/J42 was so much better than the J33 used on the **F9F-3** that all the -3s were converted to **F9F-2s** by installing the British-designed engine. The Panther was a sleek fighter with straight wings, a high tail and fixed fuel tanks at the wingtips. The wings folded over the fuselage for carrier stowage. There was a 'stinger' type tail hook under the jet pipe and a dive brake under the forward fuselage. The pilot sat on a Martin-Baker ejection seat under a bubble canopy with excellent visibility. In the nose was a quartet of 20-mm M3 cannon and (from the **F9F-2B** version on) the wings had hardpoints for six rockets and/or two bombs of up to 1,000 lb (454 kg). Earlier machines were later refitted with hardpoints and the 'B' suffix was dropped. Some Panthers had their armament replaced with cameras as the **F9F-2P** reconnaissance version. The total Panther production was 1,231.

The **F9F-4** was longer and had a revised tail. It was powered by the Pratt & Whitney J48, a version of the

An F9F-5P is escorted by two F9F-5s on a reconnaissance mission over Korea. All were from USS Bon Homme Richard. (Philip Jarrett collection)

Rolls-Royce Tay. It actually appeared after the similar and most numerous version, the **F9F-5**, which entered service from November 1950. The F9F-5 had a total of eight hardpoints and could carry 500-lb (227-kg) bombs on any of them for a total external load of 3,465 lb (1572 kg).

When the Korean War broke out in June 1950 the Panther was the most numerous aircraft on USN carrier decks. Together, VF-51 F9F-2 pilots Leonard Plog and E W Brown shot down a Yak-9 fighter for the first kill by a Navy jet on 3 July. During the war five MiG-15s were shot down by Panthers. From April 1951 Panthers were mostly involved in close air support work.

Active duty USN and USMC squadrons retired Panthers in 1956 and they left the reserves in 1958. In the same year Argentina purchased 24 refurbished F9F-2s for (land-based) naval squadrons. Although they saw no combat, the Panthers patrolled the border with Chile during a 1965 confrontation.

Panthers varied little in appearance between versions. This was the first F9F-5. The Panther later evolved into the swept-wing F9F-6 Cougar. (Philip Jarrett collection)

Specification: Grumman F9F-5 Panther
Type: single-seat carrier-borne fighter
Powerplant: one (engine power missing) Pratt & Whitney J48-P-8 turbojet
Dimensions: span 38 ft 0 in (11.58 m); length 38 ft 10 in (11.83 m); height 12 ft 3 in (3.73 m); wing area 250 sq ft (23.22 m²)
Weights: empty 10,147 lb (4603 kg); max. loaded 20,600 lb (9344 kg)
Performance: max. speed 604 mph (972 km/h); initial climb rate 6,000 ft (1829 m) per minute; service ceiling 44,600 ft (13600 m); range 1,300 miles (2092 km)
Armament: four 20-mm cannon in nose, hardpoints for up to 2,000lb (908 kg)

Mikoyan-Gurevich MiG-15 'Fagot'

Soviet Union
December 1947

Based, like the F-86 Sabre, on the results of German swept-wing research and British engine technology, the Mikoyan-Gurevich MiG-15 was the Soviet Union's first really successful jet fighter and led the way to the famous family of MiG interceptors.

MiG's initial design was similar in layout to the Focke-Wulf Ta 183, but was stalled until Britain supplied the USSR with several Rolls-Royce Nene engines, which Klimov copied as the RD-45. The first prototype **S-01** flew with a Nene engine on 30 December 1947 and the production **MiG-15** a year later. The armament was three cannon in the nose, one 37-mm N-37 and two 23-mm NS-23. The pilot had an ejection seat, a bubble canopy and a high-mounted tailplane. The first MiG-15s entered service in 1949 and were given the NATO code-name 'Fagot'.

North Korean MiGs and USAF Sabres met in many dogfights during the Korean War of 1950–53. Most of the MiGs were flown by Russian pilots, with Yevgeny G. Pepelyaev the top-scoring of over 50 Soviet aces in Korea, with 23 victories. A further six Chinese and two North Korean aces have been acknowledged.

The MiG-15 was faster-climbing and had a higher ceiling and better acceleration than the Sabre, allowing it to make effective zoom attacks from

Avia of Czechoslovakia built the MiG-15 as the S.102 and the MiG-15bis as the S.103 (seen here). Over 3,000 'Fagots' were built in three countries. (TRH Pictures)

The MiG-15 was supplied to many Soviet client states such as Czechoslovakia and to allied Third-World nations and Finland. (TRH Pictures)

above, but the superior training of the F-86 pilots and faster-firing armament was instrumental in the high kill ratio in fighter combat. Nevertheless, the MiGs destroyed many B-29s and other aircraft as well as over 70 Sabres. The improved **MiG-15bis** was delivered from 1949 and also saw combat in Korea.

Well over 3,000 single-seaters were built in the Soviet Union and Eastern Europe, to which can be added an unknown large number supplied to China. It was long believed that China's Fagots were locally built as the **Shenyang J-2**, but in fact all were supplied from by the USSR. Czech-built MiG-15s and MiG-15bis models were produced as the **S.102** and **S.103** and Polish aircraft were **Lim-1** and **Lim-2**s, respectively. Minor variants included the **MiG-15P** with radar and the reconnaissance **MiG-15bisR.**

The most important version numerically was the **MiG-15 UTI** 'Midget' two-seater, which had an elongated canopy and a second seat for an instructor. Over 5,000 were built and were often retained as conversion trainers for the MiG-17 after single-seat Fagots were retired.

Some of the last known single-seaters in service were a dozen used by Albania up to about 1999.

Specification: MiG-15
Type: single-seat fighter
Powerplant: one Klimov RD-45F turbojet rated at 5,005 lb (22.26 kN) thrust
Dimensions: span 33 ft 1 in (10.08 m); length 32 ft 11.25 in (10.04 m); height 12 ft 1.67 m (3.70 m); wing area 221.75 sq ft (20.60 m²)
Weights: empty 7,767 lb (3523 kg); max. take-off 10,941 lb (4963 kg)
Performance: max. speed 652 mph (1050 km/h); climb to 16,405 ft (5000 m) in 2 minutes 30 seconds; service ceiling 48,640 ft (14825 m); range 730 miles (1175 km)
Armament: two 23 mm NS-23 cannon and one 37-mm N-37 cannon

Mikoyan-Gurevich MiG-17 'Fresco'

Soviet Union
January 1950

The **MiG-17** was a development of the MiG-15, designed in parallel with the MiG-15bis but incorporating a new thin wing and other aerodynamic refinements. Although very similar in appearance, the MiG-17 was longer in span but slightly shorter. The new wing had more sweepback and three prominent fences. In side view, the only obvious visual difference was prominent bulges over the larger air brakes. The **SI-2** prototype flew in January 1950, production was ordered in September 1951 and operational capability with the Soviet VVS was achieved in October 1952. NATO gave the MiG-17 the reporting name 'Fresco'. The armament was the same as the MiG-15's, namely two 23-mm and one 30-mm cannon.

The developed **MiG-17F** version was fitted with the VK-1F turbojet with afterburner and first flew in September 1951. The rear fuselage and air brakes were redesigned and the cannon could be supplemented by 190-mm or 210-mm rockets. The radar-equipped **MiG-17PF** appeared in 1952. The 30-mm cannon was replaced with a third 23-mm weapon.

In Vietnam, the MiG-17 was the main fighter equipment of the North Vietnamese People's Air Force (NVAF) from 1964. Although far less sophisticated than the USAF fighters, the US rules of engagement brought them into turning combat with the nimble MiGs. NVAF records credit over 60 victories to the pilots of the 921st and 923rd Fighter Wings. Top NVAF Fresco ace was Nguyen Van Bay

The MiG-17PF with its bi-part radar in the intake trunk and upper lip represented a major leap ahead of the basic MiG-15 airframe design. (Philip Jarrett collection)

with seven kills. In April 1972 Van Bay led one of the few offensive actions by the NVAF, an attack on US destroyers, causing serious damage to the USS *Higbee*. Over 8,000 MiG-17s were built in the USSR and large numbers were exported, particularly to African nations. Many Egyptian and Syrian MiGs were destroyed in the Six-Day War, mostly on the ground.

China built 767 **Shenyang J-5**s, a licence-built MiG-17F. These shot down at least eight Taiwanese aircraft in 1957–8 and later a few straying USAF fighters. Chinese-built examples were supplied to Albania, North Korea, Sudan and Tanzania. The only two-seat variants are thought to be 1,000 Chinese conversions, built as the **Chengdu JJ-5** or **FT-5** between 1966 and 1986. Similar in appearance to the MiG-15 UTI, the FT-5 was supplied to Sri Lanka and Pakistan. About 1,000 MiG-17Fs were also built in Poland as the **Lim-5** and **Lim-6**. Polish MiG-17s were retired in about 1992, but a few may remain in service with Cuba, Algeria and Yemen. The MiG-17 was mainly used as a fighter-bomber in its later years.

Mozambique was one of many Soviet 'client states' to receive MiG-17s. This one was flown to South Africa by a defector and evaluated by the SAAF. (Aerospace Publishing)

Specification: Mikoyan-Gurevich MiG-17F Fresco C
Type: single-seat fighter
Powerplant: one Klimov VK-1F turbojet rated at 5,732 lb (29.50 kN) thrust
Dimensions: span 31 ft 7 in (9.63 m); length 36 ft 11.5 in (11.26 m); height 12 ft 5.5 in (3.8 m); wing area 243.27 sq ft (22.6 m²)
Weights: empty 8,664 lb (3930 kg); max. take-off 13,380 lb (6069 kg)
Performance: max. speed 684 mph (1100 km/h); climb to 16,405 ft (5000 m) in 2 minutes 36 seconds; service ceiling 54,460 ft (16600 m); range (ferry) 1,255 miles (2020 km)
Armament: three NR-23 23-mm cannon

Douglas F4D Skyray

A contract to study the feasibility of delta-winged fighters was awarded to several US aircraft manufacturers in 1947, with Douglas winning the contract to build a prototype in June. Using the results of German research, Ed Heinemann and C S Kennedy eschewed a pure delta for a highly swept wing with rounded tips and no tailplane. Pitch control was provided by large elevons and pitch trimmers on the trailing edge. The engine was the Westinghouse J40, but the design allowed for a choice of engines, which was fortunate given the short and disappointing career of the J40. Due to problems with the J40, the prototype **XF4D-1** flew with an Allison J35 of 5,000 lb (22.25 kN) thrust on 23 January 1951. During testing, the J40 was abandoned and the 10,200 lb (45.37 kN) thrust J57 substituted, creating a potent interceptor but delaying service entry until April 1956. The first **F4D-1** Skyray unit to serve aboard ship was VF-74, and the first USMC unit was VMF(AW)-115. The impressive climb rate of the Skyray led to one unit being allocated to North American Air Defense Command (NORAD) alongside USAF and Canadian interceptors.

The Skyray could be refuelled in flight using a modified drop tank equipped with a fixed probe,

Despite its rather blunt appearance, the Skyray was one of the highest-performing fighters of its day, with an exceptional climb rate. (TRH Pictures)

The only production version of the Skyray was the F4D-1 as seen here. The bomb-shaped object is a Douglas-designed navigation package. (Philip Jarrett collection)

although this entered service late in the aircraft's career. The nose of the 'Ford' housed an APQ-50A search and single-target track radar to guide it within firing distance of its early AIM-9 Sidewinder or rocket pod armament.

Production ended in 1958 with 419 F4D-1s produced. In 1962, the F4D-1 was redesignated **F-6A**, but by then was in service with only three front-line units. The last fleet Skyrays were retired in 1964, but examples were used for various test programmes.

Although the F4D was deployed to Taiwan in 1958 and to Guantanamo Bay, Cuba, in 1962 during the Taiwan Straits and Cuban missile crises, respectively, none ever saw combat action.

The improved F4D-2 was cancelled, but the much-revised F4D-2N was built as the **F5D Skylancer**, which was longer and stronger and fitted with a new thinner wing. The armament was much the same as before with the addition of AIM-7 Sparrow I radar-guided missiles. Only four **XF5D-1s** were built, as the Navy chose to concentrate on fewer fighter types. Faster and longer-ranged than the Skyray, despite having essentially the same engine, two were used in several research programmes with NASA until 1970.

Specification: Douglas F4D-1 Skyray
Type: single-seat carrier-based interceptor
Powerplant: one P&W J57-P-8 turbojet giving 10,200 lb (45.37 kN) thrust dry, 16,000 lb (71.17 kN) thrust in afterburner,
Dimensions: span 33 ft 5 in (10.21 m); length 45 ft 5 in (13.84 m); height 13 ft 0 in (3.96 m); wing area 557 sq ft (51.75 m²)
Weights: empty 16,024 lb (7268 kg); loaded 28,000 lb (12701 kg)
Performance: max. speed 652 mph (1049 km/h) climb rate 18,000 ft (5486 m) per minute; service ceiling 55,000 ft (16764 m); range 600 miles (966 km)
Armament: four 20-mm cannon, four 2.75-in rocket pods or four AAM-N-7 Sidewinders

Dassault Mystère

Following the straight-winged Ouragon (Hurricane) of 1949, France's first indigenous jet fighter, Marcel Dassault began work on a swept-wing successor, the MD 452 Mystère (Mystery). The single **Mystère I** was created by attaching a 30-degree wing and modified tail to an Ouragon. This was followed by 40 **Mystère II** pre-series aircraft equipped with licence-built British Nene or Tay engines, or the SNECMA Atar 101. The 90 **Mystère IIC**s, which had greater tail sweepback than the Mystère I, were powered by the non-afterburning Atar 101D-2 or D-3 engine of 6,173 lb (27.46 kN) thrust. By the time the last Mystère IIC was delivered in 1957, they were already being relegated to the advanced training role. The **Mystère IIIN** was a one-off with lateral intakes and a nose radome, although radar was never fitted.

The definitive **Mystère IV** was similar in appearance to the Mystere II, but with thinner wings swept to 32 degrees and a new, oval-section fuselage containing a Tay engine. After the first 50, Hispano Verdon (licence-built Tay) engines were substituted. Under the NATO assistance programme, the US paid for the first 225 Mystères, followed by 100 bought with French funds.

The prototype Mystère IV first flew on 28 September 1952. The first production aircraft flew in May 1954 and entered Armée de l'Air service as the Mystère IVA in 1955, seeing action over Suez in 1956. The 59 Israeli Mystère IVAs also saw action at this time, claiming seven MiG-15s, MiG-17s and Vampires,

The prototype Mystère IV shows off its clean (if portly) lines. Early Mystère IVs were powered by British-built Rolls-Royce Tays. (TRH Pictures)

and again in 1967, mainly in a ground-support role. India's 110 Mystère IVs, delivered from 1957, also saw action against Pakistan in 1965.

As an interceptor, the Mystère IV was replaced by the Mirage III in the early 1960s, but carried on in the ground-attack role until 1975 when replaced by the Jaguar. The last operational trainers were retired in 1980. Indian Mystères were retired during 1973.

The Avon-powered Mystère IVB was cancelled in favour of the **Super Mystère B2** with the afterburning Atar 101G and a rocket pack as well as cannon armament. The Super Mystère could also carry AS.30 AGMs and Sidewinder AAMs. The career of the 180 French examples spanned from 1957 to 1977. Israel used its 36 'Sambad' Super Mystères from 1958, upgrading them with Pratt & Whitney J52s and local avionics in the early 1970s. These aircraft saw combat in 1973, when they defeated MiG-19s in a number of encounters. A dozen Israeli Super Mystères were sold to Honduras in 1977, where they were used until at least 1989.

The Mystère IVA had a short career as a front-line fighter. This one flew on in private hands in the 1980s until damaged in an accident. (Author)

Specification: Super Mystère B2
Type: single-seat fighter
Powerplant: one 7,716-lb (34.4-kN) Hispano-Suiza Verdon 350 turbojet
Dimensions: span 34 ft 5.75 in (10.51 m); length 45 ft 9 in (13.95 m); height 14 ft 11.25 in (4.55 m); wing area 378.36 sq ft (35.15 m²)
Weights: empty 15,282 lb (6932 kg); max. take-off 20,558 lb (9325 kg)
Performance: max. speed 645 mph (1038 km/h); initial climb 10,827 ft (3300 m) per minute; service ceiling 55,750 ft (17000 m); range 540 miles (870 km)
Armament: two 30-mm DEFA cannon, 35 68-mm rockets, up to 2,000 lb (908 kg) of bombs, rockets, AS.30 AGMs or AIM-9 Sidewinder AAMs

Hawker Hunter

United Kingdom
July 1951

Designed as as replacement for the Gloster Meteor, the Hawker Hunter was the backbone of RAF Fighter Command the late 1950s and was exported to many friendly nations.

After two official specifications failed to produce results, Hawker designed their own fighter in 1948 and the Air Ministry issued a specification around it. This **P.1067**design was an attractive swept-wing fighter with a blown canopy and intakes in the wing roots. The prototype Hunter first flew on 20 July 1951 with a 6,500-lb (28.91-kN) Avon 103 engine and was flown supersonically (in a dive) in April 1952.

The Hunter **F 1** entered service in July 1954 but suffered many teething problems and was quickly superseded by the **F 4** from June 1955. With a strengthened wing, the F 4 could carry rockets and bombs to supplement its four 30-mm cannon. The **F 2** and **F 5** were developed in parallel with the Armstrong Whitworth Sapphire engine, but were produced in limited numbers. The F 5 was mainly used in the Middle East and saw action in Suez and Aden. The definitive fighter version was the **F 6** with the 'big bore' Avon 203 and (on most) a 'dog tooth' on the wing leading edge. The arrival of the Lightning saw the interceptor Hunters phased out in 1963, but in the ground attack role, the **FGA 9** lasted until 1970. The Royal Navy used similar **FGA 11**s into the late 1980s to test shipboard defensive systems. Royal Navy **T 8M**s had Blue Fox radar to train Sea Harrier pilots.

The Hunter was the mount of a number of aerobatic teams, including the RAF's 'Blue Diamonds' who flew F 6s in 1961 and 1962. (TRH Pictures)

India was the first export customer, taking 16 ex-RAF F 6s in 1957, followed by many **F 66** and **T 66** trainers and other refurbished aircraft as **FGA 56A**s.

Other export customers included Chile, Denmark, Iraq, Jordan, Kenya, Kuwait, Lebanon, the Netherlands, Oman, Peru, Qatar, Rhodesia (Zimbabwe), Saudi Arabia, Singapore, Somalia, Sweden and Switzerland. The Swiss bought 100 **F 58**s and later reconditioned 60 ex-RAF aircraft as **F 58A**s. These served up until 1994.

Jordanian and Iraqi Hunters fought against Israel in 1967 and 1973, scoring some victories although generally the losers in most combats. Again in the India–Pakistan wars of 1965 and 1971, India's Hunters had some successes, but usually lost out to the PAF's F-104s and F-86s. Few Hunters were ever equipped with air-to-air missiles, but some Swiss aircraft were modified to carry AGM-65B Maverick AGMs. Although long-since replaced elsewhere, a few Indian and Zimbabwean Hunters may have made it into service past 2000.

Two-seat Hunters (this is a T.7) served with the RAF into the 1990s, lastly as trainers for the Buccaneer, which had no dual-control version. (TRH Pictures)

Specification: Hawker Hunter F 6
Type: single-seat fighter
Powerplant: one Rolls-Royce Avon 203 rated at 10,000 lb (44.48 kN) static thrust
Dimensions: span 33 ft 8 in (10.2 m); length 45 ft 11 in (14 m); height 13 ft 2 in (4.01 m); wing area 340 sq ft (31.6 m²);
Weights: empty 12,760 lb (5795 kg); max take-off 17,750 lb (8062 kg)
Performance: max. speed 715 mph (1150 km/h);climb to 45,000 ft (13,725 mph) in 7 minutes 30 seconds; service ceiling 51,500 ft (15707 m); range 1840 miles (2960 km);
Armament: four 30-mm cannon

McDonnell F3H Demon

In May 1948 the US Navy issued a request for proposals for a carrier-based day fighter that had equal or superior performance to the high-performance Air Force fighters of the time. It was to be powered by the new Westinghouse J40 turbojet and have 45-degree wing sweep. The McDonnell company responded with their first swept-wing fighter design, which was ordered as the **XF3H-1** in January 1949.

The XF3H-1 flew on 7 August 1951 with a Westinghouse J40-WE-6 initially without afterburner as the afterburning WE-8 version was not yet available. Even at 10,500 lb (44.5 kN) this was twice as powerful as any other Navy engine of the time. The prototype Demon proved to have poor stability, poor forward visibility and a low roll rate. These faults were corrected on the initial production **F3H-1N**, but the poor reliability and performance of the J40 meant that most of the 58 built never flew and were sent to shore bases for use as ground trainers. The Navy decided that the J40 was not worth persisting with and new versions were produced with the 9,700-lb (43.16 kN) Allison J71-A-2E. With afterburning the J71 gave 14,250-lb (63.41 kN) and was much more reliable, but the Demon was still underpowered for its

The Demon was somewhat of a failure, but a big leap in technology for the Navy. The F3H-2M could carry four AIM-7 Sparrow I missiles. (Philip Jarrett collection)

Like most 1950s fighters, the Demon was short-ranged and usually flew with auxiliary fuel tanks. This F3H-2N also carries faired rocket pods. (TRH Pictures)

weight. The throttle response of the J71 was so poor that afterburner was often needed to get aboard the carrier. The radar-equipped **F3H-2** (redesignated **F-3B** after 1962) was the main production version and had two important missile-carrying derivatives. There were 80 **F2H-2M**s with AIM-7A/B Sparrow I air-to-air missile capability. After 1962, the few remaining examples were given the unusual designation **MF-3B**. The **F3H-2N** (**F-3C**) was equipped to carry four AIM-9B Sidewinder infra-red guided missiles.

Eleven USN squadrons were equipped with Demons. Although the Demon never saw aerial combat, in March 1958 VF-122 Demons fired their guns at a Chinese beach target during tensions between Communist China and Taiwan, and also flew combat air patrol (CAP) sorties. VF-213 flew cross-deck operations from *Ark Royal* in 1957.

The Demon was the first swept-wing naval fighter and contributed features to the subsequent F4H Phantom II. Despite its many faults, the Demon was the only true all-weather Navy fighter for a number of years and could fly missions when the Skyrays, Tigers and Bearcats were confined to the carrier deck. The last of 519 Demons built were retired in 1964.

Specification: McDonnell F3H-2 Demon
Type: single-engined carrier-based interceptor
Powerplant: one 9,700 lb (43.16 kN) thrust Allison J71-A-2E turbojet
Dimensions: span 35 ft 4 in (10.77 m); length 58 ft 11 in (17.96 m); height 14 ft 7 in (5.13 m); wing area 519 sq ft (48.22 m²)
Weights: empty 22,133 lb (10039 kg); max. take-off 33,900 lb (15377 kg)
Performance: max. speed 693 mph (1116 km/h); initial climb rate 12,410 ft (3783 m) per minute; service ceiling 42,650 ft (13000 m); range 1,470 miles (2366 km)
Armament: four 20-mm cannon

Gloster Javelin

United Kingdom
November 1951

The Gloster Javelin was conceived in 1947 as a high-altitude night-fighter for the RAF and seen as a counterpart to the Hunter day-fighter. The Gloster **GA.5** prototype first flew on 26 November 1951 and was selected over the de Havilland DH.110 in 1952.

Design work had been rushed before the full results of tests with aircraft such as the Fairey Delta 2 were available and as a result, the GA.5 had an unnecessarily thick wing, which reduced performance and kept it subsonic. Testing and development were marked by several crashes. The **Javelin FAW 1** entered service in 1956. The 40 Mk 1s built were followed by 30 **FAW 2**s with US-built Westinghouse APQ 43 radar rather than British AI 17.

The nickname 'Flat Iron' accurately described the Javelin's appearance with its enormous delta wing and high T-tail. The engines were two Armstrong-Siddeley Sapphires, rated at various thrusts from 8,000 lb (35.59 kN) to 11,000 lb (48.93 kN) dry and the armament was four 30-mm Aden cannon, two in each wing. The **T 3** trainer had no radar but retained cannon armament and was followed by the **FAW 4** with increased fuel tankage in the wings. The lengthened **FAW 7** was the version produced in the largest numbers with 142 delivered. This was the first

The Javelin was often known as the 'Flat Iron'. This FAW 1 was seen in 1955 at an air show to mark the jubilee of the Royal Aeronautical Establishment. (TRH Pictures)

missile-armed version with four Firestreak IR-guided AAMs and only two cannon, and entered service in 1958. The Firestreak had a range of about five miles (8 km) and a 50-lb (22.7-kg) warhead – much heavier than the contemporary Sidewinder.

Many FAW 7s were later converted to **FAW 8** standard with a refuelling probe and limited afterburners that boosted thrust to 12,300 lb (54.71 kN) above 20,000 ft (6100 m). At low altitude all they did was increase fuel consumption. Seventy-six Mk 7s were converted to definitive **FAW 9** standard in 1959. Those with probes became **FAW 9R**s.

There were 427 of all models produced. Some Mk 4s, 5s and 7s were built by Armstrong Whitworth. The Javelin is remembered for service in the Far East, where No. 60 Squadron at Tengah, Singapore, was equipped with over 30 aircraft at a time. Reputedly, one shot down a C-130 during the confrontation with Indonesia in 1964. The Javelin's career was short and the last were retired in April 1968, although one remained in use at Boscombe Down until 1976. The Javelin was the first twin-engined delta-wing aircraft and also the first British purpose-designed all-weather/night-fighter. It was the last Gloster aircraft.

A Javelin FAW 6 gets airborne from the Gloster factory airfield at Hucclecote. The Mk 6 was the same as the Mk 5 but with American radar. (TRH Pictures)

Specification: Gloster Javelin FAW 1
Type: two-seat, twin-engined all-weather fighter
Powerplant: two Armstrong-Siddeley Sapphire ASSa.6 turbojets rated at 8,000 lb (35.59 kN) thrust
Dimensions: span 52 ft (15.85 m); length 56 ft 3 in (17.15 m); height 16 ft (4.88 m); wing area 927 sq ft (86.12 m²)
Weights: empty 24,000 lb (10886 kg); max. take-off 31,580 lb (14324 kg)
Performance: max. speed 709 mph (1141 km/h); climb to 50,000 ft (15250 m) in 9.25 minutes; service ceiling 52,500 ft (16000 m); range with external fuel 950 miles (1529 km)
Armament: four 30-mm Aden cannon

North American F-100 Super Sabre

First of the 'Century Series' of USAF fighters, the F-100 Super Sabre began as a refined supersonic version of the F-86 Sabre day-fighter. North American proposed a number of iterations of the Sabre with 45 degrees wing sweep and different engines were proposed, but the design by Raymond Rice and Edgar Schmued evolved into a completely new aircraft by the time the USAF ordered two prototypes and 110 production aircraft in November 1951. Cold War urgency accelerated the normal procurement and development process and the first of two **YF-100A**s flew on 25 May 1953. It was powered by a single Pratt & Whitney J57-P-7 rated at 9,220 lb (41.01 kN) thrust and 14,800 lb (65.85 kN) thrust with afterburner.

The F-100 had a large underfuselage speed brake, a simple ranging radar in the top lip of the sharp-lipped intake and was armed with four 20-mm cannon. The number built was 203. The **F-100A** became the first USAF fighter capable of supersonic speed in level flight, but had some stability problems, mostly cured by greatly increasing the fin area on the **F-100C**.

On 20 August 1955 an F-100C achieved the first supersonic speed record at 822.135 mph (1322.815 km/h). There were 476 F-100Cs built, of which a third served with the USAF in Europe and Morocco. The **TF-100C** prototype two-seat combat trainer became the **F-100F**, of which 339 were built.

The main production version was the **F-100D**, with

The F-100D was the most important Super Sabre variant. It was the first USAF fighter to be supersonic in level flight when flown 'clean' as seen here. (Philip Jarrett collection)

1,274 built. It was a dedicated fighter-bomber with more wing and tail area and a refuelling probe.

From 1964 F-100s were operated in the Vietnam War and were used exclusively for ground attack, although it is now believed that one MiG fell to the guns of a 'Hun' pilot. In the war 242 were lost to all causes, all losses to enemy action being due to anti-aircraft guns. The F-100D was the main version used in Vietnam, F-100Cs serving only with ANG squadrons on temporary rotations to the theatre. (After service with the ANG ended in 1979, over 200 were converted to **QF-100** target drones.)

The F-100F was the first USAF aircraft used in the 'Wild Weasel' role to detect and destroy enemy surface-to-air missile (SAM) radar systems, using sensitive detection gear and Shrike missiles.

The Super Sabre was used as the mount of both the 'Thunderbirds' and 'Skyblazers' demonstration teams. Over 500 F-100Ds and Fs were supplied to France, Turkey, Denmark and Taiwan under the Military Assistance Program.

F-100Ds were exclusively used in the ground-attack role in Vietnam. This example has a refuelling probe fixed to the starboard wing. (TRH Pictures)

Specification: F-100D Super Sabre
Type: single-seat fighter-bomber
Powerplant: one Pratt & Whitney J57-P-21 turbojet rated at 10,200 lb (45.37 kN) thrust dry and 16,000 lb (71.17 kN) with afterburner
Dimensions: span 38 ft 9.3 in (11.82 m); length 47 ft 5 in (14.44 m); height 16 ft 2.67 in (4.94 m); wing area 400 sq ft (37.16 m²)
Weights: empty 21,000 lb (9526 kg); max. loaded 28,847 (13085 kg)
Performance: max. speed 891 mph (1434 km/h); initial climb rate 18,000 ft (5846 m) per minute; service ceiling 38,700 ft (11796 m); range 1,954 miles (3144 km)
Armament: four 20-mm cannon, up to 5,000 lb (2270 kg) conventional or nuclear bombs, rockets, Bullpup and Sidewinder missiles or fuel tanks on six underwing hardpoints

Mikoyan-Gurevich MiG-19 'Farmer'

Soviet Union
January 1954

The MiG-19 (NATO code-name 'Farmer') was built to give the Soviet Union a supersonic fighter with as little fuss as possible and proceeded from a development order to its first flight on 5 January 1954 in just under six months. The design owed much to the I-360 (a modified MiG-17) of 1951.

Powered by two AM-9B turbojets, the **SM-9** prototype of the MiG-19 was easily capable of supersonic level flight, and demonstrated Mach 1.34 on an early flight.

The production **MiG-19** featured a 55-degree wing sweep and three 23-mm cannon in the wingroots and nose. The most important version was the **MiG-19S** with a 'flying tail', 30-mm cannon and a Tumansky RD-9B engine. The **MiG-19P** and **MiG-19PM** Farmers were radar- and missile-equipped interceptors with K-13 'Atoll' and K-5M 'Alkali' AAMs.

In service with Soviet Air Defence Forces by 1955, MiG-19s failed to bring down any of the U-2 spy plane overflights, and one was destroyed by a SAM during the Gary Powers shootdown incident of 1 May 1960. However, MiG-19s shot down an RB-47H electronic intelligence (Elint) aircraft near Archangel a month later on 1 June and another on 1 July. East Germany-based Farmers destroyed a number of aircraft that strayed

The MiG-19 equipped the interceptor squadrons of many air forces defending the borders of the Warsaw Pact countries. This is a Czech MiG-19S. (TRH Pictures)

The MiG-19 was widely exported to nations friendly to the USSR. Egypt was the biggest Middle East user and lost many in the Six-Day War. (TRH Pictures)

outside of the Berlin corridor. Syria and Egypt were the first non-Warsaw Pact MiG-19 users. Many of their aircraft were destroyed on the ground or in the air by Israeli fighters in June 1967. North Korea bought some MiG-19s from Iraq and later sold some to Iran, but it is not thought either nation's Farmers saw much, if any, action in the 1980–88 Iran–Iraq war. Production was low compared to other MiGs, 'only' 2,000 or so being built outside China, although this was still more than most Western jet fighters.

The Chinese **Shenyang J-6** derivative (export designation **F-6**) was built in far greater numbers than Soviet and Czech (**Avia S.105**) aircraft. Using the J-6 as a basis, Nanchang developed the **Q-5** strike aircraft with a pointed nose and lateral intakes. Pakistan took many F-6s, and their pilots claimed ten Indian aircraft in the 1971 war for one loss, while India admitted only four losses and claimed four F-6s destroyed.

North Vietnam's 54 MiG-19Ss (F-6s) destroyed seven USAF and US Navy F-4 Phantoms in May 1972. At least three MiG-19s were lost to US fighters. The F-6 saw long service in Pakistan, finally retiring in 2001, but J-6s still form the backbone of the Chinese Air Force. The trainer model is the **JJ-6** (**FT-6**).

Specification: MiG-19S

Type: single-seat twin-engined fighter
Powerplant: two Tumansky RD-9B turbojets rated at 5,732 lb (25.5 kN) thrust dry and 7,165 lb (31.87 kN) with afterburner
Dimensions: span 29 ft 6.33 in (9.00 m); length 41 ft 4 in (12.60 m); height 12 ft 9.5 in (3.90 m); wing area 269.1 sq ft (25.00 m²)
Weights: empty 11,399 lb (5172 kg); max. loaded 19,470 lb (8832 kg)
Performance: max. speed 902 mph (1451 km/h); initial climb 22,640 ft (6901 m) per minute; service ceiling 57,400 ft (17500 m); range (ferry) 1,350 miles (2200 km)
Armament: three Nr-30 30-mm cannon, plus rocket pods on underwing pylons

Lockheed F-104 Starfighter

Although the Starfighter's USAF career was relatively brief, the Luftwaffe operated F-104Gs for training at Luke AFB for many years in US markings. (TRH Pictures)

Designed by Lockheed's Kelly Johnson for lightness and simplicity as an interceptor for Air Defense Command, the F-104 Starfighter was an extremely slender aircraft, with short, thin wings. It was powered by a J79 turbojet, initially of 9,000 lb (40.03 kN) thrust. The prototype **XF-104** flew on 4 March 1954 and was followed by 17 **YF-104**s. The Starfighter had impressive speed and climb performance but a poor turn rate and some bad handling characteristics.

The USAF originally ordered 722 Starfighters but only took delivery of 296. Between 1965 and 1967, a few were based in Vietnam where one was lost to a MiG and eight to anti-aircraft artillery (AAA) and SAMs. The USAF operated 77 **F-104C**s up to mid-1975. They were also used by NASA on various duties. In December 1959, an **NF-104** with an auxiliary rocket reached 103,389 ft (31,534 m), the first aircraft to top 100,000 ft (30,480 m) entirely under its own power.

Small numbers of **F-104A**s were supplied to Pakistan and Taiwan (who passed the survivors to Jordan, who gave some to Pakistan). In 1965, Pakistan's F-104s scored four kills for two losses against Indian jets.

The F-104's USAF career was undistinguished and the story would have been short if not for the 'deal of the century' in 1958 when the first of nine NATO nations bought the Starfighter. **The F-104G** was a multi-role fighter-bomber for West Germany with a larger tail, strengthened structure and improved electronics. Five hardpoints could take up to 4,000 lb (1814 kg) of stores, including the B-43 nuclear weapon. The first 96 were ordered in 1958, and 210 were built under licence. In all, Germany received 917 F-104Gs, **RF-104G**s, **TF-104G**s and **F-104F**s and lost 270 of them in accidents. German Navy Starfighters were equipped with Kormoran anti-ship missiles. Canada co-produced 200 Orenda-powered models as the **CF-104**, bought 38 **CF-104D** two-seaters and built 140 for Greece, Norway, Spain, Taiwan and Turkey. Companies in the Netherlands, Belgium and Italy built Starfighters for an eventual European-built total of 843. The total production of all models was 2,580.

Taiwan's Starfighters (mainly As and Cs from a variety of sources) served from 1960 to 1996, and were armed with indigenous Sky Sword I and II AAMs. Mitsubishi built 210 **F-104J**s for the JASDF.

The last Starfighters in service are Italy's **F-104S** and **TF-104S** models, which were acquired from 1962 and have been modernised to carry the AIM-7 or the related Aspide AAM.

Italy is now the last nation to use the Starfighter. The survivors have been upgraded to ASA standard with Aspide missile capability. (Author's collection)

Specification: F-104C Starfighter

Type: single-seat fighter-bomber
Powerplant: one General Electric J79-GE-19 turbojet rated at 17,900 lb (79.62 kN) thrust with afterburner
Dimensions: span 21 ft 9 in (6.63 m); length 54 ft 8 in (16.66 m); height 13 ft 5 in (4.09 m); wing area 196.1 sq ft (18.22 m²)
Weights: empty 12,760 lb (5788 kg); max. take-off 27,853 lb (12634 kg)
Performance: max. speed 1,150 mph (1850 km/h); max. climb 54,000 ft (16459 m) per minute; service ceiling over 50,000 ft (15240 m); range 850 miles (1370 km)
Armament: one 20-mm M61A1 Vulcan cannon and two AIM-9 Sidewinder AAMs

McDonnell F-101 Voodoo

United States
September 1954

Design work began on the **XP-88** 'penetration fighter' at McDonnell Aircraft as early as 1945. A contract for two prototypes was awarded in June 1946. When it first flew in October 1948, the XF-88 was powered by two 3,000 lb (13.35 kN) thrust Westinghouse XJ-34-WE-13 turbojets without afterburner and featured a swept wing with root intakes, and a raised tail with a mid-mounted fin at the end of a long fuselage. The second prototype was the **XF-88A** with afterburner and cannon, while the first prototype became the **XF-88B** test aircraft with a nose-mounted turboprop (as well as jets) and in 1953 became the first propeller aircraft to exceed Mach 1. Although it was judged the best of competing designs, funding problems meant no production orders were forthcoming. McDonnell's E.M. Flesh improved on the design and in May 1953 the USAF ordered this revised version as the **F-101 Voodoo**.

There was no Voodoo prototype as such, but the **F-101A** strike aircraft (first flight 29 September 1954) was much revised with a new wing, a high-mounted tailplane and Pratt & Whitney J57-P-53 engines with 16,000 lb (71.17 kN) thrust in afterburner. The armament was four M39 cannon, with provision for an external load, usually a single nuclear weapon.

Canada was the main user of the Voodoo in the fighter role. Its CF-101Bs and Fs were armed with conventional Falcon and nuclear-tipped Genie missiles. (Author's collection)

Despite its 'fighter' designation, the F-101A was more of a strike aircraft, and was armed with cannon and a nuclear weapon. (TRH Pictures)

The RF-101A reconnaissance aircraft had a 'chisel' camera nose and retained nuclear capability. Taiwan received eight of the 35 built.

The **F-101B** was the first production fighter version, with two seats, a weapons bay for AIM-4 Falcon AAMs in semi-recessed stowage and internally carried AIR-2 (MB-1) Genie unguided nuclear rockets. The first of 479 F-101Bs entered service in January 1959. About half were completed as or converted to dual-control **F-101F** standard. The last Bs and Fs left ANG service in 1981, but 112 were transferred to Canada from 1968 as the **CF-101B** and **CF-101F**.

The **RF-101C** was the only version to see combat other than Taiwan's **RF-101A**s. Twenty-eight were lost in action in Vietnam, one of them to a MiG-21. In Europe and elsewhere, the RF-101C fulfilled nuclear alert as well as reconnaissance duties. Other reconnaissance conversions were the single-seat **RF-101G** and **RF-101H**. The **F-101C** was in virtually all respects identical to the F-101A, but had structural improvements and a revised fuel system, giving better afterburner performance. The F-101C's mission was to perform nuclear strikes, and the 47 built served mainly with squadrons in England.

Specification: F-101B Voodoo
Type: two-seat twin-engined interceptor
Powerplant: two Pratt & Whitney J57-P-55 turbojets rated at 14,880 lb (6.19 kN) thrust
Dimensions: span 39 ft 8 in (12.09 m); length 67 ft 4.75 in (20.54 m); height 18 ft (5.49 m); wing area 386 sq ft (34.19 m²)
Weights: empty 28,970 lb (13141 kg); max. take-off 52,400 lb (23,768 kg)
Performance: max. speed 1,221 mph (1965 km/h); initial climb rate 36,500 ft (11133 m) per minute; service ceiling 54,800 ft (16705 m); range 1550 miles (2494 km)
Armament: two MB-1 Genie nuclear-tipped AAMs and four AIM-4 Falcon AAMs or six AIM-4s

Vought F-8 Crusader

In 1952 the USN issued a requirement for its first carrier-based fighter capable of sustained supersonic flight. Russ Clark's team at Vought designed an aircraft with a long, slender fuselage, a high-mounted wing and a single tail and was awarded a prototype contract in May 1953. The engine was to be the highly successful Pratt & Whitney J57 and the armament was four cannon, two AIM-9s and a 16-shot rocket pack in the speed brake. An unusual feature was the hinged wing that could be raised to vary its incidence for carrier take-offs and landings, allowing operation at lower speeds. The **XF8U-1** Crusader prototype flew on 25 March 1955 at Edwards AFB.

During testing, early Crusaders broke many speed records and memorable flights included John Glenn's 1957 Los Angeles-to-New York flight, completed in three hours and 23 minutes.

The first **F8U-1**s (redesignated **F-8A** in September 1962) entered the USN fleet in March 1957, followed by the all-weather **F8U-1E** (**F-8B**) and the **F8U-2** (**F-8C**) with ventral fins and four AIM-9s. The **F8U-2N** (**F-8D**) had the uprated J57-P-20 of 18,000 lb (80.07 kN) thrust in afterburning, better radar and no rockets.

The **F8U-1P** (**RF-8A**) reconnaissance platform was very important in monitoring Soviet missile deployments during the Cuban Missile Crisis of 1962. Photo F-8s were unarmed, with a suite of cameras in the nose. The last **RF-8G**s were retired in 1987.

There were 286 **F8U-2NE** (**F-8E**) models with all-weather APQ-92 radar. The F-8E scored 11 out of a total of

France flew the Crusader from its aircraft carriers for over 35 years, finally retiring them in 2000. Note the castoring nosewheel. (Author's collection)

18 Crusader victories over North Vietnamese MiGs, all in the 1966–8 period. Twenty-one F-8s were lost to enemy action, three to MiGs.

In all, 1,261 Crusaders were built, but there were several remanufactured versions, including the **F-8J** (from F-8Es), **F-8K** (F-8B) and **F-8L** (F-8C). The Philippines operated 25 **F-8H** models and others in the US for training including the sole two-seat **TF-8A**.

The **XF8U-3 Crusader III** was a highly modified version with a J75 engine of 29,500 lb (131.22 kN) thrust with afterburning, a new intake and large ventral fins. Although capable of Mach 2.2, the F8U-3 was rejected in favour of the F4H-1 Phantom II.

Forty-two **F8E(FN)**s were delivered to the French Aéronavale in July in 1964–5. They were flown from the carriers *Clemenceau* and *Foch* and and could carry Matra 530 and Magic AAMs. In the early 1990s 17 were updated as the **F-8P** (for *prolongé* or prolonged), which improved reliability and efficiency but did not equip them fully for modern operations.

The 'Crouze' was finally retired in December 1999 and is slowly being replaced by the Dassault Rafale.

The RF-8G was the main unarmed reconnaissance version of the Crusader. It sported cameras in the nose and lower fuselage. (TRH Pictures)

Specification: Vought F-8E Crusader
Type: single-seat carrier-borne interceptor
Powerplant: one P&W J57-P-20A turbojet rated at 10,700 lb (47.61 kN) thrust dry and 18,000 lb (80.07 kN) thrust with afterburner
Dimensions: span 35 ft 8 in (10.87 m); length 54 ft 3 in (16.53 m); height 15 ft 9 in (4.80 m); wing area 375 sq ft (34.84 m²)
Weights: empty 17,836 lb (8090 kg); max. take-off 34,100 lb (15467 kg)
Performance: max. speed 1,135 mph (1839 km/h); climb rate 21,000 ft (6400 m) per minute; service ceiling 58,000 ft (17680 m); range 1,425 miles (2293 km)
Armament: four 20-mm Mk 12 cannon, four AIM-9 AAMs, up to 5,000 lb (2270 kg) bombs

Convair F-102 Delta Dagger

United States
June 1955

The Convair Delta Dagger was born of a 1950 USAF requirement for a missile-armed 'interim interceptor', although the company had been working on delta-wing designs based on German research for several years. The company's rocket/ramjet-powered **XP-92** proposal was a radical design, little more than a tube with delta wing and tail surfaces, the pilot sitting in the intake cone. It was deemed necessary to first build a less complex jet-powered experimental aircraft with a conventional cockpit. This Model 7-002 (later **XF-92A**) first flew on 19 September 1948 and was the first pure delta-winged aircraft to fly. The P/F-92 project was cancelled, but Convair designed the larger **YF-102** around the MX-1179 missile system (later the AIM-4 Falcon) to have a weapons bay and a conical nose. First flying on 24 October 1953, the YF-102 refused to go supersonic in testing and a panic programme produced the **YF-102A** by December 1954. This incorporated 'area rule', under which the fuselage was narrowed adjacent to the widest part of the wing – the so-called 'Coke bottle' fuselage.

The production **F-102A** Delta Dagger finally took to the air on 24 June 1955, powered by the 11,000 lb (48.93 kN) dry thrust Pratt & Whitney J57. The production F-102s were armed with up to six AIM-4

The F-102 had a fairly short front-line career, but served with many Air National Guard units such as the 'Happy Hooligans' of the 178th Fighter Squadron. (Philip Jarrett)

Several squadrons of F-102s operated with US Air Forces in Europe (USAFE). They were also exported to Greece and Turkey. (Via Robert F. Dorr)

radar-guided or infra-red missiles in an internal bay and 12 or 24 rockets in the weapons bay doors. One or two AIM-26 nuclear Falcons with a 1.5-kiloton warhead could be carried. Service began with the 327th FIS of Air Defense Command in April 1956. After 25 aircraft were built the height of the tailfin was increased. A side-by-side two-seat conversion trainer with full armament was built as the **TF-102A**.

Delta Daggers were initially used for air defence of the Continental USA, Alaska and Hawaii but were also based in Europe and on Okinawa. One unit defended US bases in Vietnam, flew B-52 escort and was involved in a limited ground-attack role using rockets against buildings and watercraft. One was shot down by a MiG-21 in February 1968. By 1977 the last F-102s were phased out of ANG service and 213 of them became **PQM-102** and **QF-102** pilotless drones, which were destroyed in missile tests and in exercises. In all, exactly 1,000 F-102s had been produced, 111 of them two-seaters.

Delta Daggers were exported to Greece and Turkey. They saw some action in 1974 over Cyprus, where two Turkish F-102As may have been destroyed by Greek F-5As.

Specification: F-102A Delta Dagger
Type: single-seat delta-winged interceptor
Powerplant: one P&W J57-P-23 turbojet rated at 17,200 lb (76.50 kN) thrust with afterburner
Dimensions: span 38 ft 1.5 in (11.60 m); length 68 ft 4.67 in (20.83 m); height 21 ft 2.5 in (6.45 m); wing area 695 sq ft (64.57 m²)
Weights: empty 19,350 lb (8812 kg); max. loaded 31,500 lb (14288 kg)
Performance: max. speed 825 mph (1328 km/h); initial climb 13,000 ft (3962 m) per minute; service ceiling 55,000 ft (16765 m); range 1,350 miles (2173 km)
Armament: six AIM-4 Falcon IR or radar-guided AAMs, or AIM-26 nuclear AAMs

Saab J35 Draken

In 1949 the Swedish *Flygvapnet* issued an ambitious requirement to replace the J29 Tunnan with a fighter superior to all others then entering service around the world. To meet this challenge, Saab's Erik Bratt designed a fighter of unique configuration with a double delta wing with intakes at the roots. The pilot sat on a Martin-Baker ejection seat that was raked backwards (as on the F-16), increasing g tolerance. To test the aerodynamics of the **J 35 Draken** (Dragon), the Saab 210 **L'il** (Little) **Draken** was built as a 70 per cent scale testbed and flown in January 1952.

The first of two full-scale Draken prototypes was flown on 25 October 1955 with a Rolls-Royce Avon engine and the 90 production **J 35A**s entered service from March 1960, powered by a licence-built Avon Mk 48A designated as the Volvo RM 6B. This gave 10,780 lb (47.95 kN) thrust dry and 14,407 lb (64.09 kN) thrust with afterburner. The longer **J 35B** followed and had two small tailwheels to allow a high nose-up landing attitude which gave aerodynamic braking, aided by a drag chute. Like other Swedish fighters, the Draken was designed to operate from dispersed highway bases and be maintained by conscripts. Twenty-five J 35As were converted to **Sk 35C** trainers. The rear-seat instructor had a retractable periscope to give a forward view. Swedish and Danish Drakens intercepted and brought back the first photographs of many new Soviet fighters, bombers and patrol aircraft transiting the Baltic.

This J 35J served with the second squadron of the F10 wing at Ängelholm until 1998, making it one of the last Swedish Drakens. (TRH Pictures)

The **J 35D** with the 17,635 lb (78.44 kN) thrust RM 6C was capable of Mach 2.0 and the **J 35F** could carry AIM-4 (Swedish designation RB 27 and 28) Falcon missiles (and later Sidewinders). Two 30-mm Aden cannon were fitted in the lower wingroots.

The last Swedish Drakens were 66 **J 35J**s upgraded from J 35Fs. The strengthened **Saab 35X** with increased fuel capacity was offered on the export market and the first customer was Denmark in 1968. Danish **AX 35D**s (or **F-35**s) were dual-use interceptors and ground attackers. The **S 35XD (TF-35)** trainer and the **RF-5** for reconnaissance made up the remainder of Denmark's 46 Drakens, which were updated in the mid-1980s. Finland received the first of 42 Drakens in 1970. The first 12 were locally assembled Saab 35Xs, later supplemented by 30 ex-Swedish aircraft. Finnish Drakens served until 1998.

Austria was the last Draken customer, buying 24 surplus J 35Fs in 1987 as **J 35OE**s, armed with AIM-9P Sidewinders in 1993, after Austria amended its constitution to allow the military to operate missiles.

Austria's is the last air force to fly the Draken. Note the tail bumper wheels on this J 35OE seen on a 1997 deployment to RAF Waddington. (Author)

Specification: Saab J35F Draken
Type: single-seat interceptor fighter
Powerplant: one Volvo Flygmotor RM 6C turbojet rated at 17,262 lb (76.79 kN) thrust with afterburner
Dimensions: span 30 ft 10 in (9.4 m); length 50 ft 4.3 in (15.35 m); height 12 ft 9 in (3.89 m); wing area 529.6 sq ft (49.2 m²)
Weights: empty 16,369 lb (7425 kg); max. take-off 27,998 lb (12700 kg)
Performance: max. speed 1,320 mph (2125 km/h); max. climb rate 39,370 ft (12000 m) per minute; service ceiling 65,615 ft (20000 m); range 597 miles (960 km) with external fuel
Armament: one 30-mm Aden cannon in wing, four Rb 27/28 Falcon AAMs

Mikoyan-Gurevich MiG-21 'Fishbed'

Soviet Union
January 1956

The classic MiG-21 series of fighters stemmed from a 1954 design programme to develop a lightweight interceptor capable of Mach 2 and altitudes over 20000 m (65,600 ft). Debate about the merits of different wing configurations led to the swept-wing Ye-2 and delta-wing Ye-4 test aircraft in 1955. Each had a nose intake, a bubble canopy and a slender fuselage ending in a swept fin and all-moving tailplanes. The canopy consisted of a single-piece unit that hinged forward and provided a blast screen on ejection. The delta-winged Ye-5 powered by the Tumansky AM-11 turbojet of 11,243 lb (50 kN) thrust with afterburner flew on 9 January 1956 and was chosen as the basis for production. Series production of the **MiG-21F-13** began in 1960 in the USSR, soon followed by factories in Czechoslovakia and China.

Chinese MiG-21F-13s were built as the **Chengdu J-7** and were subject to much local development after the Sino-Soviet split. The export **F-7M Airguard** had a rear-hinged canopy, two cannon and up to four AAMs. Much Western equipment was fitted and the F-7M was exported to Pakistan, Iran and Zimbabwe.

The second-generation **MiG-21PF** was the afterburner-equipped development of the MiG-21P with a longer intake cone (containing radar) and a

China still operates many Chengdu J7s derived from early generation MiG-21s. This is a J7E of the '1st of August' aerobatic team. (Robert Hewson)

Aerostar and Elbit have upgraded most of the Romanian Air Force's MiG-21s to 'Lancer' standard, with new avionics and weapons. (Author)

fuselage spine and new two-piece side-hinged canopy. About 200 PFs were assembled or built by HAL in India. The **MiG-21S** series featured a longer dorsal spine containing fuel and was exported as the **MiG-21M**. The **MiG-21MF** was the most important sub-variant and had pylons for four AAMs as opposed to two on most earlier models. The multi-role R-25-300-powered **MiG-21bis** introduced improved avionics, AA-8 'Aphid' AAMs, and improved Sapphire-21 radar. With high speed and a low visual signature, the missile-equipped 'Fishbed' proved troublesome to US fighters over Vietnam from mid-1966.

In various Middle East conflicts, the MiG-21 usually came off second best in combat, with Israeli fighters claiming over 380 destroyed, although Arab Fishbed pilots have claimed more than 100 IDF kills in return.

The two-seat trainer version is the **MiG-21U** 'Mongol' with individual canopies. Sub-variants include the **MiG-21UM** and **MiG-21US**, usually with cannon pods and two weapons pylons.

Over 10,000 MiG-21s were completed in the Soviet Union alone up to 1987. Chinese developments continue, with the **F-7PG** being the latest to enter service with Pakistan.

Specification: MiG-21MF
Type: single-seat interceptor
Powerplant: one Tumansky R-13-300 turbojet rated at 8,972 lb (39.92 kN) thrust dry and 14,307 lb (63.66 kN) with afterburner
Dimensions: span 23 ft 5.7 in (7.15 m); length 51 ft 8.5 in (15.76 m); height 13 ft 6.2 in (4.125 m); wing area 247.5 sq ft (23 m²)
Weights: empty 11,795 lb (5350 kg); max. take-off 20,723 lb (9400 kg)
Performance: max. speed 1,385 mph (2220 km/h); initial climb rate 23,622 ft (7200 m) per minute; service ceiling 59,711 ft (18200 m); range (ferry) 1,118 miles (1800 km)
Armament: one GSh-23L 23-mm cannon and four K-13 IR-guided AAMs

Dassault Mirage III/5

France
November 1956

The classic Mirage series of fighters began with the **MD550 Mystère Delta**, a sub-scale delta-winged testbed flown in 1955 and later named **Mirage I**. This was followed on 18 November 1956 by the slightly larger **Mirage III**, later modified to the vertical take-off and landing (VTOL) **'Balzac V'**. The pre-production **Mirage IIIA** was the first 'full-sized' version and led to the **IIIC** interceptor for the Armée de l'Air in 1961.

The multi-role **Mirage IIIE** fighter (and equivalent **Mirage IIID** trainer) was flown in 1961 and introduced provision for an AN52 nuclear bomb. France itself operated 483 Mirage IIIs and Vs from 1963 to 1993 in interceptor, strike and reconnaissance roles.

Based on the IIIE, the prototype **Mirage IIIO** for Australia had a Rolls-Royce Avon engine, although all 100 subsequent Australian-built examples were Atar-powered. Retired in 1988, the IIIOs were sold to Pakistan. Switzerland's **IIIS**s could carry Falcon and Sidewinder AAMs and late in service received small canard foreplanes. The **Mirage IIIR** was equipped with a camera nose and retaining cannon. The **IIIRS** is still in service in Switzerland, but South Africa's **IIIRZ** is long retired. The Mirage IIIV was a greatly enlarged VTOL testbed with eight lift engines. Two were flown in 1965–6. The **Mirage 5** was essentially a ground-attack version of the IIE for Israel. The initial **Mirage 5F** had a longer, slimmer nose with an ESD Aida ranging radar and served with the Armée de l'Air when France embargoed their sale in 1967. The

Some of the last Mirage IIIs in French service were Mirage IIIRs with an undernose camera fairing. The similar Mirage IIIS still serves in Switzerland. (Author's collection)

Mirage 50 first flew in April 1979 and introduced the Mirage F1's Atar 9K-50 engine, endowing better field performance, faster acceleration, a larger weapon load and improved manoeuvrability.

Denied the Mirage 5 by France, Israel clandestinely acquired the plans and Israel Aircraft Industries (IAI) built the **Nesher** without a licence. The survivors were supplied to Argentina as the **Dagger** and were used as bombers in the Falklands War. Later they were upgraded as the **Finger**.

Israel further developed the Mirage III as the **IAI Kfir** with a similar long nose, but with the 17,900 lb (79.62 kN) thrust General Electric J-79 engine, which required larger intakes and a prominent ram-air inlet at the base of the tail. Twenty-five **Kfir-C1**s were leased to the USN and USMC as the **F-21A** to be used as adversary trainers in 1985–8. The **Kfir-C2** and **Kfir-C7** had fixed canard foreplanes. Ecuador, Colombia and Sri Lanka have acquired Kfirs. The South African **Atlas Cheetah** is a Kfir-influenced Mirage III conversion with a longer nose and indigenous AAMs.

The Mirage III and 5 have seen service with over 20 air arms, with 1,422 built plus Israeli derivatives. This is a Belgian Mirage 5BR. (Author)

Specification: Dassault Mirage IIIC
Type: single-seat interceptor fighter
Powerplant: one SNECMA Atar 9C turbojet rated at 13,228 lb (58.84 kN) thrust with afterburner
Dimensions: span 27 ft (8.22 m); length 48 ft 5 in (14.75 m); height 14 ft 9 in (4.5 m); wing area 375 sq ft (35 m²)
Weights: empty 14,495 lb (6575 kg); max. take-off 27,998 lb (12700 kg)
Performance: max. speed 1,320 mph (2112 km/h); initial climb 16,400 ft (5000 m) per minute; service ceiling 65,615 ft (20000 m); range 1,000 miles (1610 km)
Armament: two 30-mm DEFA cannon, two AIM-9 and one Matra R.530 AAM

Convair F-106 Delta Dart

In 1948 the USAF began planning for the '1954 Ultimate Interceptor', a name that reflected the intended in-service date and that the then-new but subsonic F-86D, F-89 and F-94 were interim types. The USAF was seeking an integrated weapons system rather than an aircraft with its equipment as a second thought, and the project became known as WS-201A. Hughes won the contract for the fire-control system and weapons and Convair's F-102 design was chosen as the airframe. Delays in the Hughes MA-1 system led to the adoption of the F-102A as the 'interim interceptor' in 1951 and Convair proposed an improved **F-102B** to carry the MA-1.

Renamed the **F-106 Delta Dart**, the new aircraft was similar in configuration and dimensions to the F-102 but had refined aerodynamics, a square-topped fin, completely revised intakes and a Pratt & Whitney J75-P-17 turbojet rated at 17,200 lb (76.50 kN) static thrust (24,500 lb (108.98 kN) with afterburner). Other improvements compared with the F-102 were the incorporation of an aerial refuelling receptacle and a runway arrester hook. The first **YF-106A** flew on 26 December 1956 at Edwards AFB, California, and the production **F-106A** entered service with the 539th FIS at the end of May 1959, five years after originally

Like the 'Deuce', the 'Six' saw many years' service with ANG squadrons. An F-106A from Florida's 159th Fighter Squadron is shown. (Author's collection)

The Delta Dart was the 'Ultimate Interceptor' for the USAF. This F-106A served with the 5th Fighter Interceptor Squadron (FIS), the 'Spittin' Kittens'. (Via Robert F. Dorr)

planned. An F-106A set an absolute speed record of 1,525.93 mph (2455.68 km/h) on 15 December 1959.

The MA-1 fire-control system was the first large-scale use of automation in a fighter. When linked to the SAGE (Semi-Automatic Ground Environment) system, the F-106 could be flown almost completely through its mission by ground control.

The MB-1 Genie rocket with a nuclear warhead was an unguided weapon and had a range of about 6.2 miles (10 km) and a flight duration of 12 seconds. The fire-control system guided the F-106 to a firing position on a formation of bombers and the blast of the 1.5-kiloton warhead made up for any slight inaccuracy. The Genie was retired in 1985.

Unlike the F-102, the F-106 did not serve in Europe, and it was not exported. Two **YF-106C**s with a 5-ft (1.5-m) nose extension were built. The **TF-106** (later **F-106B**) was designed with tandem seating to preserve its performance and was combat capable.

The Delta Dart was finally retired from ANG service in August 1988, but continued to serve with NASA and in the B-1B bomber programme. Of the 340 F-106As and Bs built, 173 were converted to **QF-106** drones for use in missile tests.

Specification: Convair F-106A Delta Dart
Type: single-seat delta-winged interceptor
Powerplant: one P&W J75-P-17 turbojet rated at 17,200 lb (76.50 kN) static thrust and 24,500 lb (108.98 kN) with afterburner
Dimensions: span 38 ft 3.5 in (11.67 m); length 70 ft 8.75 in (21.55 m); height 20 ft 3.5 in (6.18 m); wing area 697.8 sq ft (64.83 m²)
Weights: empty 24,318 lb (11029 kg); max. loaded 39,195 lb (17779 kg)
Performance: max. speed 1,328 mph (2137 km/h); climb 42,800 ft (13045 m) per minute; service ceiling 57,000 ft (17374 m); range 1809 miles (551 km) with full external tanks
Armament: one MB-1 Genie nuclear and four AIM-4 Falcon radar/IR-guided AAMs

English Electric Lightning

United Kingdom
April 1957

In 1948 the team behind the Canberra bomber led by Teddy Petter won the contract for a supersonic research aircraft with their English Electric **P.1** design. The English Electric **P.1A** first flew with two Sapphire Sa.5 turbojets on 4 August 1951 and went supersonic on its third flight. This was followed in late 1952 by the Shorts SB.5 aerodynamic testbed, which was flown with several wing configurations, a T-tail and a fixed undercarriage. As it happened, the low-tail P.1 formed the basis for the **P.1B**, which was the true precursor of the Lightning. The P.1B and subsequent aircraft had twin Rolls-Royce Avon engines in an under-and-over configuration and thin, highly swept mid-set wings of parallel chord with matching low-set tailplanes. The intake was in the nose with the AI 23 Airpass radar fitted in the intake shock cone. The radar could fly the aircraft to within range of the target and fire the missiles, although the system was not as sophisticated as on contemporary US fighters. The armament of the P.1B, which first flew on 4 April 1957, was a pair of Firestreak AAMs. The initial production **Lightning F 1** entered service with No. 74 Squadron in July 1960.

The F 1 was followed by the **F 1A** with an optional refuelling probe, the **F 2** with fully variable reheat (afterburner) and the two-seat **T 4** with side-by-side seating. The first 'second generation' Lightning was the **F 3**, which had improved radar, Red Top AAMs and

The Lightning was one of the highest-performing inter-ceptors of all time. This F 6 served with No. 23 Squadron in 1974. (TRH Pictures)

provision for fuel tanks in overwing mounts. The **F 3A** had an enlarged ventral fuel tank and led to the definitive **F 6**. Later F 6s added cannon in a belly pack, but proposals to integrate Sidewinder came to nought.

Although short-ranged, the Lightning had one of the fastest climb rates ever, and intercepted many Soviet bombers and patrol aircraft in the airspace around the British Isles. It also served for years in Germany in the low-level role.

After the loan of seven F 2 and T 4 models in 1966, Saudi Arabia took delivery of 35 **F 53**s and six **T 55**s from 1969 to counter Yemeni incursions and Egyptian air attacks. These could carry bombs and air-to-ground rockets on underwing pylons and were used in action in late 1969. One was lost to Yemeni ground fire.

Kuwait had less success with their 14 aircraft. Not having contracted with BAC for support, they found maintaining the complex aircraft difficult. The Lightning was finally retired from front-line RAF service in 1988 and replaced by the Tornado F 3.

In the 1970s, some Lightnings adopted camouflage for low-level operations. This F 6 carries Red Top AAMs and a refuelling probe. (Aerospatiale Matra)

Specification: Lightning F 6
Type: single-seat twin-engined interceptor
Powerplant: two Rolls-Royce Avon 301 turbojets rated at 16,360 lb (72.77 kN) thrust with afterburner
Dimensions: span 34 ft 10 in (10.62 m); length 55 ft 3 in (16.84 m); height 19ft 7 in (5.97 m); wing area 458.5 sq ft (42.97 m²)
Weights: empty 28,041 lb (12711 kg); max. take-off 42,000 lb (19047 kg)
Performance: max. speed 1320 km/h (2112 kg); climb rate 50,000 ft (15240 m) per minute; service ceiling 55,000 ft (16770 m); range 800 miles (1290 km)
Armament: two Red Top or Firestreak IR AAMs or up to 44 2-in (50-mm) rockets

McDonnell Douglas F-4 Phantom II

United States
May 1958

A true classic of the jet age, the **F-4 Phantom II** was designed as a shipboard interceptor, but was equally effective in the strike, close support and reconnaissance roles.

The McDonnell Douglas F-4 Phantom was originally designed as a shipboard interceptor for the USN and USMC. The prototype **XF4H-1** first flew on 27 May 1958 and was ordered as the **F-4B**, entering service in 1960. The USAF borrowed 29 as the **F-110** and subsequently ordered 583 **F-4C** fighters and 825 **F-4D**s optimised for air-to-ground operations. All these versions saw extensive action in Vietnam, as did the improved USN **F-4J** and the **RF-4B** and **RF-4C** unarmed reconnaissance models.

All the US aces of the Vietnam War flew Phantoms and the F-4 scored nearly 160 victories. In return, NVAF pilots claimed about 80 Phantoms. Close-range combat with nimble MiG fighters showed the need for an internal gun, leading to the definitive **F-4E** for the USAF, which first flew in June 1967. It had a 20-mm cannon under the nose and a smaller radome. Later F-4Es had manoeuvring slats on the outer wing, and these were added to F-4Js to produce the **F-4S**. The F-4B went through an electronics upgrade and became the **F-4N**. The **F-4G**

An F-4M (Phantom FGR.2) of No. 92 Squadron RAF basks in the sun. British Phantoms were unique in having Rolls-Royce Spey turbofan engines. (Author's collection)

The F-4E was the ultimate fighter Phantom. Many still serve with Turkey, some of them ex-USAF aircraft retaining their former owners' colours and serials. (Author's collection)

'Wild Weasel' anti-radar variant resulted from the conversion of 116 F-4E airframes, deleting the integral cannon and adding a radar-warning antenna. They were the last US Phantoms to see active service, in the 1991 Gulf War. In all, the USAF, USN and USMC had 4,138 Phantoms. A few still serve with test units and as **QF-4** drones.

Air Force Phantom versions were widely exported, although the Navy F-4J was the basis for the **F-4K** **(Phantom FG.1)** for the Royal Navy and the **F-4M** **(Phantom FGR.2)** for the RAF. These were the only F-4s not powered by the GE J79, having Rolls-Royce Spey turbofans. The UK is the only customer to completely retire its F-4s, as they still serve with Egypt, Germany, Greece, Iran, Israel, Japan, South Korea, Spain and Turkey, although in diminishing numbers. A total of 5,195 Phantoms were built.

Several nations have upgraded their F-4s. Germany's **F-4F**s can now carrry AMRAAMs. Japan built 125 of its 140 **F-4EJ** and RF-4EJ Phantoms, now upgraded to **F-4EJ Kai** and RF-4EJ Kai standard with APG-73 radar and new weapons. Israel's **Kurnass** upgrade has also been adopted by Turkey as the **Phantom 2000**. Greece is also upgrading its F-4Es.

Specification: F-4E Phantom II
Type: two-seat twin-engined strike fighter
Powerplant: two 17,900 lb (79.62 kN) GE J79-GE-17A afterburning turbojets
Dimensions: span 38 ft 5 in (11.71 m); length 63 ft (19.20 m); height 16 ft 5.5 in (5.02 m); wing area 530 sq ft (49.25 m²)
Weights: basic empty 30,328 lb (13757 kg); max. take-off 61,795 lb (28030 kg)
Performance: max. level speed 2390 km/h (1,485 mph); max. rate of climb 61,400 ft (18715 m) per minute; service ceiling 62,250 ft (18975 m); radius 786 miles (1266 km)
Armament: one M61 20-mm cannon, four AIM-7 and four AIM-9 AAMs, up to 16,000 lb (7258 kg) of conventional or nuclear bombs

Sukhoi Su-15 'Flagon'

Developed as a pure interceptor to replace the Su-11, a fighter in traditional Soviet form with a nose intake, the **Sukhoi Su-15** deviated by having a large radome and lateral intakes, although it was otherwise similar. The **T-58** prototype had a mid-mounted delta wing with square tips, swept-back tail surfaces and a large bubble canopy. It made its first flight on 30 May 1962. The T-58 was followed by a large number of pre-series aircraft and entered service as the Su-15 (NATO code-name **'Flagon A'**) in 1967. Designed as a high-performance bomber destroyer, the 'Flagon' was capable of Mach 2.4 and had no internal gun, initially relying on armament of two R-23 (AA-3 'Anab') AAMs.

The **'Flagon D'** was the first model built in large numbers and had a 'cranked' wing and was initially known to NATO as the **Su-21**, although this was never a true Soviet designation. The **Su-15T 'Flagon E'** had a new Taifun radar, which proved a failure in service and only a few were built. The **Su-15TM 'Flagon F'** of 1972 had a more aerodynamic ogival radome housing revised Taifun M radar and improved R-98M missiles. This was the major production version and featured R-13F-300 turbojets of 14,500 lb (64.5 kN) thrust with afterburner. An additional pair of pylons were added, allowing for two infra-red R-23TE (AA-3 'Anab') and two radar-guided R-23RE AAMs to be carried. A twin cannon pack containing 23-mm GSh-23 cannon pods was added with this version. The **Su-15UT 'Flagon C'** was a two-seat combat-capable trainer based on the

A Sukhoi Su-15TM 'Flagon F' carrying R-60 (AA-8 'Aphid') air-to-air missiles inboard and K-8 (AA-3 'Anab') AAMs on the outer pylons. (Philip Jarrett collection)

'Flagon D/E'. The instructor had a separate canopy and a periscope for forward vision. The **'Flagon G'** was the two-seat version of the 'Flagon F'. An unusual one-off was the **Su-15VD** with three vertical lift engines mounted in the centre fuselage and flown as a technology demonstrator in 1967.

The 'Flagon' came to international prominence when an Su-15TM shot down a Boeing 747 flying as Korean Air Lines flight KAL 007 in September 1983 using two missiles. An Su-15 also damaged and forced down a KAL Boeing 707 in April 1978 with cannon fire near Murmansk. The type was involved in many interceptions of Western reconnaissance aircraft over the Baltic and Soviet Far East.

Although the 'Flagon' was not supplied to Warsaw Pact countries or exported, with the dissolution of the Soviet Union, some were transferred to Georgia and Ukraine, but appear to have seen little or no service. Azerbaijan may have acquired four during or before 1997. All Russian Su-15s were withdrawn under the Conventional Forces in Europe (CFE) treaty by 1992.

The Su-15M 'Flagon E' was introduced in the early 1970s. Total production amounted to about 1,500 aircraft of the series. (Philip Jarrett collection)

Specification: Sukhoi Su-15 'Flagon A'
Type: Twin-engined interceptor
Powerplant: two Tumansky R-13F2-300 afterburning turbojets rated at 31,460 lb (139.95 kN) thrust
Dimensions: span 28 ft 3 in (8.62 m); length 70 ft 3 in (21.41 m); height 16 ft 6 in (5.00 m); wing area 394 sq ft (36.6 m²)
Weights: empty 25,000 lb (11340 kg); max. take-off 35,275 lb (16000 kg)
Performance: max. speed 1,385 mph (2320 km/h); initial climb rate 45,000 ft (13730 m) per minute; service ceiling 60,700 ft (18500 m); range 901 miles (1,450 km)
Armament: two R-98M 'Anab', two R-60 'Aphid' AAMs, one GSh-23L gun pod

Northrop F-5 Freedom Fighter/Tiger II

United States
May 1963

In 1954 the US government initiated a study for a simple lightweight fighter to be supplied via the Military Assistance Program. Northrop's private-venture **N-156C** design made its first flight on 30 July 1959, and was selected in 1962. The **F-5A Freedom Fighter** prototype flew in May 1963. A corresponding two-seat **F-5B** trainer entered service in April 1964, four months ahead of the F-5A. Northrop also developed the reconnaissance **RF-5A**, equipped with four nose-mounted cameras.

The USAF used F-5As in Vietnam under the Skoshi Tiger programme where they proved a useful close-support aircraft. Otherwise, the US made little use of the type. First generation F-5s were exported to Brazil, Greece, Jordan, Morocco, the Philippines, Saudi Arabia, South Korea, Spain, Thailand, Turkey, Venezuela and Yemen. Improved versions were built by Canadair as the **CF-5A** and **CF-5D** and were later upgraded by Bristol Aerospace. Some were later sold to Botswana. The Royal Netherlands air force ordered 105 **NF-5A**s and **NF-5B**s with leading-edge manoeuvre flaps and Doppler radar.

The second-generation **Tiger II** had uprated J85 engines, an integrated fire control system, additional fuel and a larger, modified wing with leading edge root

The NF-5A served alongside F-104s in the Dutch Air Force (KLu) for many years before both types were replaced by the F-16. (Author's collection)

The Royal Thai Air Force (RTAF) is one of several Southeast Asian users of the F-5E Tiger II. This low-cost fighter had outstanding export success. (Author's collection)

extensions (LERXes) and manoeuvring flaps. The **F-5E** is the single-seat variant and was first flown on 11 August 1972. The combat-capable **F-5F** trainer had a lengthened fuselage and was first delivered to the USAF in 1973, mainly to train foreign users. F-5E/Fs were later used for aggressor training with the USAF and still fly with the USN and USMC.

Some 1,300 F-5E/Fs were supplied to 20 air forces. Current operators are Bahrain, Botswana, Brazil, Chile, Honduras, Indonesia, Iran, Jordan, Kenya, Malaysia, Mexico, Morocco, Saudi Arabia, Singapore, South Korea, Sudan, Switzerland, Taiwan, Thailand, Tunisia, USN/USMC, Venezuela and Yemen.They were also built under licence in South Korea, Switzerland and Taiwan. Iranian F-5Es destroyed many Soviet-built Iraqi-fighters between 1980 and 1987.

Many F-5 upgrade programmes are now available. Chile, Brazil, Indonesia, Singapore, Taiwan and Turkey have all modernised their aircraft with new radars, cockpit systems and weapons.

A specialised **RF-5E Tigereye** reconnaissance version, retaining full combat capability, first flew in 1978. The **F-5G** (later **F-20 Tigershark**) was a private-venture attempt in the 1980s to build a well-equipped lightweight export fighter for nations unable to afford the F-16, but it failed to win any orders.

Specification: Northrop F-5E Tiger II
Type: twin-engined fighter-bomber
Powerplant: two 5,000 lb (22.24 kN) thrust GE J85-GE-21B afterburning turbojets
Dimensions: wing span 28 ft (8.53 m) with tip-mounted AAMs; length 47 ft 4.75 in (14.45 m); height 13 ft 4.5 in (4.08 m)
Weights: empty 9,558 lb (4349 kg); max. take-off 24,664 lb (11187 kg)
Performance: max. level speed 1,056 mph (1700 km/h); max. rate of climb at sea level 34,300 ft (10455 m) per minute; service ceiling 51,800 ft (15590 m); combat radius 875 miles (1405 km) with two AIM-9 AAMs
Armament: two M39A2 20-mm cannon; max. ordnance 7,000 lb (3175 kg)

Mikoyan Gurevich MiG-25/31

Soviet Union
September 1964

The Mikoyan-Gurevich **MiG-25** (NATO code-name 'Foxbat') was developed to counter the high-flying Mach 3 North American B-70 strategic bomber, which itself was destined never to enter production. It featured advanced construction techniques, using tempered steel for most of the airframe with titanium for the leading edges. The prototype **Ye-155P-1** first flew on 9 September 1964, powered by a pair of 22,500 lb (100 kN) thrust Mikulin R-15B-300 turbojets.

Production of the refined **MiG-25P 'Foxbat-A'** fighter began in 1969, and it entered service in 1973. The definitive **MiG-25PD 'Foxbat-E'** featured a new RP-25 look-down/shoot-down radar, an IRST, more powerful R-15BD-300 turbojets and provision for a large 1,166-Imp gal (5300-litre) belly tank. About 370 surviving 'Foxbat-As' were brought up to PD standard, as the **MiG-25PDS**. Some MiG-25PDSs were fitted with a 10-in (250-mm) nose plug to allow installation of a retractable refuelling probe, taking the overall length to 78 ft 11.67 in (24.07 m). **The MiG-25PU 'Foxbat-C'** conversion trainer lacks radar and has a new instructor's cockpit stepped down in an elongated nose in front of the standard cockpit. The instructor's position replaces the radar and the student has the same view as on a standard 'Foxbat'.

MiG-25 fighters were exported to Algeria, Iraq, Libya and Syria, and also remain in small-scale service in Russia and a handful of former Soviet states. At least two Iraqi MiG-25PFs were shot down by USAF

Despite its outward similarity, the MiG-31 'Foxhound' is a completely revised, much more sophisticated interceptor than the MiG-25 'Foxbat'. (TRH Pictures)

fighters in the Gulf War, but one claimed the only Iraqi aerial victory when it destroyed a USN F/A-18 on the first night of the war.

The **MiG-31 'Foxhound'** was developed to counter the threat posed by new low-level strike aircraft and cruise missiles, complementing the Su-27 in service and using its ultra-long-range capability to fill gaps in Russia's ground-based radar chain. A two-seat derivative of the MiG-25 'Foxbat' airframe, the 'Foxhound' introduced an all-new structure, a new wing planform with small LERXes, Soloviev D-30F-6 turbofans and a new undercarriage. **The Ye-155MP** prototype flew on 16 September 1975 and series production of 280 MiG-31s began in 1979.

The MiG-31 featured a flat belly with four missile recesses for its primary armament, which consisted of R-33 (AA-9 'Amos') AAMs. The improved **MiG-31M** interceptor variant was built in prototype form only. It could carry six R-37 long-range AAMs and its radar could engage six targets simultaneously. Development was abandoned due to lack of funding.

The MiG-25 was widely used as a reconaissance platform This MiG-25RBT 'Foxbat B' has an elongated nose for a signals intelligence (Sigint) system. (Aerospace Publishing)

<table>
<tr><td colspan="2">Specification: MiG-25PDS 'Foxbat-E'</td></tr>
</table>

Specification: MiG-25PDS 'Foxbat-E'
Type: twin-engined interceptor
Powerplant: two 24,691 lb (109.83 kN) thrust Tumansky R-15BD-300 turbojets
Dimensions: wing span 45 ft 11.75 in (14.02 m); length 78 ft 1.75 in (23.82 m); height 20 ft 0.25 in (6.10 m)
Weights: normal take-off 76,894 lb (34920 kg); max. take-off 80,952 lb (36720 kg)
Performance: max. level speed Mach 2.8 (1,864 mph, 3000 km/h); climb to 65,615 ft (20000 m) in 8 minutes 54 seconds; service ceiling 67,915 ft (20700 m); range 1,075 miles (1730 km)
Armament: four or six AA-6 'Acrid', AA-7 'Apex' or AA-8 'Aphid'AAMs

Dassault Mirage F1

France
December 1966

The Mirage F1 was Dassault's successor to its highly successful Mirage III/5 delta series and was developed to meet an Armée de l'Air requirement for an all-weather interceptor. Although powered by a version of the SNECMA Atar 9 engine as used on the Mirage III, the F1 forsook the delta configuration for a high-mounted wing and conventional tail surfaces. The prototype first flew on 23 December 1966 and was followed by the initial production **Mirage F1C**, delivered from May 1973. The 83 initial aircraft were followed by 79 **Mirage F1C-200**s with fixed refuelling probes (necessitating a small fuselage plug). The Armée de l'Air also received 20 **Mirage F1B** tandem-seat trainers, which retained full combat capability.

Dassault converted 64 F1C-200s to serve as dedicated tactical reconnaissance platforms. These **Mirage F1CR-200**s are equipped with an infra-red linescan unit, undernose cameras and centreline pods for side-looking airborne radar (SLAR) and other sensors.The Mirage **F1CT** (T-Tactique) was a logical product of the shortfall in French ground-attack capability and a surplus of air defence fighters following Mirage 2000C deliveries. From 1991, 55 Mirage F1Cs were converted to F1CT standard and given expanded tactical capability with a laser

Mirage F1Cs were initially delivered to the Armee de l'Air without missile armament. By 1976, Matra R.530 missiles were available. (CEV)

The F1B is the two-seat trainer version of the Mirage F1 fighter for the French Air Force. It is fully combat-capable. (Author's collection)

rangefinder, improved RWR and chaff/flare dispensers. F1CTs were most often deployed with the French units based in Africa.

The Mirage F1 has been widely exported. F1Cs were sold to South Africa (**F1CZ**, now withdrawn), Morocco (**F1CH**), Jordan (**F1CJ**), Kuwait (**F1CK**, **F1CK2**, now withdrawn), Greece (**F1CG**) and Spain (**F1CE**). The Mirage **F1A** was a simplified version for day visual attack missions, equipped with the Aida II ranging radar in a reprofiled nose. It was sold to Libya (**F1AD**) and South Africa (**F1AZ**) now withdrawn).

The Mirage **F1E** (and corresponding Mirage **F1D** trainer) was an upgraded multi-role fighter/attack version for export, with an inertial navigation system (INS) and head-up display (HUD). F1Es were exported to Ecuador (**F1JA/E**), Iraq (**F1EQ**), Jordan (**F1EJ**), Libya (**F1ED**), Morocco (**F1EH** and **F1EH-200**), Qatar (**F1EDA** and **F1DDA**) and Spain (**F1EE-200**).

Iraqi F1s were destroyed in significant numbers by Iranian fighters in 1980–88 and by US and Saudi aircraft in 1991. In return, half a dozen victories were scored against Iran's fighters, including at least one F-14A. South African Air Force (SAAF) Mirages destroyed several Angolan MiG-17s in the 1980s.

Specification: Dassault Mirage F1C
Type: single-seat fighter
Powerplant: one 15,785 lb (70.21 kN) thrust SNECMA Atar 9K-50 afterburning turbojet
Dimensions: span 30 ft 6.75 in (9.32 m); length 50 ft 2.5 in (15.30 m); height 14 ft 9 in (4.50 m); wing area 269.11 sq ft (25.0 m²)
Weights: empty 16,314 lb (7400 kg); max. take-off 35,715 lb (16200 kg)
Performance: max. speed 1,453 mph (2338 km/h); climb rate 41,930 ft (12780 m) per minute; service ceiling 65,615 ft (20000 m); combat radius 264 miles (425 km)
Armament: two DEFA 553 30-mm cannon, max. ordnance 13,889 lb (6300 kg), including R.530/Super 530F, AIM-9 or Magic AAMs

Saab JA37 Viggen

Saab's System 37, the **Viggen** (Thunderbolt) was developed as a relatively low-cost Mach 2 fighter for the Swedish Flygvapnet capable of deployed short-field operations. The design pioneered the use of flap-equipped canards with a stable delta-wing configuration. The selected RM8A turbofan was based on the commercial Pratt & Whitney JT8D-22 and equipped with a thrust reverser and Swedish-designed afterburner.

The initial **AJ 37** Viggen all-weather attack variant featured sophisticated navigation/attack and landing systems and the PS-37 multi-role radar. The first of seven Viggen prototypes initially flew on 8 February 1967 and deliveries of the first of 109 AJ 37s began in 1971. The primary armament comprised Saab Rb 04E anti-ship missiles (replaced by the far more capable long-range Rbs 15) and licence-built AGM-65 Maverick air-to-surface missiles (ASMs). Several AJ 37-based variants were developed. The **SF 37** was tasked with all-weather day and night overland reconnaissance. It is equipped with various optical and IR cameras, and carries podded sensors. The **SH 37** was modified for all-weather sea surveillance and patrol with a secondary maritime strike role. It has a modified radar, ventral night reconnaissance and long-range camera

With it's canard delta configuration, the Viggen was advanced for its day. This JA 37 serves with F17 at Ronneby in southeast Sweden. (Author)

This JA 37 Viggen of F16 wears a particularly patriotic colour scheme. The Viggen is being phased out as Gripen deliveries progress and defence cuts take effect. (F16)

pods. A tandem two-seat **SK 37** trainer was also developed with a stepped rear cockpit fitted with a bulged canopy and twin periscopes.

The next-generation **JA 37** Jakt Viggen (Fighter Viggen) was developed as a dedicated interceptor. It introduced a new pulse-Doppler look-down/shoot-down PS-47 radar, new avionics, an uprated and modified RM8B engine and a ventral 30-mm cannon. The main armament was two Rb 71 (Sky Flash) semi-active radar-homing AAMs, together with two Rb 24s (AIM-9 Sidewinders). A modified AJ 37 was flown as the JA 37 prototype on 27 September 1974. Overall production of this variant was 149, taking total Viggen sales to 330, although at one time 800 were proposed. JA 37s entered service in 1978. A number have now undergone the **JA 37 Mod D** upgrade, giving them AIM-120 AMRAAM capability.

The advent of the JAS 39 Gripen brought about a rationalisation of the Viggen fleet. The attack/recce Viggens were upgraded to a new 'multi-role' standard. AJ 37s became **AJS 37**s, SF 37s became **AJSF 37**s and SH37s became **AJSH 37**s. A number of SK 37s have also been radically modified to serve as **SK 37E** EW/SEAD aircraft, known as 'Eriks'.

Specification: Saab JA 37 Viggen

Type: single-seat interceptor fighter
Powerplant: one 28,110 lb (125.04 kN) thrust Volvo Flygmotor RM8B turbofan
Dimensions: span 34 ft 9.25 in (10.60 m); length 53 ft 9.75 in (16.40 m); height 19 ft 4.25 in (5.90 m); wing area 561.89 sq ft (52.20 m²)
Weights: normal take-off 33,069 lb (15000 kg); max. take-off 37,478 lb (17000 kg)
Performance: max. speed 1,321 mph (2126 km/h); climb to 32,800 ft (10000 m) in 1 minute 40 seconds; service ceiling 60,000 ft (18290 m); radius 622 miles (1000 km) plus
Armament: one 30-mm Oerlikon KCA cannon; max. ordnance 13,000 lb (5897 kg)

Mikoyan-Gurevich MiG-23 'Flogger'

Soviet Union
July 1967

The Mikoyan-Gurevich **MiG-23** was developed as a MiG-21 replacement, with greater range and firepower and incorporating the new 'swing-wing' or variable geometry technology for better low-speed handling. After the first flight of the **MiG-23-11** on 10 July 1967, the initial **MiG-23S** was ordered into production. The MiG-23 had a single Tumansky R-27F turbojet rated at 22,046 lb (98.07 kN) thrust in afterburner, lateral intakes and a pointed radome containing Sapfir 21 radar. A large ventral fin gave lateral stability and was hinged to allow ground clearance on landing. Only 50 were built.

The **MiG-23M** and export MiG-23MF (NATO code-name 'Flogger-B') had 'High Lark' pulse-Doppler radar, infra-red search and tracking (IRST), AA-7 'Apex' missiles, and a shortened rear fuselage. Some remain in use with Bulgaria, Cuba, India, Romania and Syria. In Soviet service, the down-graded **MiG-23MS** 'Flogger-E' was an export version with 'Jay Bird' radar, and no beyond visual range (BVR) missile, and remains in service with Algeria, Libya and perhaps Syria. The Soviet Frontal Aviation forces used the MiG-23M for battlefield air superiority and ground attack. Air-to-air armament was typically a pair of R-23 (AA-7 'Alamo') and a pair of R-60 (AA-8 'Aphid') short-range AAMs.

The lightweight **MiG-23ML** 'Flogger-G' introduced airframe, engine, radar and avionics improvements. Examples remain in service in Angola, Bulgaria, Cuba, Iraq, North Korea, Syria and Yemen. The **MiG-23P** was

MiG-23MF. The large missiles are R-23s (AA-7 'Apex') and the small ones are R-60s AA-8 'Aphids'. (TRH Pictures)

a dedicated interceptor for the Air Defence Forces (PVO). The final **MiG-23MLD** 'Flogger-K' fighter variant is still used by Belarus, Kazakhstan and Bulgaria. This version had automatic leading-edge slats, large chaff dispensers and swivelling outer wing pylons. In all, over 25 nations operated MiG-23s. Few if any remain in service with Russian forces. **The MiG-23UB** 'Flogger-C' two-seat trainer version first flew in 1968 and was delivered to all operators.

In air combat, Iraqi MiG-23s had some success against Iranian F-4 Phantoms in 1980–88, but the Flogger has been defeated in all aerial encounters with USAF and USN aircraft. A small number of confirmed kills were scored against Israeli F-4s and A-4s in 1974 and 1981 and other claims were made, but the kill ratio is strongly in favour of Israel's fighters, particularly over Lebanon in 1982.

The attack-dedicated **MiG-23B/BN** 'Flogger-F' had an upgraded navigation/attack system and a derated R-29B-300 engine and led to the **MiG-27** ground-attack aircraft series.

The 'Flogger' has become a rare breed in Europe. The Czech Air Force's MiG-23MLs have been retired, but Bulgaria and Romania still fly the type. (Author)

Specification: MiG-23ML 'Flogger-G'
Type: single-seat fighter/ground attacker
Powerplant: one 28,660 lb (127.49kN) thrust Tumansky R-35-300 afterburning turbojet
Dimensions: span 45 ft 10 in (13.97 m) spread; length 54 ft 9.5 in (16.70 m); height 15 ft 9.6 in (4.82 m); wing area 402 sq ft (37.35 m²)
Weights: empty 22,487 lb (10200 kg); max. take-off 39.242 lb (17800 kg)
Performance: max. speed 1,553 mph (2500 km/h); max. climb rate 47,244 ft (14400 m); service ceiling 60,695 ft (18500 m); combat radius 715 miles (1150 km)
Armament: one GSh-23 23-mm cannon, max. ordnance 6,613 lb (3000 kg)

Grumman F-14 Tomcat

United States
December 1970

Intended as a successor to the F-4 Phantom in the fleet air defence role, the Grumman **F-14A** Tomcat was conceived to engage and destroy targets at extreme range using the AWG-9 fire control system and AIM-54 Phoenix missiles. It remains the US Navy's standard carrier-based interceptor. The first development aircraft made its maiden flight on 21 December 1970. Deliveries to the US Navy began in October 1972, with the first operational cruise in 1974. F-14s covered the evacuation of Saigon in 1975, but saw no combat at this time.

Problems with the F-14A's TF-30 turbofan were a key factor in the development of re-engined and upgraded Tomcat variants. One airframe was fitted with F401-PW-400s and tested as the **F-14B** as early as 1973–4. This aircraft later re-emerged as the F-14B Super Tomcat, equipped with F101DFE engines. This engine was developed into the GE F100-GE-400 turbofan, which was selected to power improved Tomcat variants. Two re-engined variants were proposed: the **F-14A(Plus)** was to be an interim type, while the **F-14D** would introduce advanced digital avionics. Subsequently, the F-14A(Plus) was redesignated as the **F-14B**, 38 new-build examples being joined by 32 F-14A rebuilds by 1988. These incorporated a modernised fire control system, new radios, upgraded RWRs and various cockpit changes.

The first new-build F-14D made its first flight on 9 February 1990. The F-14D added digital radar

A pair of VF-14 'Tophatters' F-14As carrying LANTIRN Pods and 500-lb bombs. This squadron has now transitioned to the F/A-18F Super Hornet. (Author)

processing and displays to the AWG-9, resulting in a designation change to APG-71, and a dual undernose TCS/IRST sensor pod. Other improvements include NACES ejection seats and new RWR equipment. Defence cuts meant the service only received 37 new-build aircraft, with deliveries beginning in 1990. Deliveries of F-14D rebuilds totalled 110, ending in 1995. A proposed **Tomcat 21** strike-fighter lost out to the F/A-18E/F Super Hornet.

US Navy F-14s destroyed Libyan Su-22s and MiG-23s in encounters over the Gulf of Sidra in the 1980s, but were credited with only one helicopter in the 1991 Gulf War. Iran received 79 F-14As and has managed to keep about 25 airworthy despite lack of spares. In the Iran–Iraq war, Iran's F-14s scored around 42 kills for one loss to Iraqi fighters.

In late 1990 the F-14's air-ground potential began to be exploited as the '**Bombcat**' entered the fleet, although with 'dumb' bombs only. Since then, precision weapons have been cleared and used over Bosnia, Kosovo and Afghanistan.

An F-14B of VF-11 'Red Rippers' lands aboard the USS John F. Kennedy after flying a mission over Afghanistan. (Author)

Specification: Northrop Grumman F-14D
Type: twin-engined, two-seat, carrier-based fleet defence/strike fighter
Powerplant: two 23,100 lb (102.75 kN) thrust GE F110-GE-400 turbofans
Dimensions: span (spread) 64 ft 1.5 in (19.54 m); length 62 ft 8 in (19.10 m); height 16 ft (4.88 m); wing area 565 sq ft (52.49 m²)
Weights: empty 41,780 lb (18,951 kg); max. take-off 74,349 lb (33,724 kg)
Performance: max. speed 1,241 mph (1997 km/h); max. climb rate over 30,000 ft (9145 m) per minute; ceiling over 53,000 ft (16150 m); combat radius 1,239 miles (1994 km/h)
Armament: one 20-mm cannon; four AIM-9s, four AIM-7s and six AIM-54 AAMs

McDonnell Douglas F-15A/C Eagle

United States
July 1972

The **F-15 Eagle** is viewed as the world's best air superiority fighter and interceptor, particularly in BVR air-to-air missions. It was designed by McDonnell Douglas for the USAF's 1968 FX requirement, which called for a long-range air superiority fighter to replace the F-4. McDonnell won the competition and first flew a prototype **F-15A** on 27 July 1972, followed by a prototype **F-15B** two-seat trainer in July 1973.

The F-15 has an advanced aerodynamic design with large lightly loaded wings conferring high agility. It features a sophisticated avionics system and its APG-63 radar introduced a genuine look-down/shoot-down capability. Radar-guided AIM-7 AAMs form the primary armament, augmented by AIM-9 AAMs. Although still in use, the AIM-7 has now been superseded by the far more capable AIM-120 AMRAAM. The USAF is also preparing to introduce the latest AIM-9X off-boresight short-range missile.

The USAF received 360 production F-15As and 58 F-15Bs from 1976. Most remaining F-15A/Bs now serve with ANG units. The only foreign F-15A/B operator is Israel, which currently operates a force of about 50 A/Bs. Israeli Eagles (including two-seaters) scored nearly 60 kills against Syrian fighters in the period 1979–82. Saudi F-15s destroyed two Iranian F-4s during the Iran–Iraq war

USAF Eagles are based in the USA, England and Okinawa. This Kadena-based F-15C attended the 1988 William Tell fighter meeting at Tyndall in Florida. (Author's collection)

The Eagle was designed as an 'air superiority fighter' and has been victorious in many combats in the Middle East with US, Israeli and Saudi air forces. (Author)

and two Iraqi Mirage F1s in the Gulf War. USAF Eagle pilots were credited with 35 kills against Iraq's jets and helicopters. In March 1999, USAF F-15Cs shot down four Serbian MiG-29s over Kosovo with AIM-120s.

The **F-15C**, an improved and updated F-15A, was the definitive production version. The two-seat **F-15D** was a similarly improved F-15B. First flying on 26 February 1979, the F-15C introduced uprated F100 engines and provision for conformal fuel tanks (CFTs). Initial deliveries were made in September 1979 and F-15C/Ds later replaced F-15A/Bs with three wings. The F-15 Multistage Improvement Program (MSIP) was initiated in February 1983, with the first production MSIP F-15C produced in 1985. The final 43 were fitted with a Hughes APG-70 radar. The USAF is now fitting all its F-15A/Cs with the upgraded APG-63(V)1 radar.

F-15C/Ds were delivered to the USAF, Israel and Saudi Arabia. The equivalent **F-15J/DJ** is Japan's principal air superiority fighter. Most of the JASDF's 213 planned Eagles have been licence-built by Mitsubishi.

The first of these aircraft entered service in April 2001. During 2000 18 special F-15Cs were fitted with the APG-63(V)2 Active Electronically Scanned Array (AESA) radar.

Specification: F-15A Eagle
Type: twin-engined air superiority fighter
Powerplant: two 25,000-lb (111.2 kN) P&W F100-PW-100 turbofans
Dimensions: span 42 ft 10 in (13.05 m); length 63 ft 9 in (19.43 m); height 18 ft 5.5in (5.63 m); wing area 608 sq ft (56.48 m²)
Weights: operating empty 27,000 lb (12247 kg); max. take-off 56,000 lb (25402 kg)
Performance: max. level speed more than 1,650 mph (2655 km/h); max. rate of climb at sea level more than 50,000 ft (15240 m) per minute; ceiling 60,000 ft (18290 m); radius 1,222 miles (1967 km) (interception mission)
Armament: one 20-mm Vulcan cannon, four AIM-7 and four AIM-9 AAMs

General Dynamics F-16 Fighting Falcon

The **F-16 Fighting Falcon** is the benchmark modern combat aircraft. It was conceived as a lightweight 'no frills' fighter for air-to-air combat. The first **YF-16** service-test prototype's maiden flight was on 2 February 1974. In 1975 it won a competitive USAF evaluation against the Northrop YF-17. The production F-16A had an enlarged wing, greater fuel capacity and a deeper nose to house the APG-66 radar. The F-16 was the first 'fly-by-wire' fighter, commanded by a sidestick in the cockpit.

The first **F-16A** and **F-16B** trainer deliveries to the USAF began in 1979. These 94 aircraft were built to **F-16 Block 1** standard, powered by the F100-PW-200 engine. They were followed by 197 **F-16 Block 5**s and 312 **Block 10**s. Block 5 and Block 10 F-16A/Bs were exported to Belgium, Denmark, Israel, the Netherlands and Norway.

The **F-16A/B Block 15** introduced the larger 'big tail' fin and wider tailplanes. The APG-66 radar was improved and new electronic warfare (EW) and identification friend or foe (IFF) systems were fitted. Export sales were made to Belgium, Denmark, Egypt, Israel, the Netherlands, Norway, Pakistan and Venezuela.

A specialist USAF interceptor version, armed with the AIM-7 missile, was developed as the **F-16 Block 15 ADF** (air defense fighter). The **F-16 Block 15 OCU** added some features of the F-16C/D, including the F100-PW-220E engine and has been delivered to

Norway is one of 20 nations to operate the F-16. Its F-16As operate in the anti-shipping role with Penguin missiles as well as in the air defence role. (Lockheed Martin)

Belgium, Denmark, Indonesia, Netherlands, Norway, Pakistan, Portugal and Thailand.

The European F-16s are now undergoing the **F-16 MLU** (mid-life update) bringing them up to Block 50 standard, with AIM-120 AMRAAM and precision weapons capability.

The **F-16C/D** is a development of the F-16A/B with structural, avionics and systems modifications. Cockpit changes include a wide-angle HUD and an improved data display. The first F-16C flew on 19 June 1984 and the initial production-standard **F-16 Block 25** aircraft was acquired solely by the USAF.

The **F-16C/D Block 30** introduced the General Electric F110-GE-100 engine as an alternative powerplant. Block 30 exports went to Greece, Israel and Turkey. The F-16C/D Block 32 was powered by an uprated F100-PW-220 engine and delivered to Egypt and South Korea. The F-16C/D **Block 40** and **Block 42** Night Falcons were supplied to the USAF, Bahrain, Egypt, Israel and Turkey. The **Block 50/52** has gone to South Korea, Singapore and Turkey.

The Netherlands was one of the first and most important export customers for the F-16. An F-16A MLU of No. 322 Squadron destroyed a MiG-29 over Kosovo in 1999. (KLu)

Specification: Lockheed Martin F-16C Block 52

Type: single-seat fighter
Powerplant: one 29,100 lb (129.4 kN) thrust GE F110-GE-129 IPE afterburning turbofan
Dimensions: span 31 ft (9.45 m); length 49 ft 4 in (15.03 m); height 16 ft 8.5 in (5.09 m); wing area 300 sq ft (28.9 m²)
Weights: empty 18,917 lb (8581 kg); max. take-off 27,099 lb (12292 kg)
Performance: max. speed over 1,320 mph (2125 km/h); max. climb rate 50,000 ft (15250 m) per minute; ceiling 50,000 ft (15240 m); ferry range 2,619 miles (4215 km)
Armament: one M61 Vulcan 20-mm cannon, max. ordnance 15,591 lb (7072 kg)

Mikoyan-Gurevich MiG-29 'Fulcrum'

Soviet Union
October 1977

The Mikoyan-Gurevich **MiG-29** (NATO code-name 'Fulcrum') was developed to meet a 1971 requirement for a lightweight fighter to replace Frontal Aviation MiG-21s, MiG-23s and Su-17s in the battlefield air superiority and ground-attack roles. Design work began in 1974, and the first prototype flew on 6 October 1977. Deliveries began in 1983.

The baseline MiG-29 **'Fulcrum-A'** carries two BVR AA-10 'Alamo-As' inboard and four short-range AA-8 'Aphid' or AA-11 'Archer' IR-homing missiles outboard, backed by an internal 30-mm cannon. The MiG-29 has an N-019 pulse-Doppler radar and a passive IRST system. More than 450 single-seat 'Fulcrums' are estimated to be in service with the VVS, and other former Soviet states including Belarus, Kazakhstan, Moldova, Turkmenistan, Ukraine and Uzbekistan. The aircraft was also acquired by Bangladesh, Bulgaria, Cuba, the Czech Republic, Germany, Hungary, India, Iran, Iraq, North Korea, Malaysia, Peru, Poland, Romania, Slovakia, South Yemen, Syria and Yugoslavia. MiG-29s have been evaluated by Israel and by the USA.

The 'Fulcrum' represented a massive technological leap for Soviet fighter design and was much vaunted

The MiG-SMT's enlarged spine contains avionics and a fuel tank. A small number of this model have been produced by conversion of earlier Fulcrums. (Author)

The Czech Republic passed some of its early-model MiG-29s to Slovakia when the two countries separated, and later sold others to Poland. (Author)

in the West for its excellent manoeuvrability without fly-by-wire controls. In actual combat, however, the MiG-29 has not fared well. No kills were recorded against allied aircraft in the Gulf War or over the former Yugoslavia. During fighting between Ethiopia and Eritrea in 1998–9, four to six were destroyed by Ethiopian Su-27s using R-73 missiles.

The **MiG-29UB** trainer has no radar, but retains the IRST and has a weapons system simulator, allowing the instructor to generate HUD, IRST and radar symbology in the front cockpit. An improved single-seater (Model 9-13, known to NATO as the **'Fulcrum-C'**) introduced a bulged spine, housing additional fuel and an active jammer. None have been exported outside the former USSR, except a handful of Moldovan aircraft bought by the USA.

The **MiG-29M** was an advanced derivative with revised structure, increased fuel and genuine multi-role capability. This reached the prototype stage, as did the carrier-borne **MiG-29K**. It is likely that India will purchase MiG-29Ks to equip the carrier *Gorshkov* purchased from Russia. A handful of modernised **MiG-29SE** aircraft entered service in Russia, and the **SD** formed the basis of the **MiG-29N** for Malaysia.

Specification: MiG-29 'Fulcrum A'
Type: twin-engined, single-seat fighter
Powerplant: two 18,298 lb (81.39 kN) thrust Klimov RD-33 afterburning turbofans
Dimensions: span 37 ft 3.25 in (11.36 m); length 56 ft 10 in (17.32 m); height 15 ft 6.2 in (4.73 m); wing area 409.04 sq ft (38.0 m²)
Weights: empty 24,030 lb (10900 kg); max. take-off 40,785 lb (18500 kg)
Performance: max. speed 1,519 mph (2445 km/h); max. climb rate 64,961 ft (19800 m) per minute; service ceiling 55,775 ft (17000 m); ferry range 1,305 miles (2100 km)
Armament: one GSh-301 30-mm cannon, max. stores of 6,614 lb (3000 kg), including up to six AAMs

Dassault Mirage 2000

The Dassault **Mirage 2000** was chosen in December 1975 to be the next-generation fighter for the Armée de l'Air and the first of five prototypes took to the air on 10 March 1978. With the Mirage 2000, Dassault returned to the delta configuration, using negative longitudinal stability and a fly-by-wire flight control system to eliminate many of the shortcomings of a conventional delta. As such, the Mirage 2000 has the Mirage III/5 series' large internal volume and low drag, but has improved agility, slow-speed handling and lower landing speed. The first of 37 production **Mirage 2000C**s made its maiden flight on 20 November 1982 and deliveries began in April 1983. All early production **2000C-S2**, and **-S3** aircraft had SNECMA M53-5 engines, and introduced successive improvements to the Thomson-CSF RDM radar. The Mirage **2000C-S4** and **-S5** introduced the uprated M53-P2 powerplant and the RDI radar optimised for look-down/shoot-down intercepts with two Matra Super 530D AAMs.

Export versions of the RDM-equipped, M53-P2-powered variant have been delivered to Abu Dhabi (**Mirage 2000EAD**, 22 aircraft), Egypt (**Mirage 2000EM**, 16), Greece (**Mirage 2000EG**, 36), India (**Mirage 2000HS**, locally known as Vajra, 46) and Peru (**Mirage 2000P**, 10).

The **Mirage 2000B** tandem two-seat trainer first flew in August 1983. It loses some internal fuel and both cannon in order to accommodate the second

The Mirage 2000-5 has new multifunction RDY radar, and can launch the Mica AAM, seen here on the underfuselage pylons. On the wings are Matra Magics. (Dassault)

cockpit. Abu Dhabi's two-seat trainers are known as **Mirage 2000DAD**s, India's are **Mirage 2000TH**s and Peru's are **Mirage 2000DP**s. The reconnaissance-configured **Mirage 2000R** has a radar nose and carries podded sensors. Abu Dhabi has acquired eight Mirage **2000RAD**s.

The upgraded **Mirage 2000-5** introduces the Rafale's five-screen cockpit display, Mica AAMs, RDY multi-mode radar, and advanced self-protection suite and additional avionics. The 2000-5 is aimed largely at the export market, and significantly improves the basic aircraft's combat capability. France is also acquiring the **Mirage 2000-5F** through the conversion of 37 of its existing 2000Cs. The first conversion flew on 26 February 1996. The first export customer for the -5 was Taiwan, who ordered 60 **Mirage 2000-5EI**s (including 12 **2000-5DI** trainers), delivered from 1997. Other orders have come from Qatar (12 **Mirage 2000-5EDA/DDA**s). Abu Dhabi and Greece are acquiring a further improved version, the **Mirage 2000-5 Mk II**, also known as the **Mirage 2000-9**.

Greece is acquiring a total of 36 Mirage 2000EG and BG fighters. All will be supplied or upgraded to Mirage 2000-5 standard. (Dassault)

Specification: Dassault Mirage 2000-5
Type: single-seat interceptor
Powerplant: one 21,384 lb (95.12 kN) thrust SNECMA M53-P2 turbofan
Dimensions: span 29 ft 11.5 in (9.13 m); length 47 ft 11.25 in (14.36 m); height 17 ft 0.75 in (5.20 m); wing area 441.33 sq ft (41.0 m²)
Weights: empty 16,534 lb (7500 kg); max. take-off 37,478 lb (17000 kg)
Performance: max. speed 1,453 mph (2338 km/h); climb rate 55,971 ft (17060 m) per minute; service ceiling 59,055 ft (18000 m); range (ferry) 2072 miles (3335 km)
Armament: two 30-mm DEFA 554 cannon; 13,890-lb (6300-kg) ordnance

McDonnell Douglas F/A-18 Hornet

United States
November 1978

The F/A-18 Hornet was a more sophisticated navalised derivative of the Northrop YF-17 Cobra, which was developed in its final form in partnership with McDonnell Douglas (now Boeing). The first of 11 pre-production aircraft made its maiden flight on 18 November 1978 and the production of 371 **F/A-18A**s followed. A two-seater version was initially designated **TF-18A**, before becoming the **F/A-18B**. Basically identical to the F/A-18A, provision of a second seat in tandem was accomplished with a six per cent cut in fuel capacity.

The F/A-18 was revolutionary, introducing a genuinely multi-role capability and the first truly modern fighter cockpit. The pilot has three multi-function displays (MFDs) and true hands on throttle and stick (HOTAS) controls, which can switch easily from the air-to-ground role to air-to-air or defence suppression duties. The F/A-18's dogfighting capability is remarkable. The advanced wing design with large slotted LERXes confers excellent high-Alpha capability and turn performance.

F/A-18A/Bs were exported to Australia, Canada (as the **CF-188**) and Malaysia. US Navy Hornets scored two kills against Iraqi MiG-21s in the Gulf War, but have had few air combat opportunities so far. In the

An F/A-18C of VFA-131 'Wildcats' readies for launch from the USS John F. Kennedy in the Arabian Sea carrying a pair of 1,000-lb JDAM bombs. (Author)

The F/A-18 has the ability to switch roles within a single mission. In the Gulf War, Hornets scored kills without having to dump bombs and continued to the target. (Author)

Gulf and over Yugoslavia, US and Canadian Hornets undertook many bombing missions, and carrier-based USN and USMC aircraft were heavily used in Operation Enduring Freedom over Afghanistan in 2001/2002.

The improved **F/A-18C** was first flown in September 1986. An expanded weapons capability introduced the AIM-120 AMRAAM, imaging IR AGM-65 missiles and other weapons. The F/A-18C also features an avionics upgrade with new AN/ALR-67 radar homing and warning system (RHAWS), provision for the AN/ALQ-165 airborne self-protection jammer (ASPJ) and improvements to mission computer equipment. After 137 baseline F/A-18Cs had been delivered, production switched to a night-attack capable version. Export customers are Kuwait, Finland and Switzerland (the latter two nations with fighter role-only **F-18C**s).

The two-seat **F/A-18D** trainer is broadly similar to the single-seat F/A-18C. However, the USMC has developed a sophisticated two-crew combat-capable version, the **Night Attack F/A-18D** (originally known as the F/A-18D+). F/A-18Ds can also be fitted with the ATARS reconnaissance system nose.

Specification: Boeing F/A-18C Hornet
Type: twin-engined, carrier-based fighter
Powerplant: two 17,700 lb (78.73 kN) thrust General Electric F404-GE-402 turbofans
Dimensions: span over AAMs 40 ft 5 in (12.31 m); length 17.07 m (56 ft); height 15 ft 3 in (4.66 m); wing area 400 sq ft (37.16 m²)
Weights: empty 23,050 lb (10455 kg); max. take-off 51,900 lb (23541 kg)
Performance: max. speed over 1,190 mph (1915 km/h); max. climb rate 45,000 ft (13715 m) per minute; service ceiling 50,000 ft (15250 m); radius over 460 miles (740 km)
Armament: one M61A1 20-mm cannon, max. ordnance load 15,500 lb (7031 kg), including AIM-9 and AIM-120 AAMs

British Aerospace Sea Harrier

D eveloped from the RAF's Harrier GR.Mk 3, the **Sea Harrier FRS.Mk 1** introduced a redesigned forward fuselage and nose fitted with a Ferranti Blue Fox radar, a new canopy and raised cockpit for improved view, and a 21,492 lb (96.3 kN) thrust Pegasus Mk 104 engine. Avionics changes included the addition of an auto-pilot, a revised navigation/attack system and a new HUD. An initial order was placed in 1975 for 24 FRS.Mk 1s and a single **T. Mk 4A** trainer. The first operational squadron (No. 899 Squadron) was commissioned in April 1980 and two units (Nos. 800 and 801 Squadrons) were subsequently deployed during the Falklands War, where they served with distinction, scoring 23 confirmed victories.

Post-Falkland attrition replacements and further orders subsequently took total Royal Navy procurement up to 57 FRS.Mk 1s and four trainers (including three **T.Mk 4N**s). Improvements included revised wing pylons for the carriage of four AIM-9Ls (on twin launch rails), larger-capacity drop tanks and the installation of an improved Blue Fox radar and RWR. In 1978, the Indian Navy became the second Sea Harrier operator, ordering a total of 24 **FRS.Mk 51**s and four **T.Mk 60** trainers.

A mid-life update was initiated in 1985 to refine the Sea Harrier as a more capable interceptor. BAe (now BAE Systems) converted two FRS.Mk 1s to serve as **FRS.Mk 2** prototypes, with the first flying in September 1988. Despite the addition of an extra

The Sea Harrier FRS.1 found fame in the Falklands War. In the mid-1980s, they were upgraded to take dual Sidewinder launchers. (British Aerospace)

equipment bay and a recontoured nose to house the Blue Vixen multi-mode pulse-Doppler radar (giving compatibility with the AIM-120 AMRAAM), the FRS.Mk 2 is actually nearly 2 ft (0.61 m) shorter overall due to the elimination of the FRS.Mk 1's pitot probe. The cockpit introduces new multi-function cathode ray tube (CRT) displays and HOTAS controls. The FRS.Mk 2 designation was changed to **F/A.Mk 2** in May 1994 and then to the current **FA.Mk 2** in 1995.

Two development aircraft were built, with the first flying in September 1988, followed by 33 conversions. Another 18 new-build FA.Mk 2s were also acquired, and delivered between 1995 and 1998. Seven T Mk 4/4N trainers have been converted to Sea Harrier **T.Mk 8** standard to train FA.Mk 2 pilots. FA.Mk 2s saw action over Bosnia in the mid-1990s. Plans now call for the 'SHAR' to be retired in 2004 pending arrival of new large carriers and the F-35 JSF.

The Sea Harrier F/A.2 introduced Blue Vixen radar and AIM-120 AMRAAM capability. The refuelling probe is a non-retractable bolt-on fit. (Royal Navy)

Specification: BAE Systems Sea Harrier FA.Mk 2
Type: single-seat STO/VL carrier fighter
Powerplant: one 21,500 lb (95.64 kN) thrust Rolls-Royce Pegasus Mk 106 turbofan
Dimensions: span 25 ft 3 in (7.70 m); length 46 ft 6 in (14.17 m); height 12 ft 2 in (3.71 m); wing area 202.10 sq ft (18.6 m²)
Weights: empty 14,585 lb (6616 kg); max. take-off 26,200 lb (11884 kg)
Performance: max. speed 711 mph (1144 km/h); max. climb rate 50,000 ft (15240 m) per minute; service ceiling 51,000 ft (15545 m); combat radius 460 miles (750 km)
Armament: two 30-mm ADEN cannon, max. ordnance 8,000 lb (3629 kg)

Panavia Tornado Air Defence Variant

United Kingdom
October 1979

The **Panavia Tornado**, initially known as the **Multi-Role Combat Aircraft** (MRCA), was designed to fulfil a tri-national requirement for a strike, interdiction, counter-air, close air support, reconnaissance and maritime attack aircraft. The prototype flew on 14 August 1974. The UK-specific **Tornado ADV** (Air Defence Variant) was optimised for long-range, all-weather interception. Its primary mission is the defence of the UK Air Defence Region and UK maritime forces, with an important out-of-area commitment. The ADV was designed around the Marconi Al.Mk 24 Foxhunter radar and an armament of four Sky Flash AAMs and four Sidewinders. One 27-mm cannon was retained, but the other was removed to make room for a fully retractable inflight refuelling probe. The radar suffered development problems and delays, before being brought to an acceptable standard by 1990. Carrying the primary missile armament semi-recessed under the fuselage necessitated a lengthened airframe and increased internal fuel capacity.

The first of three prototypes flew on 27 October 1979 and these were followed by 18 interim Tornado F 2s with RB.199 Mk 103 engines. These early aircraft initially flew with lead ballast in place of radar and

The swing-wing Tornado F 3 provided air defence for the UK and the Falkland Islands. This unarmed F 3 is from No. 43 Squadron based at Leuchars in Scotland. (Author)

performed only conversion training duties until January 1988. Plans for their conversion to operational standards as **F 2A**s were never implemented, and they were scrapped.

The definitive **Tornado F 3** first flew in November 1985. BAe produced 144 aircraft (38 with dual-controls), including a cancelled Omani order for eight aircraft, which were transferred to the RAF before completion. Some 24 more were built for Saudi Arabia from 1989, but a second Saudi batch was cancelled. Twenty-four ex-RAF Tornado F 3s were leased to Italy from 1995 as a stop-gap measure, pending the availability of the Eurofighter Typhoon.

The Tornado F 3 introduced Mk 104 engines and a second INS. A Tornado Capability Sustainment Programme launched in 1996 will provide a MIL STD 1553B databus and an enhanced main computer. It will also integrate the AIM-120 AMRAAM and the short-range ASRAAM. Five front-line RAF units operate the Tornado F.Mk 3, and the type has seen extensive operational service in the Middle East and the Balkans. A detachment is based at Mount Pleasant Airport to provide air defence for the Falkland Islands.

No. 11 Squadron is one of five UK air defence squadrons equipped with the Tornado ADV. Other users are Saudi Arabia and Italy. (Author)

Specification: Panavia Tornado F.Mk 3
Type: twin-engined, two-seat interceptor
Powerplant: two 16,520 lb (73.48 kN) thrust Turbo-Union RB.199-34R Mk 104 turbofans
Dimensions: span (spread) 45 ft 7.5 in (13.91 m); length 61 ft 3.5 in (18.68 m); height 19 ft 6.25 in (5.95 m); wing area 286.33 sq ft (26.60 m²)
Weights: empty 31,970 lb (14502 kg); max. take-off 61,700 lb (27986 kg)
Performance: max. speed 1,453 mph (2338 km/h); max. climb rate unknown; operational ceiling about 40,000 ft (12192 m); combat radius over 1,151 miles (1852 km)
Armament: one 27-mm Mauser cannon, four Sky Flash/AMRAAMs , four AIM-9L/Ms

Sukhoi Su-27 'Flanker'

Soviet Union
April 1981

Sukhoi began work on a new long-range heavy fighter for Frontal Aviation in 1969. This was to be a highly manoeuvrable aircraft, with long range, heavy armament and modern sensors, capable of intercepting low-flying or high-level bombers, and of out-fighting the F-15. The requirement was re-drafted to cover two separate but complementary designs, one heavy and with a long range, and the other a cheaper, lower-cost tactical fighter.

Sukhoi was awarded a contract to develop the heavy aircraft, as the **T10**. The **T10-1** prototype (later designated '**Flanker-A**' by NATO) flew on 20 May 1977, but testing revealed serious problems and the type underwent a total redesign. The planned seventh prototype (T10-7) was completed as the **T10S-1** '**Flanker-B**' with a redesigned wing, undercarriage and fuselage, and a spine-mounted air brake, and flew on 20 April 1981. An early T10S was stripped and lightened and fitted with uprated engines. As the **P-42** this aircraft set a series of time-to-height records between 1986 and 1988. The new configuration formed the basis of the production **Su-27 'Flanker-B'**, which entered service in 1985.

The 'Flanker-B' has an advanced pulse-Doppler radar, backed up by an IRST system and a laser rangefinder. This allows the Su-27 to detect, track and engage a target without using radar. The Su-27 is also compatible with a helmet-mounted target designation system. The prototype **Su-27UB 'Flanker-C'** trainer

The Chinese Air Force (PLAAAF) is to receive locally built Su-27s as the J-11. This, however is an Su-27UBK, delivered from Russian production. (Robert Hewson)

featured a lengthened fuselage with stepped tandem cockpits under a single canopy and larger tailfins and air brake and first flew on 7 March 1985.

About 600 Su-27s have been built, and about 395 of these were in service with the Russian air forces, serving with Frontal Aviation and the PVO air defence force. Most of the remainder served in small numbers with former Soviet republics, including Armenia, Azerbaijan, Belarus, Georgia, Ukraine, Uzbekistan. Some of these aircraft have been sold on, to Angola and Ethiopia. Ethiopian Su-27s destroyed about six Eritrean MiG-29s in 1998/9. Fifty new-build export **Su-27SK**s and two-seat **Su-27UBK**s have been delivered to the People's Republic of China, where 200 more are to be built under licence as the **Shenyang J-11**. Some 12 aircraft have also been delivered to Vietnam.

The **Su-27PU** (later **Su-30**) was designed to fulfil a requirement for a long-range fighter-interceptor with inflight refuelling. India has ordered **Su-30MKI**s with canard foreplanes, thrust-vectoring engines and advanced air-to-ground precision weapon capability.

The 'Flanker' is a powerful and impressive aerobatic performer. Getting airborne here is an Su-27B from the Ukrainian Air Force's 831 IAP. (Author)

Specification: Sukhoi Su-27 'Flanker-B'
Type: twin-engined, single-seat interceptor fighter
Powerplant: two 27,557 lb (122.58 kN) thrust NPO Lyul'ka AL-31F turbofans
Dimensions: span 48 ft 2.75 in (14.70 m); length 71 ft 11.5 in (21.94 m); height 19 ft 5.5 in (5.93 m); wing area 667.4 sq ft (62.0 m²)
Weights: empty 39,021 lb (17700 kg); max. take-off 66,138 lb (30000 kg)
Performance: max. speed 1,553 mph (2500 km/h); max. climb rate 60,039 ft (18300 m) per minute; service ceiling 59,055 ft (18000 m); combat radius 932 miles (1500 km)
Armament: one 30-mm GSh-30-1 cannon, max. ordnance 13,228 lb (6000 kg)

Dassault Rafale

France
July 1986

Dassault's *Avion de Combat Experimentale* (ACX), evolved as an early 1980s technology demonstrator for a national combat aircraft programme even before France's withdrawal from the EFA (Eurofighter) project in August 1985. The **Rafale A** ACX testbed was first flown on 4 July 1986. It established and proved the basic design, configuration and performance of the definitive Rafale, or ACT (*Avion de Combat Tactique*), as well as its fly-by-wire control system and mainly composite structure. The Rafale is powered by a pair of SNECMA M88-2 turbofans, with the more powerful M88-3 now under development. The Rafale's RBE2 multi-mode electronically scanned radar is one of the first phased-array fighter radars to be developed in the West, and will be fully integrated with the IRST/FLIR sensor package above the nose. The Rafale will also be fitted with the Spectra RF/laser/IR self-protection system.

The Armée de l'Air's generic '**Rafale D**' (*discret*, 'stealth') family is four per cent smaller than the prototype Rafale A, and uses 'low-observable' (stealthy) elements in its airframe. In addition to these design techniques, Dassault may also have developed a classified 'active stealth' system to further reduce the aircraft's radar cross-section.

The Armée de l'Air is acquiring a total of 212 Rafales, with the first to be delivered in 2003, split 60:40 between the Rafale B (shown here) and C. (Dassault)

The naval Rafale M is the first version to enter service. A detachment has seen operational service over Afghanistan from the carrier Charles de Gaulle. (Dassault)

The **Rafale C** is the Armée de l'Air's production-standard single-seat multi-role combat version, and a prototype first flew on 19 May 1991. The **Rafale M** is the Aéronavale's single-seat carrier-borne fighter, modified for carrier operations with an arrester hook, a 'jump strut' nosewheel leg and no forward centreline pylon. The prototype Rafale M first flew on 12 December 1991. The **Rafale B** was originally planned as a straightforward dual-control trainer, but is now being developed into a fully operational version. The prototype flew on 30 April 1993.

The Rafale's development and acquisition plans have been very badly hampered by budget restrictions. The first aircraft to enter service will be the Aéronavale's 60 Rafale Ms – the first production-standard example flew on 6 July 1999. An experimental Rafale M unit was formed in 2001 and conducted operations over Afghanistan from the carrier *Charles de Gaulle* in 2002. The two-seat **Rafale BM** will enter service in 2007. The initial **Rafale M-F1** air defence aircraft will be replaced by the multi-role **Rafale M-F2** in 2004/05. Deliveries of the full-standard **Rafale M-F3** will begin in 2007, and all 60 Rafale Ms will be in service by 2012.

Specification: Dassault Rafale C
Type: twin-engined, single-seat fighter
Powerplant: two 19,555 lb (86.98 kN) SNECMA M88-2 turbofans
Dimensions: span 35ft 9.25 in (10.90 m) over wingtip missiles; length 50 ft 2.5 in (15.30 m); height 17 ft 6.75 in (5.34 m); wing area 484.39 sq ft (45.0 m²)
Weights: empty 19,973 lb (9060 kg); max. take-off 47,399 lb (21500 kg)
Performance: max. speed 1,321 mph (2125 km/h); climb rate unknown; service ceiling approx 65,620 ft (20000 m); combat radius 655 miles (1055 km)
Armament: one 30-mm DEFA 791B cannon, max. 17,637 lb (8000 kg) of ordnance

Saab JAS 39 Gripen

Following the cancellation of the Saab B3LA light-attack/advanced trainer project in 1979, Saab began to develop the **JAS 39 Gripen** (Griffin) as an advanced lightweight multi-role successor to the Viggen. The JAS designation (Jakt Attack Spaning – fighter, attack, reconnaissance) underlined the fact that one aircraft (and one pilot) would be able to undertake all the combat tasks of the mission-specific Viggen family. The Gripen was designed to carry the advanced Ericsson PS-05/A multi-mode radar, integrated with the D80 mission computer. The cockpit featured the Ericsson EP-17 display system with three monochrome screens and a wide-angled HUD. The Gripen uses a highly developed version of Sweden's tactical airborne datalink system that allows rapid real-time exchange of complex mission data between aircraft and ground stations. Power was supplied by the Volvo RM12 turbofan, an improved licence-built version of the General Electric F404. Above all, the Gripen was designed to be rapidly deployable and easily maintainable. It was intended to use Sweden's Bas 90 system of dispersed 2,624-ft (800-m) long roadstrips, and to be re-armed, refuelled and maintained in the field by a team of just five ground personnel.

Five **JAS 39A** prototypes were built, with the first flying on 9 December 1988. The first production Gripen flew in December 1992. The development programme was slowed by the loss of two aircraft in

The Gripen was designed for the particular conditions of Sweden, but with one eye on the export market. South Africa and Hungary are the first customers. (Saab)

1989 and 1993. These incidents led to a redesign of the Gripen's pioneering digital fly-by-wire system.

The Gripen was declared fully operational with, F7 Wing on 1 November 1997. The second Gripen wing, F10, is now fully equipped. The Swedish air force will acquire a total of 204 Gripens, including 28 two-seat combat-capable **JAS 39B**s. Sweden's Gripens are being delivered in three batches, each with improving levels of capability. Advanced simulators have allowed pilot conversion without use of dual-control trainers.

The ultimate Batch Three evolution (designated **JAS 39C** and **JAS 39D**) will be delivered from 2003 to 2007. These 64 aircraft will have a full colour cockpit with enlarged displays, air-to-air refuelling capability and upgraded computer systems. Future Gripen upgrade options include a re-engining plan and conformal fuel tanks to extend range. In 1998 South Africa ordered 25 Gripens for delivery beginning in 2007. Hungary is to lease 14 Gripens from Sweden and the Czech Republic has contracted for the purchase of 28 Gripens, to be operational by 2005.

The Gripen is replacing the Viggen in Flygvapnet service. Here one of F10 Wing's new JAS 39As poses with the unit's last JA 37, marked 'The Show Must Go On'. (Author)

Specification: SAAB JAS 39A Gripen
Type:single-seat fighter
Powerplant: one 18,100-lb (80.5-kN) Volvo Aero RM12 turbofan, Volvo Flygmotor RM-12 afterburning turbojet
Dimensions: wing span 27 ft 6.75 in (8.40 m); length 46 ft 3 in (14.10 m); height 14 ft 9 in (4.50 m); wing area 323 sq ft (30 m²)
Weights: operating empty 14,600 lb (6622 kg); maximum take-off 28,600 lb (13000 kg)
Performance: Max. speed 1,321 mph (2126 km/h); altitude and climb rate unavailable; combat radius approximately 800 km (497 miles)
Armament: one 27-mm Mauser BK 27 cannon, max. ordnance 4500 kg (9,920 lb)

Eurofighter EFA2000 Typhoon

Germany/Italy/Spain/UK
March 1994

The Eurofighter consortium was officially formed in June 1986 by Britain, Germany and Italy (soon joined by Spain) to produce an air superiority fighter for service from the late 1990s. This followed the issue of an outline Air Staff Target by the four partners, and France, in 1983. The Eurofighter design drew heavily on BAe's Experimental Aircraft Programme (EAP), and a number of other technology demonstrator programmes. The **EAP** technology demonstrator first flew in August 1986 and amassed invaluable data before its retirement in May 1991. The Eurofighter copied EAP's unstable canard delta layout, adding active digital fly-by-wire flight controls, advanced avionics, multi-function cockpit displays, carbon-fibre composite construction and extensive use of aluminium-lithium alloys and titanium.

The new ECR-90 multi-mode pulse-Doppler look-up/look-down radar was selected for development in May 1990, building on the proven and highly regarded Blue Vixen used by the Sea Harrier. The radar is supplemented by an IRST. Integrated defensive aids comprise missile approach, laser and radar warning systems, wingtip ESM/ECM pods, chaff/flare dispensers and a towed radar decoy.

Eight EFA prototypes were ordered in late 1988

The first prototype EFA2000 flew in Germany in 1994. It has now been joined by six more prototypes and three initial production aircraft. (Eurofighter)

DA-7 is the Italian single-seat prototype and is fitted with the EJ200 engines. Italy has ordered 130 Eurofighters and flew its first production aircraft in 2002. (Alenia)

(though this total was subsequently reduced to seven). In 1992, Germany demanded major cost-reductions, triggering major project reviews and leading to long delays and threats of withdrawal before they decided to procure a smaller number of standard aircraft, stripped of their advanced defensive aids, and re-christened as the **Eurofighter 2000**. Later batches of the RAF's EFA 2000s will not have the gun, as a cost-saving measure. The original requirement for 765 EFAs (250 each for the RAF and the Luftwaffe, 165 for the Italian Air Force (MMI) and 100 for the Ejercito del Aire) was cut back and now stands at 620 (232 for the RAF, 180 for the Luftwaffe, 121 for Italy and 87 for Spain). The name **Typhoon** was adopted for export aircraft (and for the RAF's Eurofighters) in 1998. Greece has become the first non-partner nation to order the Typhoon, agreeing to purchase 60 with 30 options, and Austria ordered 24 in July 2002.

The prototype EFA 2000 made its long-awaited first flight on 27 March 1994 from Manching, Germany. Further prototypes have been built and flown for each of the participating nations for a total of seven, including four two-seaters.

Specification: Eurofighter Typhoon
Type: twin-engined single-seat fighter
Powerplant: two 20,250 lb (90 kN) thrust Eurojet EJ200 turbofans
Dimensions: span 34 ft 5.5 in (10.50 m); length 47 ft 7 in (14.50 m); height 13 ft 1.5 in (4.00 m); wing area 538.2 sq ft (50 m²)
Weights: empty 21,495 lb (9750 kg); max. take-off 46,297 lb (21000 kg)
Performance: max. speed 1,321 mph (2125 km/h); climb to 35,000 ft (10670m) in 2 minutes; service ceiling 55,000 ft (16775 m); range 863 miles (1390 km)
Armament: one Mauser Mk 27 27-mm cannon, max. ordnance 14,330 lb (6500 kg)

Boeing F/A-18E/F Super Hornet

When the US Navy was forced to cancel the General Dynamics A-12 long-range, stealthy attack aircraft, it still faced the problem of replacing its A-6 Intruders and early-model F/A-18 Hornets. The solution was to develop an improved version of the Hornet, albeit one that would be substantially different to existing aircraft. This **Super Hornet** was first proposed in 1991 and the engineering and manufacturing development (EMD) contract was awarded to McDonnell Douglas in June 1992. Single-seat Super Hornets were given the designation **F/A-18E**, while the two-seat version became the **F/A-18F**.

The Super Hornet is based on the basic F/A-18C airframe, but is longer and heavier with increased wing area, larger tail surfaces and extended leading-edge extensions. Many elements, such as the engine intakes, have been redesigned to make the aircraft stealthier. The Super Hornet can carry more fuel than earlier Hornets, and has a much higher landing weight limit, allowing greater 'bringback' of unexpended ordnance to the carrier. The final production standard aircraft will be fitted with the AESA electronically scanned radar and a very advanced mission computer fit and digital cockpit.

The Super Hornet EMD contract covered seven prototypes, five F/A-18Es and two F/A-18Fs. The first Super Hornet (an E) made its maiden flight on 29 November 1995. Carrier trials began in mid-1996 and low-rate initial production was approved in March

The F/A-18F will replace the F-14 in the fleet defence role. This is the first aircraft, seen during carrier trials aboard the **John C. Stennis** *in January 1997.* (McDonnell Douglas)

1997 (the same year that Boeing took over the programme from McDonnell Douglas).

During flight tests the F/A-18E/F encountered a number of unexpected problems, and suffered much criticism for poor handling and a lack of performance.

In November 1999 the F/A-18E/F passed its critical Operational Evaluation, and achieved its initial operating capability in 2000. The first active squadron is VFA-122, which was established at NAS Lemoore, in January 1999. When Tomcat units VF-14 and VF-41 returned from operations over Afghanistan in early 2002, they began the transition to the F/A-18E and F/A-18F, respectively. The US Navy hopes to eventually acquire 222 Super Hornets. Boeing is now offering a suppression of enemy air defences (SEAD) version of the F/A-18E/F to replace the EA-6B Prowler, dubbed the **F/A-18C2W** (or **F/A-18G**) 'Growler'. Boeing is even promoting the 'Super Bug' as a tanker to replace the S-3B Viking in this role. Malaysia is one of several potential export customers.

Boeing hopes to sell the US Navy an 'EA-18G Growler' version based on the F/A-18F to replace the EA-6B Prowler in the electronic attack role. (Boeing)

Specification: F/A-18E Super Hornet
Type: twin-engined, carrier-based fighter
Powerplant: two 22,000 lb (97.9 kN) thrust General Electric F414-GE-400 afterburning turbofans
Dimensions: span over wingtip AAMs 40 ft 8.5 in (13.62 m); length 60 ft 1.25 in (18.31 m); height 16 ft (4.88m); wing area 500 sq ft (46.45 m²)
Weights: empty 29,574 lb (13,387 kg); max. take-off 66,000 lb (29940 kg)
Performance: max. speed over Mach 1.8 climb not known; service ceiling 50,000 ft (15250 m); radius over 400 miles (740 km)
Armament: one M61A1 20-mm cannon, max. ordnance load 17,750 lb (8051 kg)

Lockheed Martin/Boeing F-22 Raptor

United States
September 1997

Designed as an 'Air Dominance Fighter', the **F-22** began from studies during the 1970s into low-observable (LO) technologies, or 'stealth', and progressed to the ATF (Advanced Tactical Fighter) programme launched by the USAF in April 1980. This was spurred by Soviet fighter developments that threatened to out-perform the F-15 Eagle, and the outline requirement was for 750 new aircraft. After an evaluation of seven manufacturer's proposals, Lockheed's **YF-22** and Northrop's YF-23 designs were selected for competitive evaluation (demonstration/validation, or dem/val) in October 1986. Lockheed teamed with Boeing and General Dynamics to refine (in fact, completely redesign) the aircraft and to share development cost and expertise. The revised YF-22 (unofficially named Lightning II) first flew on 29 September 1990. A second prototype first flew on 30 October, but was damaged beyond repair after a flight control system failure in April 1992.

The Lockheed/Boeing team won the dem/val competition in April 1991. The first of these nine engineering and manufacturing development (EMD) **F-22A** Raptors (Raptor 4001) flew on 7 September 1997 and the second followed on 26 June 1998.

Many fundamental aspects of the F-22's design,

Alignment of fins and intakes and mounting of the wing and horizontal tail in the same plane all contribute to the F-22's low radar cross-section. (Boeing)

The F-22 Raptor will replace the F-15 Eagle as the USAF's main fighter aircraft, but in much smaller numbers than originally envisaged. (Boeing)

such as its internal weapons bays and same-plane wing and tailplane, are intended to minimise its radar cross-section and make it 'stealthy'. Radar absorbent materials are used throughout. The lower weapons bay can carry up to six AIM-120C AMRAAMs, with two AIM-9X Sidewinders in the side bay. A pair of GBU-32 JDAM bombs can be fitted in place of four of the AMRAAMs. A 20-mm Vulcan cannon fires from a 'shoulder' compartment on the right-hand upper fuselage and is covered by a door when not in use. The F-22 is the first aircraft to be designed from the outset for vectored-thrust control and for 'supercruise' (sustained supersonic flight without afterburner).

The APG-77 active array radar combines with sensors mounted around the airframe to create 'sensor fusion', presenting the pilot with an all-around 'big picture' of the air battle. A powerful datalink allows information to be passed between members of a flight and advanced warning and control (AWAC) platforms.

Plans to acquire 648 F-22s were cut back to 339 and now stand at 295. A lack of funds halted plans for a two-seat **F-22B** trainer in 1996. The F-22 is scheduled to enter service in 2005.

Specification: F-22A Raptor
Type: twin-engined 'Air Dominance' fighter
Powerplant: two 35,000 lb (156 kN) thrust Pratt & Whitney F119-PW-100 thrust vectoring turbofans
Dimensions: span 44 ft 6 in (13.56 m); length 62.1 ft (18.90 m); height 16 ft 5 in (5.02m); wing area 840 sq ft (78 m²)
Weights: empty 31,670 ft (14365 kg); max. take-off 60,000 lb (27216 kg)
Performance: max. speed Mach 2; max. climb rate not available; service ceiling not available; combat radius not available
Armament: one M61A1 Vulcan 20-mm cannon, up to six AIM-120C AMRAAM and two AIM-9X Sidewinder AAMs

Index

Aircraft listed by manufacturer, name and designation

A5M Claude (see Mitsubishi)
A6M Zero-Sen 'Zeke' (see Mitsubishi)
A-36A Apache (see North American P-51)
Airacobra (see Bell P-39)
Airco D.H.1 and D.H.2: **3**
Albatros D.I to D.V biplanes: **9**
Anteater (see Dornier Do 335)
Apache (see North American P-51)
Arado 68: **25**
Atlas Cheetah (see Dassault Mirage III/5)
Avia
    S.92 (see Messerschmitt Me 262)
    S.105 (see Mikoyan-Gurevich MiG-19)
    S.199 (see Messerschmitt Bf 109)

Balzac V (see Dassault Mirage III/5)
B.E.2 (see Royal Aircraft Factory)
Bearcat (see Grumman F8F)
Beaufighter (see Bristol)
Bell: P-39 Airacobra/P-63 Kingcobra: **42**
Bf 109 (see Messerschmitt)
Black Widow (see Northrop P-61)
Boeing
    F4B/P-12: **18**
    P-26 Peashooter: **22**
    F/A-18E/F Super Hornet: **109**
Bombcat (see Grumman F-14)
Bristol
    F.2 Fighter: **10**
    Bulldog: **17**
    Beaufighter: **44**
British Aerospace Sea Harrier: **103**
Bulldog (see Bristol)

Camel (see Sopwith)
Chaika (see Polikarpov biplane fighters)
Chance-Vought F4U Corsair: **49**
Chengdu
    J-7 (see Mikoyan-Gurevich MiG-21)
    JJ-5 (see Mikoyan-Gurevich MiG-17)
Claude (see Mitsubishi A5M)
Convair
    F-102 Delta Dagger: **84**
    F-106 Delta Dart: **88**
Corsair (see Chance-Vought F4U)
CR.30 to CR.42 Falco (see Fiat)
Crusader (see Vought F-8)
Curtiss
    Hawk biplanes: **16**
    P-40 Hawks: **36**

D.520 (see Dewoitine)
Dagger (see Dassault Mirage III/5)
Dassault
    Mystère: **75**
    Mirage III/5: **87**
    Mirage F1: **94**
    Mirage 2000: **101**
    Rafale: **106**
De Havilland: Mosquito fighters: **53**
Delta Dagger (see Convair F-102)
Delta Dart (see Convair F-106)
Demon (see Hawker biplane fighters)
Demon (see McDonnell F3H)
Dewoitine D.520: **35**
D.H.1 and D.H.2 (see Airco)
D.I to D.V biplanes (see Albatros)
Do 335 Pfeil (see Dornier)

Dornier: Do 335 Pfeil: **66**
Douglas: F4D Skyray: **74**
Draken (see Saab J35)
Dr.I Triplane (see Fokker)
D.VII (see Fokker)
D.XXI (see Fokker)

Eagle (see McDonnell Douglas F-15A/C)
EFA2000 Typhoon (see Eurofighter)
E.I to E.IV (see Fokker)
Eindeckers (see Fokker E.I to E.IV)
English Electric Lightning: **89**
Eurofighter EFA2000 Typhoon: **108**

F.1 Camel (see Sopwith)
F.2 Fighter (see Bristol)
F-4 Phantom II (see McDonnell Douglas)
F-5 Freedom Fighter/Tiger II (see Northrop)
F-7M Airguard (see Mikoyan-Gurevich MiG-21)
F-8 Crusader (see Vought)
F-14 Tomcat (see Grumman)
F-15A Reporter (see Northrop P-61)
F-15A/C Eagle (see McDonnell Douglas)
F-16 Fighting Falcon (see General Dynamics)
F-22 Raptor (see Lockheed Martin/Boeing)
F-86 Sabre (see North American)
F-94 Starfire (see Lockheed P-80)
F-100 Super Sabre (see North American)
F-101 Voodoo (see McDonnell)
F-102 Delta Dagger (see Convair)
F-104 Starfighter (see Lockheed)
F-106 Delta Dart (see Convair)
F/A-18 Hornet (see McDonnell Douglas)
F/A-18E/F Super Hornet (see Boeing)
F2F (see Grumman FF to F3F)
F3F (see Grumman FF to F3F)
F3H Demon (see McDonnell)
F4B/P-12 (see Boeing)
F4D Skyray (see Douglas)
F4F Wildcat (see Grumman)
F4U Corsair (see Chance-Vought)
F5D Skylancer (see Douglas F4D)
F6F Hellcat (see Grumman)
F7F Tigercat (see Grumman)
F8F Bearcat (see Grumman)
F9F Panther (see Grumman)
'Fagot' (see Mikoyan-Gurevich MiG-15)
Falco (see Fiat CR.30 to CR.42)
'Farmer' (see Mikoyan-Gurevich MiG-19)
Fiat
    CR.30 to CR.42 Falco: **23**
    G.50 Freccia: **34**
Fighting Falcon (see General Dynamics F-16)
Finger (see Dassault Mirage III/5)
'Fishbed' (see Mikoyan-Gurevich MiG-21)
'Flagon' (see Sukhoi Su-15)
'Flanker' (see Sukhoi Su-27)
'Flogger' (see Mikoyan-Gurevich MiG-23)
Focke-Wulf Fw 190: **43**
Fokker
    E.I to E.IV Eindeckers: **4**
    Dr.I Triplane: **14**
    D.VII: **15**
    D.XXI: **30**
Folgore (see Macchi MC.202)
'Foxbat' (see Mikoyan-Gurevich MiG-25)
'Foxhound' (see Mikoyan-Gurevich MiG-31)
'Frank' (see Nakajima Ki-84)

Freccia (see Fiat G.50)
Freedom Fighter/Tiger II (see Northrop F-5)
'Fresco' (see Mikoyan-Gurevich MiG-17)
'Fulcrum' (see Mikoyan-Gurevich MiG-29)
Fury (see Hawker biplane fighters)
Fw 190 (see Focke-Wulf)

G.50 Freccia (see Fiat)
General Dynamics F-16 Fighting Falcon: **99**
'George' (see Kawanishi N1K)
Gladiator (see Gloster)
Gloster
    Gladiator: **26**
    Meteor: **56**
    Javelin: **78**
Goblin 1 (see Grumman FF to F3F)
Gripen (see Saab JAS 39)
Grumman
    FF to F3F: **21**
    F4F Wildcat: **39**
    F6F Hellcat: **62**
    F8F Bearcat: **65**
    F7F Tigercat: **67**
    F9F Panther: **71**
    F-14 Tomcat: **97**

Ha-112 Buchon (see Messerschmitt Bf 109)
Hart (see Hawker biplane fighters)
Hawk biplanes (see Curtiss)
Hawker
    biplane fighters: **19**
    Hurricane: **29**
    Typhoon and Tempest: **46**
    Sea Fury: **69**
    Hunter: **76**
Hayabusa 'Oscar' (see Nakajima Ki-43)
Hayate 'Frank' (see Nakajima Ki-84)
He 219 'Uhu' (see Heinkel)
Heinkel: He 219 'Uhu': **63**
Hien 'Tony' (see Kawasaki Ki-61)
Hornet (see McDonnell Douglas F/A-18)
Hunter (see Hawker)
Hurricane (see Hawker)

I-16 (see Polikarpov)
I-153 (see Polikarpov)

J2M Raiden 'Jack' (see Mitsubishi)
J8M1 (see Messerschmitt Me 163)
J35 Draken (see Saab)
JA37 Viggen (see Saab)
'Jack' (see Mitsubishi J2M)
JAS 39 Gripen (see Saab)
Javelin (see Gloster)
Ju 88 (see Junkers)
Junkers 88 fighters: **45**

Kawanishi N1K Kyofu 'George': **59**
Kawasaki
    Ki-45-KAI Toryu 'Nick': **52**
    Ki-61 Hien 'Tony'/Ki-100: **54**
Kfir (see Dassault Mirage III/5)
Ki-43 Hayabusa 'Oscar' (see Nakajima)
Ki-45-KAI Toryu 'Nick' (see Kawasaki)
Ki-61 Hien 'Tony'/Ki-100 (see Kawasaki)
Ki-84 Hayate 'Frank' (see Nakajima)
Ki-100 (see Kawasaki Ki-61)
Kingcobra (see Bell P-39)
Kittyhawk (see Curtiss P-40 Hawks)
Komet (see Messerschmitt Me 163)

Kyofu 'George' (see Kawanishi N1K)

Lavochkin fighters: **47**
Lightning (see English Electric)
Lightning (see Lockheed P-38)
Lim-1 and Lim-2 (see Mikoyan-Gurevich MiG-15)
Lim-5 and Lim-6 (see Mikoyan-Gurevich MiG-17)
Lockheed
    P-38 Lightning: **38**
    P-80 Shooting Star: **68**
    F-104 Starfighter: **81**
Lockheed Martin/Boeing F-22 Raptor: **110**

Macchi: MC.202/MC.205 Veltro: **50**
McDonnell
    F3H Demon: **77**
    F-101 Voodoo: **82**
McDonnell Douglas
    F-4 Phantom II: **90**
    F-15A/C Eagle: **98**
    F/A-18 Hornet: **102**
Martlet (see Grumman F4F)
MC.202 Folgore (see Macchi)
MC.205 Veltro (see Macchi MC.202)
Me 163 Komet (see Messerschmitt)
Me 262 (see Messerschmitt)
Messerschmitt
    Bf 109: **28**
    Bf 110: **32**
    Me 163 Komet: **57**
    Me 262: **60**
Meteor (see Gloster)
MiG-3 (see Mikoyan-Gurevich)
MiG-15 'Fagot' (see Mikoyan-Gurevich)
MiG-17 'Fresco' (see Mikoyan-Gurevich)
MiG-19 'Farmer' (see Mikoyan-Gurevich)
MiG-21 'Fishbed' (see Mikoyan-Gurevich)
MiG-23 'Flogger' (see Mikoyan-Gurevich)
MiG-25 'Foxbat' (see Mikoyan-Gurevich)
MiG-29 'Fulcrum' (see Mikoyan-Gurevich)
MiG-31 'Foxhound' (see Mikoyan-Gurevich)
Mikoyan-Gurevich
    MiG-3: **48**
    MiG-15 'Fagot': **72**
    MiG-17 'Fresco': **73**
    MiG-19 'Farmer': **80**
    MiG-21 'Fishbed': **86**
    MiG-23 'Flogger': **96**
    MiG-25 'Foxbat': **93**
    MiG-29 'Fulcrum': **100**
    MiG-31 'Foxhound': **93**
Mirage 2000 (see Dassault)
Mirage F1 (see Dassault)
Mirage III/5 (see Dassault)
Mitsubishi
    A5M Claude: **27**
    A6M Zero-Sen 'Zeke': **41**
    J2M Raiden 'Jack': **55**
Mosquito fighters (see de Havilland)
Mustang (see North American P-51)
Mystère (see Dassault)

N1K Kyofu 'George' (see Kawanishi)

Nakajima
    Ki-43 Hayabusa 'Oscar': **37**
    Ki-84 Hayate 'Frank': **64**
Nesher (see Dassault Mirage III/5)
'Nick' (see Kawasaki Ki-45-KAI)
Nieuport
    11 to 17: **5**
    28: **13**
Nimrod (see Hawker biplane fighters)
North American
    P-51 Mustang: **61**
    F-86 Sabre: **70**
    F-100 Super Sabre: **79**
Northrop
    P-61 Black Widow: **58**
    F-5 Freedom Fighter/Tiger II: **92**

'Oscar' (see Nakajima Ki-43)
Otsu 'Oscar' (see Nakajima Ki-43)

P.7a to P.24 (see PZL)
P-12 (see Boeing F4B)
P-26 Peashooter (see Boeing)
P-38 Lightning (see Lockheed)
P-39 Airacobra (see Bell)
P-40 Hawk (see Curtiss)
P-47 Thunderbolt (see Republic)
P-51 Mustang (see North American)
P-61 Black Widow (see Northrop)
P-63 Kingcobra (see Bell P-39)
P-80 Shooting Star (see Lockheed)
Panavia Tornado Air Defence Variant: **104**
Panther (see Grumman F9F)
Peashooter (see Boeing P-26)
Pfeil (see Dornier Do 335)
Phantom II (see McDonnell Douglas F-4)
Polikarpov
    I-16: **24**
    biplane fighters: **33**
Pup (see Sopwith)
PZL P.7a to P.24: **20**

Rafale (see Dassault)
Raiden 'Jack' (see Mitsubishi J2M)
Raptor (see Lockheed Martin/Boeing F-22)
Reporter (see Northrop P-61)
Republic: P-47 Thunderbolt **51**
'Rex' (see Kawanishi N1K)
Royal Aircraft Factory
    B.E.2: **2**
    S.E.5 and SE.5a: **11**

S.102 and S.103 (see Mikoyan-Gurevich MiG-15)
Saab
    J35 Draken: **85**
    JA37 Viggen: **95**
    JAS 39 Gripen: **107**
Sabre (see North American F-86)
Scout (see Sopwith)
S.E.5 and S.E.5a (see Royal Aircraft Factory)
Sea Fury (see Hawker)
Sea Gladiator (see Gloster Gladiator)
Sea Harrier (see British Aerospace)

Sea Hurricane (see Hawker Hurricane)
Seafire (see Supermarine Spitfire)
Shenyang
    J-2 (see Mikoyan-Gurevich MiG-15)
    J-5 (see Mikoyan-Gurevich MiG-17)
    J-6 (see Mikoyan-Gurevich MiG-19)
    J-11 (see Sukhoi Su-27)
Shiden 'George' (see Kawanishi N1K)
Shiden-Kai (see Kawanishi N1K)
Shooting Star (see Lockheed P-80)
Skylancer (see Douglas F4D)
Skyray (see Douglas F4D)
Sopwith
    Pup: **6**
    Scout: **6**
    Triplane: **8**
    F.1 Camel: **12**
Spad S.VII to S.XIII: **7**
Spitfire (see Supermarine)
Starfighter (see Lockheed F-104)
Starfire (see Lockheed P-80)
Su-15 'Flagon' (see Sukhoi)
Su-27 'Flanker' (see Sukhoi)
Sukhoi
    Su-15 'Flagon': **91**
    Su-27 'Flanker': **105**
Super Hornet (see Boeing F/A-18E/F)
Super Mystère (see Dassault Mystère)
Super Sabre (see North American F-100)
Supermarine Spitfire: **31**

Ta 152 (see Focke-Wulf Fw 190)
Tempest (see Hawker Typhoon)
Thunderbolt (see Republic P-47)
Tigercat (see Grumman F7F)
Tigereye (see Northrop F-5)
Tigershark (see Northrop F-5)
Tomahawk (see Curtiss P-40 Hawks)
Tomcat (see Grumman F-14)
'Tony' (see Kawasaki Ki-61)
Torbeau (see Bristol Beaufighter)
Tornado Air Defence Variant (see Panavia)
Toryu 'Nick' (see Kawasaki Ki-45-KAI)
Triplane (see Sopwith)
Typhoon (see Eurofighter EFA2000)
Typhoon (see Hawker)

'Uhu' (see Heinkel He 219)

Veltro (see Macchi MC.202)
Viggen (see Saab JA37)
Voodoo (see McDonnell F-101)
Vought F-8 Crusader: **83**

Wildcat (see Grumman F4F)
Wildcat II (see Grumman F6F)

XFF-1 (see Grumman FF to F3F)

Yak-1 to Yak-9 (see Yakovlev)
Yakovlev: Yak-1 to Yak-9: **40**

'Zeke' (see Mitsubishi A6M)
Zero-Sen 'Zeke' (see Mitsubishi A6M)